Wade

Decorative

Ware

Volume Two: Third Edition

By
Pat Murray

W. K. Cross
Publisher

The Charlton Press

Toronto, Ontario • Palm Harbor, Florida

The National Library of Canada has catalogued this publication a follows:

Murray, Pat.
    The Charlton standard catalogue of Wade

Biennial.
2nd ed.
Previously published under title: Pre-war and more Wades.
Issues for 2002-   have title: Charlton standard catalogue Wade.
ISSN 1203-4681
ISBN 0-88968-224-0 (v. 2 : 3rd edition)

    1. George Wade and Son—Catalogs. 2. Miniature pottery—England Catalogs. 3. Figurines—England—Catalogs. I. Charlton Pres II. Title

NK8473.5.W33M8   738.8'2   C95-932732-0

**Printed in Canada
in the Province of Ontario**

The Charlton Press

EDITORIAL

Editor	**W. K. Cross**
Assistant editor	**Jean Dale**
Graphic technician	**Davina Rowan**

ACKNOWLEDGEMENTS

The Charlton Press wishes to thank those who have helped with the third edition of *The Charlton Standard Catalogue of Wade, Volume Two., Decorative Wares.*

Speical Thanks

The publishers and author would like to thank Jeremy and George Wade for allowing Pat and Gordon to visit and photograph their private collection, Peter and Lesley Chisholm for treating them as family while photographing their models, and to Janet and Brian Robinson of New Zealand for their many photographs and researched information.

Contributors To The Third Edition

Lloyd Barnes; John Beatty; Sarah Bernotas; Pamela Brain; Margaret Brebner; Peter Brooks; Mr. and Mrs. A Clark, K & P Collectables; Ellen Clayton; Father David Cox; Linda Cox; Mr. and Mrs. P. Cronin; Potteries Specialist Auctions, Stoke-on-Trent, England; Frank Davis; Peter Elson; Catherine Evans; Janet and Mike Evans, Yesterdays; Elizabeth Everill; Nancy Fronczac; Bill Gilson; Mary Lee Graham; Mr. and Mrs. V. Harvey; Val and Dave Holman; Anne Howard; Marion and Gareth Hunt, Ivy Rose Antiques, Sydney; Murray Jacques; Cyndy Katrynuk; Patty Keenan; R. J. Kent; Andrew Key; Esther Kramer; John Lawless; Dave Lee; Jane and Tina Lister; Michael Lynch; Jo-ann and Don Mandryk; C. Marshall; Mr. MacGregor; Mr. McEwen; Christian Menard; Metropolitan Toronto Reference Library, Toronto, Ontario; Kevin Murfitt; Daniel Murray; Molly and Pete Newman; Mark Oliver, Phillips, London, England; Mrs. H. Palmer; Brian and Pam Powell; Pat Powell; June and Geoff Rance; Robin Riley; Cynthia Risby; Janet and Brian Robinson; Margaret Rosetiques; Jean and Ron Sears; Mr. and Mrs. Simmonds; Joyce and Leonard Steers; Saxon Kiya Stoof; Stroud Public Library, Stroud, Ontario; Annabel and Keith Sutherland; Thelma and Jeff Swinhoe; Peter Vincent; David and Molly Wade; Carol and Valerie of Wade Watch; Kim and Derek Watson; Robert Williamson; Steve and Deb Wilson; Annie and Steve Windsor; Mary and Steve Yager; and many thanks to all those who have helped with information and photographs for this book and preferred to remain anonymous.

A SPECIAL NOTE TO COLLECTORS

We welcome and appreciate any comments or suggestions in regard to The Charlton Standard Catalofue of Wade, Volume Two, Decorative Ware. If any errors or omissions come to your attention, please write to us, or if you would like to participate in pricing or supply previously unavailable data or information, please contact Jean Dale at (416) 488-1418, or e-mail us at chpress@charltonpress.com.

DISCLAIMER

While every care has been taken to ensure accuracy in the compilation of the data in this catalogue, the publisher cannot accept responsibility for typographical errors.

The Charlton Press

P.O. Box 94, Thornhill, Ontario L3T 3N1
Telephone: (416) 488-1418 Fax: (416) 488-4656
Telephone: (800) 442-6042 Fax: (800) 442-1542
www.charltonpress.com e-mail: chpress@charltonpress.com

THE INTERNET AND PRICING

Over three years ago we wrote a column for the introduction of our guides dealing with the Internet and the impact it would have on the collecting industry. In this column we gave the reasons why the Internet would affect collectables and their selling price, and also how it would impact and change the way collectors acquire items for their collections.

All this is certainly happening. The industry is now in the sea of change. On the World Wide Web it makes no difference what you collect - coins, stamps, ceramics, art pottery, glass, books - all and sundry are impacted. Naturally, the Van Gogh's are not, but leaving out the high priced items or the exotics, all collectables are and will be affected.

The Web has lowered the transaction cost between the buyer and the seller to a point where land-based sellers (dealers, auction houses) cannot compete under the old rules.

Collectables and collections used to flow through the old supply chain: estate or non-collector/picker/dealer/collector/land auction/dealer/collector. Naturally, the chain could be interrupted or jumped when convenient.

The new chain which moves items at a much faster rate, and at a much lower cost, maybe outlined as follows: estate, non-collector, picker, collector, dealer/on-line auction/dealer/collector.

Retail stores and malls have closed. Collectable/Antique Fairs and Shows are losing dealers simply because collectors are changing their buying habits. Collectable Shows are too long and too drawn out. High-end Antique/Decorator Shows still can support long openings, for besides being fairs, they are a form of entertainment.

The following is a chart of the number of items, by type, that appear on a major on-line auction site:

Category	Items Daily	Items Projected To Yearly Basis
Coins	6,000	2,190,000
Disney	37,500	13,687,500
Harry Potter	2,300	839,500
Lalique	650	237,250
Moorcroft	250	91,250
Royal Doulton	3,500	1,277,500
Royal Worcester	600	219,000
Stamps	12,750	4,654,000
Star Wars	19,000	6,935,000

As you can see, the numbers are staggering. This major site advertises "over 5 million items for sale." That is over 1.8 billion items yearly.

Of course, these are not all collectables but one can become easily dismayed by such numbers. Turning to a positive point of view, it also signifies tremendous interest and awareness in things collectable. This major on-line auction has sites in Australia, Austria, Canada, France, Germany, Italy, Japan, the United Kingdon and the United States. Three years ago it was only the United States. What happens now, will the rest of the world (China, India) join in? When they do, the interest and awareness will only continue to build.

Certainly, collecting is a function of disposable income, but that is also improving worldwide. What is happening to prices? We, Charlton, come from a numismatic background, based in the 1960s, 70s and 80s. Our experience derives from a market that has seen wild gyrations in the supply and demand for over a forty-year period. Equating the numismatic market to the collectable market, what appears to be happening in the collectable field is exactly what occurred in the great coin melts of the late sixties to early eighties. The flood gates opened - attics, basements, garages, storage rooms, grandma's and grandpa's houses all disgorged their (coins) goodies. Today's collectables are being rushed to an on-line auction site (the melting pot), where they may be disposed of regardless of price.

How long will this go on? In the coin market, the melts lasted (as long as the precious metal prices rose) nearly 20 years. The rise in the intrinsic value of coins drew all and sundry out onto the market, identical to what is now happening to the on-line auctions and all collectables.

Everyone is rushing, looking for the next item to list on the on-line auction. When some item makes a tremendous splash (at a very high price), the hunt is on to find another like it.

With supply rising, prices will fall. Competition in the early stages will not be demand driven, but supply driven. With more competition, prices will fall. So what's the forecast?

Now, remember, this is over a long time period. Prices will move down from highs of the late-nineties, into lows for the mid-2000, and then rise again in mid-2010. The time frame mentioned may be over-estimated for we do deal with an infinite supply and the rate at which items change hands is certainly rapid.

Our guide prices will, over time, have the look of a large saucer-shaped curve for prices will rise.

Now this will not apply across the board, for what is now scarce will probably remain scarce. However, some will turn from scarce to plentiful as the flood changes the supply. The reverse will also be true, some things that are thought to be plentiful will be found to be scarce. There is one certainty: it will be an interesting time.

CONTENTS

HOW TO USE THIS CATALOGUE

The Listings

On the pages that follow Wade models are listed, illustrated, described and priced.

The measurements of the models are given in millimetres. Most items are measured according to their **height**. For relatively flat objects—ashtrays, dishes and some plaques—the measurement listed is the **diameter** of a round item, the **side** of a square or the **longest length** of a rectangle or oval. For a few items, such as boxes, some candlesticks, some plaques and posy bowls; both height and width are provided.

Although the publisher has made every attempt to obtain and photograph all models listed, several pieces, naturally, have not come into the publisher's possession.

A Word on Pricing

The purpose of this catalogue is to give readers the most accurate, up-to-date retail prices for Wade models in the United States, Canada and the United Kingdom.

To accomplish this The Charlton Press continues to access an international pricing panel of Wade experts who submit prices based on both dealer and collector retail price activity, as well as current auction results in U.S., Canadian, and U.K. markets. These market figures are carefully averaged to reflect accurate valuations for the Wade models listed herein in each of these three markets.

Please be aware that prices given in a particular currency are for models in that country only. The prices published herein have not been calculated using exchange rates—they have been determined solely by the supply and demand within the country in question.

A necessary word of caution. No pricing catalogue can be, or should be, a fixed price list. This catalogue should be considered as a guide only, one that shows the most current retail prices based on market demand within a particular region.

Current models, however, are priced differently. They are priced according to the manufacturer's suggested retail price in each of the three market regions. It should be noted, however, that it is likely that dealer discounting from these prices will occur.

The prices published herein are for items in mint condition.

Collectors are cautioned that a repaired or restored piece may be worth as little as 50 percent of the value of the same model in mint condition. Those collectors interested strictly in investment potential must avoid damaged items.

All relevant information must be known about an item in order to make a proper valuation. When comparing auction prices to catalogue prices, collectors and dealers should remember two important points. First, to compare "apples and apples," be sure that auction prices include a buyer's premium, if one is due. Prices realised for models in auction catalogues may not include this additional cost. Secondly, if an item is restored or repaired, it may not be noted in the listing, and as a result, the price will not be reflective of that same piece in mint condition.

INTRODUCTION

History

In the early 1930s, Wade consisted of three potteries—A.J. Wade Ltd., George Wade & Son Ltd. and Wade Heath and Co. Ltd.—with Wade Ulster (Ireland) being acquired in the mid 1940s. At first the company mainly produced gas burners for domestic lighting, although a small amount of gift ware was made as well. Later, Wade's chief output was insulating products, bobbins, thread guides and tiles. The company even made cone heads for guided missiles in the early 1960s.

At the onset of World War II, the government permitted the production of essential ceramics only. All gift ware production came to an end, with parts of the potteries being used as emergency food stores for the duration of the war. Afterwards the potteries were engaged in replacing the essential ceramics that had been destroyed by bombing. By the early 1950s, the George Wade Pottery began producing small collectable figures and animals.

Between 1955 and 1969 Wade Heath and Company Limited worked with Reginald Corfield (Sales) Ltd., of Redhill, Surrey (under the trademark of Regicor London), to produce a range of promotional and point-of-sale advertising ware. These earthenware products were produced by Wade Heath at its Royal Victoria Pottery in Burslem.

In 1958 the three English Wade potteries were restructured under the name Wade Potteries Ltd., later renamed Wade PLC. Wade (Ulster) Ltd. was renamed Wade Ireland in 1966.

The association with Reginald Corfield was discontinued in October 1969, and Wade Heath formed its own product, design and marketing company, called Wade PDM (PDM also stood for point of sale, design and marketing). This company specialises in advertising products for the distilling, brewing and tobacco industries, although it is not limited to those areas. It has become one of the leading suppliers of advertising products in the U.K.

In 1989 Wade PLC was taken over by Beauford PLC and renamed Wade Ceramics Ltd., in mid 1999 Beauford sold Wade Ceramics to Edward Duke (who was formally Beauford's chief executive) Alan Cooper and Paul Farmer, who were formally Wade Managing Director and Marketing Manager.

Wade Ireland was renamed Seagoe Ceramics by Beauford PLC in 1989, and continued to manufacture domestic tableware until 1993, when it reverted back to the production of industrial ceramics. Seagoe Ceramics is still owned by Beauford PLC.

The Production Process

The earthenware and Irish porcelain items in this book are made from a hard, solid china, sturdy enough to stand up to regular domestic use. They are produced from a mixture of ball clay, used for its plasticity, china clay, which gives the item a white body and plasticity, and china stone, used as a bonding agent.

Wade's porcelain, or bone china, items differ from earthenware in that they are of a lighter weight, thinner and are translucent. For these models a mixture of china clay, china stone and animal bone, which gives strength and transparency to the pieces, is used.

These materials are mixed in large vats of water, producing a thick sludge or "slip." The slip is passed into a filter to extract most of the water, leaving large flat "bats" of porcelain clay,

approximately two feet square and three inches thick. The clay bats are dried and then ground into dust ready for the forming process. Paraffin is added to the dust to assist in bonding and as a lubricant to remove the formed pieces from the steel moulds. Once pressed into the required shape, the clay articles are allowed to dry, then all the press marks are removed by sponging and "fettling," the scraping off of surplus clay with a sharp blade.

One or more ceramic colours is applied to the model, which is then sprayed with a clear glaze that, when fired, allows the colours underneath to show through. This process is known as underglaze decoration. On-glaze decoration—which includes enamelling, gilding and transfer printing—can also be done after the article has been glazed and fired.

Insuring Your Collection

As with any other of your valuables, making certain your models are protected is very important. It is paramount that you display or store any porcelain items in a secure place, preferably one safely away from traffic in the home.

Your models are most likely covered under your basic homeowner's policy. There are generally three kinds of such policies—standard, broad and comprehensive. Each has its own specific deductible and terms.

Under a general policy your models are considered part of the contents and are covered for all of the perils covered under the contractual terms of your policy (fire, theft, water damage and so on). However, since some models are extremely delicate, breakage is treated differently by most insurance companies.

There is usually an extra premium attached to insure models against accidental breakage by or carelessness of the owner. This is sometimes referred to as a "fine arts" rider. You are advised to contact your insurance professional to get all the answers.

In order to help protect yourself, it is critical that you take inventory of your models and have colour photographs taken of all your pieces. This is the surest method of clearly establishing, for the police and your insurance company, any items lost or destroyed. It is also the easiest way to establish their replacement value.

Backstamps

Most of the ink stamps used are black, although some Wade Heath and Wade marks are red, grey, green, brown or orange. The earliest ink stamps found in this book, which were used in the early 1930s, have a lion included in the stamp, along with "Wade England" or "Wadeheath England."

From the mid 1930s, the lion was omitted from the backstamp and often the design name - such as Flaxman Ware or Orcadia Ware - was included. Toward the end of the 1930s, the name *Wadeheath* was split in two to make *Wade Heath*; by the end of World War II, the *Heath* was dropped, leaving a Wade backstamp.

Beginning in the mid 1950s, Wade Ireland also used ink stamps to mark its models.

Transfer-printed Backstamps were introduced in 1953, and from that date onwards, they were used by both the English Wade potteries. Wade Ireland did use transfer prints, but they are not as common as ink stamps or their impressed and embossed backstamps.

BACKSTAMPS

INK BACKSTAMPS

TRANSFER PRINT BACKSTAMPS

TRANSFER PRINT BACKSTAMPS

IMPRESSED BACKSTAMPS

EMBOSSED BACKSTAMPS

Impressed and embossed backstamps are incorporated into the mould. It is very difficult to identify the dates of items marked with these backstamps, because when these models were reissued, sometimes as long as 20 years later, the same backstamp appeared. It is often impossible to tell which items were issued first, unless different colours were used on the reissue. This is often the case with Wade Ireland, which issued and reissued some of their popular lines two or three times, all of which carry the identical impressed or embossed backstamp.

FURTHER READING

Pre-War and More Wades, 1st Edition 1991 by Pat Murray
The Charlton Standard Catalogue of Wade Volume One General Issues, 2nd edition 1996; 3rd edition, 1999, by Pat Murray
The Charlton Standard Catalogue of Wade Volume Two Decorative Ware, 2nd edition 1996, by Pat Murray
The Charlton Standard Catalogue of Wade Volume Three Tableware, 2nd Edition 1998, by Pat Murray
The Charlton Standard Catalogue of Wade Volume Four Liquor Containers, 2nd ed. 1996, 3rd edition 1999, by Pat Murray
The Charlton Standard Catalogue of Wade Whimsical Collectables, 2nd, 3rd 4th and 5th editions 1996 -2000, by Pat Murray
The Wade Collectors Handbook, 1997, by Robert Prescott-Walker
The Wade Dynasty, 1996, by Dave Lee
The World of Wade, 1988, by Ian Warner with Mike Posgay
The World of Wade book 2, 1994, by Ian Warner and Mike Posgay
The World of Wade Price Trends, 1996, by Ian Warner and Mike Posgay
Whimsical Wades, 1st edition, 1986 by Pat Murray

CLUBS and NEWSLETTERS

The Official Wade Collectors Club

Founded in 1994, The Official Wade Collectors Club provides an information service on all aspects of the company's products, past and present. A club magazine, *Wade's World*, is published four times a year with information on new products and current events that will keep the collector up-to-date on the happenings in the world of Wade. Upon joining the club, each new member will receive a free gift and invitations to special events and exclusive offers

To join the Wade Collectors Club contact the club directly at:

**The Official International Wade Collectors Club
Royal Works, Westport Road
Burslem, Stoke-on-Trent, ST6 4AP
Staffordshire, England.**

The Wade Watch

The Wade Watch is a quarterly, six-page newsletter published by Collectors Corner. To join write to:

**Collectors Corner
8199 Pierson Court
Arvada, CO 8005
U.SA.**

ASHTRAYS AND LIGHTERS

c.1935-1993

Wade did not produce many ashtrays for the giftware market; most of their ashtrays were for advertising purposes. The majority of the ashtrays in this section were made by Wade Ireland from the mid 1950s to the late 1980s. The Irish ashtrays decorated with transfer prints were produced from the late 1950s to the early 1960s and again in 1993. Except for lighter cases made for advertising ware, only five decorative lighters have been found to date.

The items in this section are listed in alphabetical order within the following sub-chapters.

Wade Heath
Wade Ireland

BACKSTAMPS

Ink Stamps

The first type of backstamp used by Wade on its ashtrays was the black ink stamp that appeared on the flowers ashtrays, produced from the mid 1930s to 1939.

Embossed Backstamps

All the ashtrays with embossed backstamps were produced by Wade Ireland from the mid 1950s to the late 1970s.

Transfer Prints

Beginning in 1953 transfer prints were the predominant backstamp used by Wade.

Impressed Backstamps

All the ashtrays with impressed backstamps were produced by Wade Ireland in the 1950s. The lighters, produced from the late 1950s to the early 1970s, also have an impressed mark.

WADE HEATH ASHTRAYS

BARREL ASHTRAYS, c.1958

Wade made two types of Barrel ashtray, a half barrel and a quarter barrel. The original price of the half barrel was 9/6d. The centre print on 1b is of a Bugatti car.

Half barrel - two silver lustre bands   Quarter barrel - Golfing crest print

Backstamp: Red transfer print "Wade England"

No.	Description	Colourways	Size	U.S.$	Can.$	U.K.£
1a	Half barrel	Amber; two silver lustre bands	53	30.00	40.00	15.00
1b	Half barrel, Bugatti car	Amber; silver lustre band; multicoloured print	150	30.00	40.00	15.00
2	Quarter barrel, golfing crest	Amber; green / white print; black lettering	38 x 153	30.00	40.00	15.00

CUBE ASHTRAYS, 1959-c.1963

A transfer print of one or more different animal's heads can be found on each side of these cube ashtrays. The same prints can also be found on the wall plates, and Countrymen tankards (See *The Charlton Standard Catalogue of Wade, Volume One, General Issues)* and Countrymen dog and horse head dishes (see page 77).

Collie   Scottie/Terrier   Horses' heads

Backstamp: Transfer print "Wade England"

No.	Description	Colourways	Size	U.S.$	Can.$	U.K.£
1a	Collie	White; multicoloured print	67	15.00	20.00	8.00
1b	Poodle/terrier/scottie/spaniel	White; black poodle; brown/white terrier; grey scottie; black spaniel	67	15.00	20.00	8.00
1c	Poodle/terrier/scottie/spaniel	White; grey poodle; brown/white terrier; grey scottie/spaniel scottie; brown spaniel	67	15.00	20.00	8.00
1d	Horse's head	White; multicoloured print	67	15.00	20.00	8.00
1e	Horses' heads	White; multicoloured print	67	15.00	20.00	8.00

WADE HEATH ASHTRAYS (cont.)

DECORATIVE ASHTRAY, 1960s

This ashtray has no cigarette rests. The sides are decorated with pointed leaves and flowers in yellow edged rectangles.

Decorative ashtray

Backstamp: Red printed "Wade England"

No.	Description	Colourways	Size	U.S.$	Can.$	U.K.£
1	Decorative ashtray	White; black bowl; multicoloured flower prints	25 x 90	5.00	8.00	3.00

EXECUTIVE DESK SET ASHTRAY, 1993

This ashtray was part of an executive desk set produced by Wade for companies to present to their business clients. It was produced in an all-over black glaze with gold edging and a gold stylised lily transfer print in the centre.

Executive ashtray

Backstamp: Unknown

No.	Description	Colourways	Size	U.S.$	Can.$	U.K.£
1	Executive ashtray	Black; gold edges, emblem	Unknown	5.00	8.00	3.00

WADE HEATH ASHTRAYS (cont.)

FLAT, NON-TIP ASHTRAY, c.1937-1939

This non-tip ashtray has a mottled Flaxman Ware glaze.

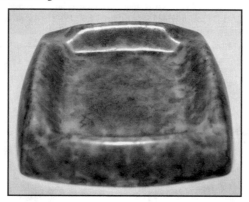

Backstamp: Ink stamp "Flaxman Wade Heath England"

No.	Description	Colourways	Size	U.S.$	Can.$	U.K.£
1	Flat, non-tip ashtray	Mottled green / brown	120	28.00	38.00	15.00

FLOWER ASHTRAYS, c.1935-1939

These dainty round ashtrays were produced as part of the second series of flowers (see section entitled Flowers). Two types of flower ashtray's have been found, No. 1 has two flowers and one cigarette rest, while No. 2 has three flowers, ([a] with pansy and primsoses, [b] with primroses) and two cigarette rests.

Flower ashtray; one cigarette rest

Flower ashtray; two cigarette rests

Backstamp: **A.** Hand written black ink "Wade England"
  B. Black ink stamp "Wade Made in England"

No.	Description	Colourways	Size	U.S.$	Can.$	U.K.£
1	Primroses, one rest	Pink tray; yellow flowers	85	26.00	36.00	15.00
2a	Pansy and primroses, two rests	Mottled green tray; blue, yellow, mauve flowers	85	26.00	36.00	18.00
2b	Primroses, two rests	Mottled grey tray; yellow, mauve; blue flowers	85	26.00	36.00	18.00

WADE HEATH ASTRAYS (cont.)

'HAPPY' ASHTRAYS, c.1939-1940

Although these ashtrays have a 1935-1937 backstamp they were actually produced c.1939-1940. Sir George Wade often toured the storerooms in the potteries and inquired about unsold stock, he would then say, "Stick 'em on something," and unsold models were combined to produce a new item. The ashtrays with their original 1935-1937 Flaxman Ware backstamp and the 1938 'Happy' dwarf pepper pot (from the Wadeheath 'Snow White' breakfast set) were unsold stock. The two were combined and reglazed in a new all-over colour to produce these novelty products.

Green non-tip ashtray

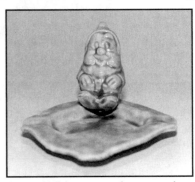

Cream with light green overglaze square ashtray

Backstamp: Black ink stamp "Flaxman Ware Hand Made Pottery By Wadeheath England"

No.	Description	Colourways	Size	U.S.$	Can.$	U.K.£
1.	'Happy' ashtray	Green	70 x 125	125.00	195.00	95.00
2.	'Happy' ashtray	Cream, light green overglaze	70 x 115	125.00	195.00	95.00

SOUVENIR ASHTRAYS, c.1953

The round ashtray has a transfer print of Niagara Falls, Canada, in the centre. A square ashtray has been seen with "Casa Loma, Toronto, Canada" in the centre.

Round ashtray - Niagara Falls print

Backstamp: Circular transfer print "Royal Victoria Pottery Wade England"

No.	Description	Colourways	Shape/Size	U.S.$	Can.$	U.K.£
1	Casa Loma, Toronto	Cream; gold rim; multicoloured print	Square/127	18.00	15.00	12.00
2	Niagara Falls, Canada	Cream/green; black print	Round/95	18.00	15.00	12.00

WADE IRELAND

IRISH PORCELAIN ASHTRAYS

A large range of Wade Ireland ashtrays was introduced and reissued throughout its 38 years of production. Only approximate dates can be given as very often the original moulds, which included impressed and embossed marks, were reissued with the same marks, with the exception of the shamrock range, and a small square ashtray found in a honey glaze. All the ashtrays are in the easily recognisable Irish Wade mottled blues and brownish-green glazes. The ashtrays are listed alphabetically by name (rim design), shape and shape number. Almost all the Wade Ireland ashtrays have a shape number (*I.P.* stands for Irish porcelain, *S.R.* for Shamrock Range).

CRINKLED EDGE ASHTRAYS

These round ashtrays are found in two sizes, they have crinkled edges and a print in the centre.

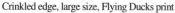

Crinkled edge, large size, Flying Ducks print   Crinkled edge, small size, Giant's Causeway print

Backstamp: **A.** Embossed circular "Irish Porcelain Made in Ireland" around a centre shamrock with a letter underneath; embossed "607" or "622"
B. Embossed circular "Made in Ireland Irish Porcelain" around a shamrock and crown design with "Wade Eire tir a dheanta" underneath; embossed "607" or "622"

Large round, (I.P. 622), c.1958-1975

No.	Description	Colourways	Shape No./Size	U.S.$	Can.$	U.K.£
1a	Blarney Castle	Blue/grey; multicoloured print	I.P.611/100	18.00	27.00	10.00
1b	Bunratty Castle	Honey; multicoloured print	I.P.611/100	18.00	27.00	10.00
1c	Flying ducks	Blue/grey; multicoloured print	I.P.611/100	18.00	27.00	10.00
1d	Irish colleen carrying peat to cottage	Grey/blue; multicoloured print; black lettering 'Ireland'	I.P.611/100	18.00	27.00	10.00
1e	Irish colleen carrying peat to cottage	Honey; multicoloured print; black lettering 'Ireland'	I.P.611/100	18.00	27.00	10.00
1f	Irish jaunting car	Grey/blue; multicoloured print	I.P.611/100	18.00	27.00	10.00
1g	Irish kitchen	Grey/blue; multicoloured print	I.P.611/100	18.00	27.00	10.00
1h	Irish passenger coach	Olive/grey; multicoloured print	I.P.611/100	18.00	27.00	10.00
1i	Stag's head	Blue/grey; multicoloured print	I.P.611/100	18.00	27.00	10.00
1j	Welsh dragon	Blue/grey; red dragon; black lettering 'Wales'	I.P.611/100	25.00	35.00	12.00

Small round, (I.P. 607), c.1958-1975

No.	Description	Colourways	Shape No./Size	U.S.$	Can.$	U.K.£
1a	Fisherman in river	Olive green/grey; multicoloured print	I.P.607/120	18.00	27.00	10.00
1b	Fisherman walking	Olive green/grey; multicoloured print	I.P.607/120	18.00	27.00	10.00
1c	Fisherman with salmon	Olive green/grey; multicoloured print	I.P.607/120	18.00	27.00	10.00
1d	Giant's Causeway	Olive green/grey; multicoloured print	I.P.607/120	18.00	27.00	10.00
1e	Irish colleen carrying peat	Olive green/grey; multicoloured print	I.P.607/120	18.00	27.00	10.00

IRISH PORCELAIN ASHTRAYS (cont.)

EVERLASTING CANDLESTICK ASHTRAY
(I.P. Unknown), c.1965

An Everlasting candle, which was produced by the Wade England pottery, was fitted in the centre of an Irish Porcelain ashtray.

Photograph not available
at press time

Backstamp: Embossed Circular "Irish Porcelain Made in Ireland" around a central shamrock

No.	Description	Colourways	Size	U.S.$	Can.$	U.K.£
1	Everlasting candlestick ashtray	Blue/grey	205	25.00	35.00	12.00

KNURLED RIM PIPE ASHTRAY
Round, (I.P. 623), c.1955

This round ashtray has a knurled pattern around the edge. There is a pear-shaped hollow on one side for a pipe to rest in and a raised plinth in the centre fitted with a piece of cork for knocking out the tobacco from a pipe.

Backstamp: Impressed "Irish Porcelain" over a large shamrock, with "Made in Ireland by Wade of Co. Armagh" printed underneath; embossed shape I.P.623

No.	Description	Colourways	Shape No./Size	U.S.$	Can.$	U.K.£
1	Pipe ashtray	Blue/green	I.P.623/153	20.00	30.00	8.00

IRISH PORCELAIN ASHTRAYS (cont.)

PLAIN RIM ASHTRAYS
Hexagonal, (I.P. 634), c.1955

These ashtrays have a plain rim and a transfer print in the centre.

Irish Colleen print

Backstamp: Impressed "Irish Porcelain" over a large shamrock, with "Made in Ireland by Wade of Co. Armagh" printed underneath; embossed I.P.634

No.	Description	Colourways	Shape No./Size	U.S.$	Can.$	U.K.£
1a	Irish colleen carrying peat	Olive/brown/pale blue; multicoloured print	I.P.634/146	18.00	27.00	10.00
1b	Irish jaunting car	Olive/brown/pale blue; multicoloured print	I.P.634/146	18.00	27.00	10.00

IRISH PORCELAIN ASHTRAYS *(cont.)*

ROSE RIM ASHTRAYS
Parallelogram, (I.P. 627), c.1972-c.1975

This unusual-shaped ashtray is half round and half square, with an embossed design of roses around the top edge and a transfer print in the centre, except for 1g which has a plain centre.

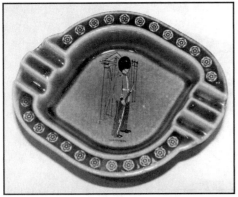

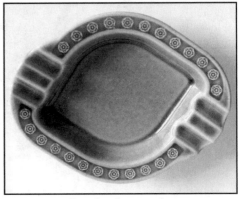

Rose rim ashtray, Guardsman print   Rose rim ashtray, no print

Backstamp: Embossed circular "Made in Ireland Irish Porcelain Wade Eire tir a dheanta" around a shamrock and crown design; embossed "627"

No.	Description	Colourways	Shape No./Size	U.S.$	Can.$	U.K.£
1a	Duck hunter	Olive green/brown; multicoloured print	I.P.627/146	24.00	37.00	12.00
1b	Flying pheasants	Olive green/brown; multicoloured print	I.P.627/146	24.00	37.00	12.00
1c	Fox hunter on horse, hat in hand	Olive green/brown; multicoloured print	I.P.627/146	24.00	37.00	12.00
1d	Fox hunter on horse, hat on head	Olive green/brown; multicoloured print	I.P.627/146	24.00	37.00	12.00
1e	Guardsman	Olive green/brown; multicoloured print;	I.P.627/146	24.00	37.00	12.00
1f	Irish kitchen	Olive green/brown; multicoloured print	I.P.627/146	24.00	37.00	12.00
1g	Plain	Olive green/brown	I.P.627/146	18.00	27.00	10.00
1h	Two fisherman by river	Olive green/brown; multicoloured print	I.P.627/146	24.00	37.00	12.00
1i	Two fisherman walking	Olive green/brown; multicoloured print	I.P.627/146	24.00	37.00	12.00

IRISH PORCELAIN ASHTRAYS (cont.)

SHAMROCKS AND IRISH-KNOT RIM ASHTRAYS

There are two sizes in the square ashtrays. The top edge of the small size ashtrays (I.P.611) are embossed with a design of shamrocks and Irish knots, with a cigarette rest at each corner. An unusual find in the small size is the 'honey' glazed ashtrays with Bunratty Castle and Irish Colleen prints, (2b and 2e).

The top edge of the large ashtrays (I.P. 626) is embossed with a design of shamrocks, and has the cigarette rests on only two of the four sides.

Large square - Bunratty Castle print   Small square - Irish colleen print

Backstamp: A. Impressed "Irish Porcelain" over a small shamrock with "Made In Ireland by Wade of Co. Armagh" underneath; embossed shape "626" or "611"
B. Embossed circular "Made in Ireland Irish Porcelain Wade Eire tire dheanta;" "626" (1971-1976)

Large square, Shamrocks, (I.P. 626), c.1955

No.	Description	Colourways	Shape No./Size	U.S.$	Can.$	U.K.£
1a	Bunratty Castle	Blue/grey; multicoloured print	I.P.626/153	24.00	37.00	12.00
1b	Fisherman in river	Blue/grey; multicoloured print	I.P.626/153	24.00	37.00	12.00
1c	Fox hunter on horse, hat in hand	Blue/grey; multicoloured print	I.P.626/153	24.00	37.00	12.00
1d	Fox hunter on horse, hat on head	Blue/grey; multicoloured print	I.P.626/153	24.00	37.00	12.00
1e	Hunter facing left	Blue/grey; multicoloured print	I.P.626/153	24.00	37.00	12.00
1f	Irish Colleen carrying peat to cottage	Blue/grey; multicoloured print; black lettering 'Ireland'	I.P.626/153	24.00	37.00	12.00
1g	Irish Jaunting Car	Blue/grey; multicoloured print	I.P.626/153	24.00	37.00	12.00
1h	Irish kitchen	Blue/grey; multicoloured print	I.P.626/153	24.00	37.00	12.00
1i	The Giant Finn MacCaul	Blue/grey; multicoloured print	I.P.626/153	24.00	37.00	12.00

Small square, Shamrocks and Irish-knots, (I.P. 611), c.1955-1989

No.	Description	Colourways	Shape No./Size	U.S.$	Can.$	U.K.£
2a	Blarney Castle	Blue/grey; multicoloured print	I.P.611/100	18.00	27.00	10.00
2b	Bunratty Castle	Honey; multicoloured print	I.P.611/100	18.00	27.00	10.00
2c	Flying ducks	Blue/grey; multicoloured print	I.P.611/100	18.00	27.00	10.00
2d	Irish Colleen carrying peat to cottage	Grey/blue; multicoloured print; black lettering 'Ireland'	I.P.611/100	18.00	27.00	10.00
2e	Irish Colleen carrying peat to cottage	Honey; multicoloured print; black lettering 'Ireland'	I.P.611/100	18.00	27.00	10.00
2f	Irish jaunting car	Grey/blue; multicoloured print	I.P.611/100	18.00	27.00	10.00
2g	Irish kitchen	Grey/blue; multicoloured print	I.P.611/100	18.00	27.00	10.00
2h	Irish passenger coach	Olive/grey; multicoloured print	I.P.611/100	18.00	27.00	10.00
2i	Stag's head	Blue/grey; multicoloured print	I.P.611/100	18.00	27.00	10.00
2j	Welsh dragon	Blue/grey; red dragon; black lettering 'Wales'	I.P.611/100	25.00	35.00	12.00

IRISH PORCELAIN ASHTRAYS *(cont.)*

SHAMROCKS AND IRISH-KNOT RIM ASHTRAYS
Triangular, (I.P.612), c.1955-c.1958, c.1972-c.1975

The top edges of these ashtrays are embossed with a design of shamrocks and Irish knots. There is a transfer print in the centre.

Irish Colleen print

Irish Jaunting-car print

Backstamp: **A.** Embossed circular "Irish Porcelain Made in Ireland" around a shamrock with a letter underneath
B. Embossed circular "Made in Ireland Irish Porcelain" around a shamrock and crown design with "Wade Eire tir a dheanta" underneath; embossed "612"

No.	Description	Colourways	Shape No./Size	U.S.$	Can.$	U.K.£
1a	Bunratty Castle	Blue/grey; multicoloured print	I.P.612/95	24.00	37.00	12.00
1b	City Hall, Belfast	Blue/grey; multicoloured print	I.P.612/95	24.00	37.00	12.00
1c	Irish colleen	Blue/grey/green; multicoloured print	I.P.612/95	24.00	37.00	12.00
1d	Irish cottage	Blue/grey/green; multicoloured print	I.P.612/95	24.00	37.00	12.00
1e	Irish jaunting car	Blue/grey/green; multicoloured print	I.P.612/95	24.00	37.00	12.00
1f	Irish passenger coach	Blue/grey/green; multicoloured print	I.P.612/95	24.00	37.00	12.00
1g	Leprechaun	Blue/grey/green; multicoloured print	I.P.612/95	24.00	37.00	12.00
1h	Stag's head	Blue/grey/green; multicoloured print	I.P.612/95	24.00	37.00	12.00

IRISH PORCELAIN ASHTRAYS (cont.)

THISTLE RIM ASHTRAYS
Round, (I.P. 628), c.1972-c.1977

These round ashtrays have an embossed design of thistles around the top edge and a transfer print in the centre.

Backstamp: Embossed circular "Made in Ireland Irish Porcelain Wade Eire tir a dheanta" around a shamrock and crown; embossed "628"

No.	Description	Colourways	Shape No./Size	U.S.$	Can.$	U.K.£
1a	Duck hunter	Blue/grey; multicoloured print	I.P.628/153	24.00	37.00	12.00
1b	Flying pheasants	Blue/grey; multicoloured print	I.P.628/153	24.00	37.00	12.00
1c	Fox hunter on horse	Blue/grey; multicoloured print	I.P.628/153	24.00	37.00	12.00
1d	Giant Finn MacCaul	Blue/grey; multicoloured print	I.P.628/153	24.00	37.00	12.00
1e	Stag's head	Blue/grey; multicoloured print	I.P.628/153	24.00	37.00	12.00
1f	Trotting horse	Blue/grey; multicoloured print	I.P.628/153	24.00	37.00	12.00

IRISH PORCELAIN LIGHTERS

MISCELLANEOUS SHAPES, c.1958-c.1980

Some of the table lighters are set in the tops of Irish Porcelain models which were originally sold as souvenirs such as the Irish Cooking pot and the Killarney Urn posy bowls. The decoration on the porcelain is either an impressed band of shamrocks or a row of knurls. The posy bowl, miniature tankard and 'stemmed' lighters are Irish Wade shapes which have not been previously recorded. The stemmed lighter has a model of the First Whimsie Crocodile attached to the base

LIGHTERS

Irish cooking pot shape

Killarney urn table lighter

Miniature tankard shape

Posy bowl table lighter

Stemmed table light with crocodile

Backstamp: **A.** Impressed "Irish Porcelain Made in Ireland" curved over a shamrock
Shape No.: I.P.95 (Kilarney Urn table lighter)
        B. Circular embossed "Irish Porcelain Made in Ireland"

No.	Description	Colourways	Shape No./Size	U.S.$	Can.$	U.K.£
1	Irish cooking pot table lighter	Grey/blue	85	20.00	35.00	12.00
2	Killarney urn table lighter	Grey/blue	IP.95/100	20.00	35.00	12.00
3	Miniature tankard table lighter	Grey/blue	100	20.00	35.00	12.00
4	Posy bowl table lighter	Grey/blue	60	20.00	35.00	12.00
5	Stemmed table lighter with crocodile	Grey/blue; greenish brown crocodile	100	30.00	45.00	20.00

SHAMROCK RANGE

SHAMROCK ASHTRAYS

The transfer prints on these ashtrays are of shamrocks.

Large ashtray with gold rim (SR17)

Small ashtray without gold rim (SR18)

Backstamp: Circular transfer print "Made in Ireland Porcelain Wade Eire tir a dheanta" around a shamrock and crown design

Large round, (SR17)

No.	Description	Colourways	Shape No./Size	U.S.$	Can.$	U.K.£
1	Shamrock ashtray	White; gold rim; green print	S.R.17/177	20.00	30.00	12.00

Small round, (SR18)

No.	Description	Colourways	Shape No./Size	U.S.$	Can.$	U.K.£
1	Shamrock ashtray	White; green print with gold edge	S.R.18/153	20.00	30.00	12.00

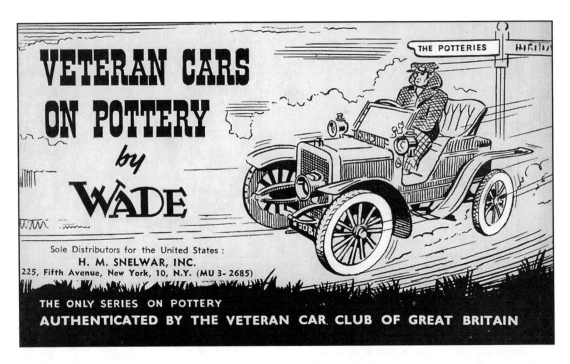

VETERAN CARS ON POTTERY by WĀDE

Sole Distributors for the United States :
H. M. SNELWAR, INC.
225, Fifth Avenue, New York, 10, N.Y. (MU 3- 2685)

THE ONLY SERIES ON POTTERY
AUTHENTICATED BY THE VETERAN CAR CLUB OF GREAT BRITAIN

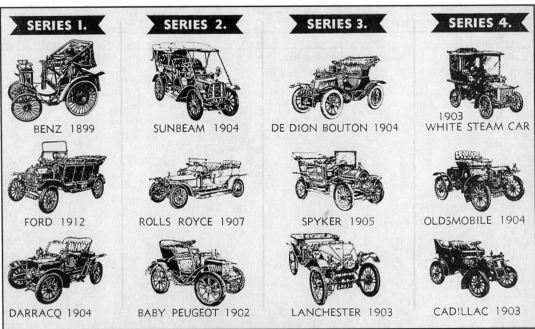

SERIES 1.	SERIES 2.	SERIES 3.	SERIES 4.
BENZ 1899	SUNBEAM 1904	DE DION BOUTON 1904	1903 WHITE STEAM CAR
FORD 1912	ROLLS ROYCE 1907	SPYKER 1905	OLDSMOBILE 1904
DARRACQ 1904	BABY PEUGEOT 1902	LANCHESTER 1903	CADILLAC 1903

BASKETS

c.1937-c.1953

Most Wade baskets were produced in all-over colours, many with embossed designs. A few were decorated with hand-painted flowers. The baskets are listed in shape-number order with all being made at the Wade Heath factory.

Wade Heath

BACKSTAMPS

Ink Stamps

The backstamps used on Wade's baskets were ink stamps such as Flaxman Wade Heath England, Harvest Ware Wade England, Wade Heath England and a handwritten Wade England. In most cases the shape number is impressed on the base.

BASKETS

SHAPE 161, BASKET WITH GOTHIC WARE DESIGN, 1940 and 1946-1953.

This basket is embossed with a design of swirling leaves and tulips. In 1940 an advertisement declared a new series of "Embossed Modelled Gothic Ornamental Ware" will be offered. The Gothic ware was first issued with a Flaxman glaze. Also, a November 1946 advertisement showing the Gothic basket in gloss colours with gold highlighting has been found.

Shape 161 - Gothic ware with Flaxman glaze   Shape 161 - Gothic ware with gloss glaze

Backstamp A. Ink stamp "Flaxman Wade Heath England"
B. Green Ink Stamp "Wade England Gothic" with impressed "161"
C. Gold printed "Wade Made in England Hand Painted Gothic" with impressed "161"

No.	Description	Colourways	Size	U.S.$	Can.$	U.K.£
1a	Gothic ware	Mottled green/orange	175	90.00	125.00	45.00
1b	Gothic ware	Cream; lilac / pink flowers; green / gold leaves; gloss	175	100.00	145.00	50.00

SHAPE 246 AND 246a, BASKETS WITH LEAF OR GOTHIC WARE DESIGNS, 1937-1939 / 1947

Five of these baskets are decorated with an embossed design of swirling leaves. The fifth basket (No. 2) is the same basic shape as the previous basket but is slightly taller and has an embossed Gothic design of swirling leaves and tulips, with a high gloss and gold highlights finish.

Shape 246 - Leaf design; Flaxman glaze   Shape 246a - Gothic ware design; high gloss glaze

Backstamp: A. Black ink stamp "Flaxman Wade Heath England"
B. Black ink stamp "Gothic Wade England"

No.	Description	Colourways	Size	U.S.$	Can.$	U.K.£
1a	Leaf design	Cream; gold rim; mottled green leaves	125	75.00	105.00	48.00
1b	Leaf design	Mottled blue/green/brown	125	65.00	95.00	38.00
1c	Leaf design	Mottled blue/yellow	125	65.00	95.00	38.00
1d	Leaf design	Mottled pale yellow/brown	125	65.00	95.00	38.00
1e	Leaf design	Mottled pale orange/green	125	65.00	95.00	38.00
2	Gothic design	Cream; gold; pink/lilac flowers; green/yellow leaves	145	85.00	120.00	58.00

BASKETS (cont.)

SHAPE 247, BASKET WITH BRICK DESIGN, c.1938

All known baskets of this design have the Flaxman glaze.

Brick design basket

Backstamp: Black ink stamp "Wade England Flaxman"

No.	Description	Colourways	Size	U.S.$	Can.$	U.K.£
1a	Brick design	Mottled blue	130	55.00	80.00	30.00
1b	Brick design	Mottled green/dark yellow	130	55.00	80.00	30.00
1c	Brick design	Mottled pale yellow	130	55.00	80.00	30.00
1d	Brick design	Mottled pale yellow/green	130	55.00	80.00	30.00

SHAPE 248, BASKET WITH VERTICAL RIB DESIGN, 1937-1939, 1953

Shape 248 was first decorated with Flaxman glazes between 1937 and 1939. The basket has a vertical rib design. A later version has been found with hand-painted flowers and leaves, dated between 1948 and 1952. The basket also appears with the colourway belonging to the Peony series.

Mottled orange and green

Backstamp: A. Black ink stamp "Flaxman Wade Heath England"
B. Black ink stamp "Harvest Ware Wade England" with impressed "248"

No.	Description	Colourways	Size	U.S.$	Can.$	U.K.£
1a	Flaxman glaze	Mottled blue/brown	130	55.00	80.00	30.00
1b	Flaxman glaze	Mottled green/pale yellow	130	55.00	80.00	30.00
1c	Flaxman glaze	Mottled orange/green	130	55.00	80.00	30.00
1d	Flaxman glaze	Mottled yellow/green	130	55.00	80.00	30.00
2	Hand-painted	Cream; large purple flowers; green leaves	130	70.00	95.00	35.00
3	Hand-painted	Cream; purple/mauve/dark red peonies	155	75.00	90.00	40.00

BASKETS (cont.)

SHAPE 250, BASKET EMBOSSED FLOWERS, 1937-1939

This basket has an embossed basket-weave and flowers design.

Basket weave with flowers

Backstamp: **A.** Black ink stamp "Flaxman Wade Heath England"
B. Black ink stamp "Wade Heath England"
C. Impressed "250"

No.	Description	Colourways	Size	U.S.$	Can.$	U.K.£
1	Basket weave and flowers	Cream; pink/mauve/yellow flowers	130	65.00	85.00	30.00

SHAPE No.: UNKNOWN, DUTCH FLOWER BASKET, c.1937-c.1939, c.1948-1953

The two ends of this large unusual shaped basket curve inward and come to a point.

Dutch flower basket

Backstamp: **A.** Black ink stamp "Flaxman Wade Heath England," c.1937-1939
B. Black ink stamp "Wade England," c.1948-1953

No.	Description	Colourways	Size	U.S.$	Can.$	U.K.£
1a	Flower basket	Mottled blue/orange	200 x 270	70.00	100.00	55.00
1b	Flower basket	Mottled green	200 x 270	70.00	100.00	55.00
1c	Flower basket	Mottled green/orange	200 x 270	70.00	100.00	55.00
1d	Flower basket	Mottled orange	200 x 270	70.00	100.00	55.00

BASKETS *(cont.)*

SHAPE No.: *UNKNOWN, WOVEN BASKET WITH ROSES, c.1937-c.1939*

This earthenware basket, probably intended as a trinket dish, was part of the first series of flowers made by Wade (see Flowers section).

Woven basket

Backstamp: **A.** Raised "British Made" and black handwritten "Wade England"
B. Raised "British Made"
C. Black handwritten "Wade England"

No.	Description	Colourway	Size	U.S.$	Can.$	U.K.£
1	Woven basket	Four pink roses on rim; pale blue basket	25 x 80	20.00	25.00	12.00

BOWLS

c.1930-1992

Wade produced many shapes in bowls, and then decorated them in various designs such as Black Frost, Gothic Ware, Harmony Ware, Orcadia Ware and the Peony Series. These bowls were part of a set that could include dishes, jugs and vases. The bowls in this section are divided into two sections and then listed in alphabetical order with shape numbers second if known.

Wade Heath
Wade Ireland

BACKSTAMPS

Handwritten Backstamp

The first backstamp Wade used on its bowls was handwritten and appeared from c.1930 to c.1935.

Ink Stamps

Ink stamps were used on bowls from 1933 to the early 1950s, after which time transfer prints were generally used.

Transfer Prints

Transfer prints were commonly used as backstamps beginning in 1953. They appear on many of Wade's bowls from 1953 to 1992.

Impressed Backstamps

The only impressed mark on the bowls appears on some of the Harmony Ware, from 1957 to the mid 1960s.

Embossed Backstamps

The only embossed backstamp used on Wade's bowls appears on the Celtic Porcelain bowl, produced in 1965.

WADE HEATH

BEACON BOWLS, 1958-1959

This set of four round bowls came boxed together. They were designed as nut or candy bowls for bridge parties. The prices below are for single bowls.

Boxed set of Beacon bowls

Backstamp: Red transfer print "Wade England"

No.	Description	Colourways	Size	U.S.$	Can.$	U.K.£
1a	Beacon	White rim; black centre	100	15.00	22.00	8.00
1b	Beacon	White rim; green centre	100	15.00	22.00	8.00
1c	Beacon	White rim; red centre	100	15.00	22.00	8.00
1d	Beacon	White rim; yellow centre	100	15.00	22.00	8.00

BLACK FROST NUT BOWLS, 1957-c.1960

In 1957 a series of ten black colourway shapes, including vases were produced with frosted white transfer prints of British wild flowers on the front and back. The flowers include mallow, scarlet pimpernel, forget-me-not, daisy and others

A variety of flower prints on Black Frost nut bowls

Backstamp: **A.** Red print "Wade England"
B. White print "Wade England"

No.	Description	Colourways	Size	U.S.$	Can.$	U.K.£
1	Black Frost	Black; white flowers; gold rim	100	15.00	22.00	8.00

WADE HEATH *(cont.)*

CHELSEA SERIES BOWLS, 1962

There are two basic bowl shapes, sloping and cup, coupled with three different feet, plain, ribbed, and ribbed with handles. These bowls are very similar in shape to the Empress series.

Chelsea ribbed foot bowl

Chelsea ribbed foot bowl, handles at base

Backstamp: Red transfer print "Wade England"

No.	Description	Colourways	Size	U.S.$	Can.$	U.K.£
1	Plain foot	Black	115	40.00	55.00	22.00
2	Plain foot/handles at base	White	115	40.00	55.00	22.00
3	Plain foot/sloping rim	Black	133	51.00	70.00	25.00
4	Ribbed foot	White	92	40.00	55.00	22.00
5	Ribbed foot	Black	115	40.00	55.00	22.00
6a	Ribbed foot	Black	130	40.00	55.00	22.00
6b	Ribbed foot	White	130	40.00	55.00	22.00
7a	Ribbed foot/handles at base	White	115	40.00	55.00	25.00
7b	Ribbed foot/handles at base	White; gold	115	50.00	70.00	35.00
8	Small foot	Black	115	30.00	40.00	18.00
9	Urn ribbed foot	Black	190	45.00	65.00	32.00

WADE HEATH (cont.)

CHINTZ ROSE BOWL, 2000

This rose bowl is decorated with the original Butterfly pattern first used in 1939 on Wadeheath Chintz tableware. See also Millennium rose bowl, page 36 and Rose bowls, page 39.

Backstamp: Gold printed "Wade England" with two lines

No.	Description	Colourways	Size	U.S.$	Can.$	U.K.£
1	Butterfly chintz	Multicoloured	85 x 160	35.00	50.00	25.00

COPPER-LUSTRE POWDER BOWLS, c.1948

These copper-lustre powder bowls were all hand decorated; therefore, each decoration will be slightly different. There are four versions of the Daisy flower, heart, pointed, round and straight edged petals. There are two styles, round and wavy bases. The original price was 2/9d.

Aster, wavy base   Daisy, round base

Backstamp: A. Green ink stamp "Harvest Ware Wade England" and impressed "Made in England"
B. Gold stamp "Wade England" and impressed "Made in England"
C. Printed "Wade Made in England Hand Painted"

No.	Description	Colourways	Size	U.S.$	Can.$	U.K.£
1	Aster, wavy base	Copper bowl, lid; pink/yellow flower; pale green leaves	45 x 105	30.00	40.00	18.00
2a	Daisy, round base	All-over copper lustre	45 x 105	30.00	40.00	15.00
2b	Daisy, round base	Copper bowl; cream lid with copper rim; mauve/ yellow flower; green leaves; brown streaks	45 x 105	30.00	40.00	18.00

WADE HEATH *(cont.)*

EMPRESS FRUIT BOWL, SHAPE 408, c.1948-c.1954

This cupped shaped footed bowl with handles off the base is similar in design to the handled Chelsea bowls. The mottled green colourway was issued c.1948, and the white c.1954.

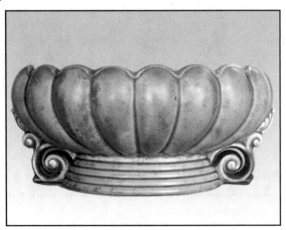

Empress fruit bowl

Backstamp: **A.** Circular ink stamp "Royal Victoria Pottery Wade England"
B. Black ink stamp "Wade England" with impressed "408"
C. Black ink stamp "Wade England"

No.	Description	Colourways	Size	U.S.$	Can.$	U.K.£
1a	Empress	Mottled green	177 x 390	250.00	350.00	105.00
1b	Empress	White	177 x 390	200.00	350.00	105.00

FALSTAFF ROSE BOWL, c.1972

Wade produced this porcelain footed rose bowl and the Falstaff Silver Plating Company produced the silver plated flower frog.

Falstaff rose bowl

Backstamp: Embossed "Wade Falstaff England"

No.	Description	Colourways	Size	U.S.$	Can.$	U.K.£
1	Falstaff rose bowl	Royal blue; silver plated frog	Unknown	60.00	80.00	25.00

WADE HEATH (cont.)

FLOWER CENTRE BOWL, c.1930-c.1935

This earthenware bowl was made to hold the flower centres produced by Wade (see Flowers section). It was part of the first series of flowers.

Photograph not available
at press time

Backstamp: Raised "British Made" with an impressed code letter and sometimes a black handwritten "Wade England" or "Made in England"

No.	Description	Colourways	Size	U.S.$	Can.$	U.K.£
1	Bowl	Black	25 x 45	10.00	15.00	5.00

GOTHIC WARE BOWLS, 1940 and NOVEMBER 1946-1953

These shallow bowls are embossed with a design of swirling leaves and tulips. In 1940 an advertisement declared a new series of "Embossed Modelled Gothic Ornamental Ware" will be offered. The Gothic ware was first issued with a Flaxman glaze. Also, a November 1946 advertisment showing the Gothic bowl in gloss colours with gold highlighting has been found.

Backstamp: Black ink stamp "Gothic Wade Heath England"

No.	Description	Colourways	Size	U.S.$	Can.$	U.K.£
1a	Gothic, Flaxman	Cream	55 x 235	60.00	80.00	30.00
1b	Gothic, Flaxman	Pale green	55 x 235	60.00	80.00	30.00
1c	Gothic, high gloss	Cream; lilac/pink flowers; green/yellow leaves; gold highlights	55 x 235	90.00	125.00	45.00
1d	Gothic, high gloss	Cream; pink flowers; pale green leaves	55 x 235	60.00	80.00	35.00

WADE HEATH (cont.)

GREAT BRITAIN BOWLS, 1959

These souvenir nut bowls are from the same moulds as the 1958 Beacon bowls.

Eros, Piccadilly Circus

London Coat of Arms

Backstamp: Green transfer print "Wade England"

No.	Description	Colourways	Size	U.S.$	Can.$	U.K.£
1a	Eros, Piccadilly Circus	Black; gold rim; white print	100	12.00	16.00	6.00
1b	London, Coat of Arms	White; red band; multicoloured print	100	12.00	16.00	6.00
1c	London, Coat of Arms	White; black band; multicoloured print	100	12.00	16.00	6.00
1d	Trafalgar Square	Black; gold rim; white print	100	12.00	16.00	6.00

WADE HEATH *(cont.)*

HARMONY WARE BOWLS, 1957-c.1962

Between 1957 and the early 1960s, Wade produced a variety of thirteen bowls, jugs and vases that were called Harmony Ware. They were decorated with transfer prints in four different designs, Carnival, Fern, Parasols and Shooting Stars, and for a short time they were also produced in solid and two-tone colours.

Shape 439, Plain-footed Bowl

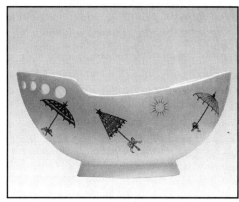

Carnival print   Parasols print

Backstamp: **A.** Red transfer "Wade England" with impressed "England" and "439"
B. Red transfer "Wade England Fern" with impressed "England" and "439"
C. Black transfer "Wade England Parasol" with impressed "England" and "439"
D. Black transfer "Wade England" with impressed "England" and "439"
E. Black transfer "Wade England" and green shooting stars with impressed "England" and "439"
F. Impressed "Wade England" and "439"

No.	Description	Colourways	Size	U.S.$	Can.$	U.K.£
1a	Carnival	White; yellow/red/green flowers	140 x 280	90.00	120.00	45.00
1b	Fern	White; black/red/fern	140 x 280	90.00	120.00	45.00
1c	Parasols	White; multicoloured parasols	140 x 280	90.00	120.00	45.00
1d	Shooting stars	White; multicoloured stars	140 x 280	90.00	120.00	45.00
1e	Solid colour	Black	140 x 280	90.00	120.00	45.00
1f	Solid colour	Green	140 x 280	90.00	120.00	45.00
1g	Solid colour	White	140 x 280	90.00	120.00	45.00
1h	Solid colour	Yellow	140 x 280	90.00	120.00	45.00
1i	Two-tone	Green/peach	140 x 280	90.00	120.00	45.00
1j	Two-tone	Grey/pink	140 x 280	90.00	120.00	45.00

WADE HEATH (cont.)

HARMONY WARE BOWLS (cont.)
Shape 440, Three-footed Bowl

Carnival print

Two-tone colourway

Parasol print

Backstamp: **A.** Red transfer "Wade England" with impressed "England" and "440"
B. Red transfer "Wade England Fern" with impressed "England" and "440"
C. Black transfer "Wade England Parasol" with impressed "England" and "440"
D. Black transfer "Wade England" with impressed "England" and "440"
E. Black transfer "Wade England" and green shooting stars with impressed "England" and "440"
F. Impressed "Wade England" and "440"

No.	Description	Colourways	Size	U.S.$	Can.$	U.K.£
1a	Carnival	White; yellow/red/green flowers	125 x 222	90.00	120.00	45.00
1b	Fern	White; black/red fern	125 x 222	90.00	120.00	45.00
1c	Parasols	White; multicoloured parasols	125 x 222	90.00	120.00	45.00
1d	Shooting stars	White; multicoloured stars	125 x 222	90.00	120.00	45.00
1e	Solid colour	Black	125 x 222	90.00	120.00	45.00
1f	Solid colour	Green	125 x 222	90.00	120.00	45.00
1g	Solid colour	White	125 x 222	90.00	120.00	45.00
1h	Solid colour	Yellow	125 x 222	90.00	120.00	45.00
1i	Two-tone	Green/peach	125 x 222	90.00	120.00	45.00
1j	Two-tone	Grey/pink	125 x 222	90.00	120.00	45.00

WADE HEATH (cont.)

HARMONY WARE BOWLS (cont.)
Shape No. 449, Shallow-footed Bowl

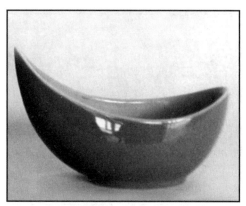

Two-tone colourway

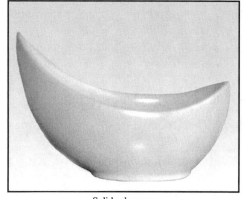

Solid colourway

Backstamp: **A.** Red transfer "Wade England" with impressed "England" and "449"
B. Red transfer "Wade England Fern" with impressed "England" and "449"
C. Black transfer "Wade England Parasol" with impressed "England" and "449"
D. Black transfer "Wade England" with impressed "England" and "449"
E. Black transfer "Wade England" and green shooting stars with impressed "England" and "449"
F. Impressed "Wade England" and "449"

No.	Description	Colourways	Size	U.S.$	Can.$	U.K.£
1a	Carnival	White; yellow/red/green flowers	62 x 105	10.00	15.00	5.00
1b	Fern	White; black/red fern	62 x 105	10.00	15.00	5.00
1c	Parasols	White; multicoloured parasols	62 x 105	10.00	15.00	5.00
1d	Shooting stars	White; multicoloured stars	62 x 105	10.00	15.00	5.00
1e	Solid colour	Copper	62 x 105	8.00	10.00	4.00
1f	Solid colour	White	62 x 105	8.00	10.00	4.00
1g	Two-tone	Green/peach	62 x 105	8.00	10.00	4.00
1h	Two-tone	Grey/pink	62 x 105	8.00	10.00	4.00

WADE HEATH (cont.)

HARMONY WARE BOWLS *(cont.)*
Shape 450, Shallow-footed Bowl

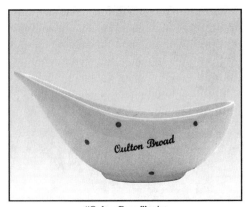

Fern print

"Oulton Broad" print

Backstamp: **A.** Red transfer "Wade England" with impressed "England" and "450"
B. Red transfer "Wade England Fern" with impressed "England" and "450"
C. Black transfer "Wade England Parasol" with impressed "England" and "450"
D. Black transfer "Wade England" with impressed "England" and "450"
E. Black transfer "Wade England" and green shooting stars with impressed "England" and "450"
F. Impressed "Wade England" and "450"

No.	Description	Colourways	Size	U.S.$	Can.$	U.K.£
1a	Carnival	White; yellow/red/green flowers	62 x 130	8.00	10.00	3.00
1b	Fern	White; black/red fern; red spots	62 x 130	8.00	10.00	3.00
1c	"Oulton Broad"	White; red spots; black lettering	62 x 130	8.00	10.00	3.00
1d	Parasols	White; multicoloured parasols	62 x 130	8.00	10.00	3.00
1e	Shooting stars	White; multicoloured stars	62 x 130	8.00	10.00	3.00
1f	Solid colour	Grey	62 x 130	8.00	10.00	3.00
1g	Two-tone	Green/peach	62 x 130	8.00	10.00	3.00
1h	Two-tone	Grey/pink	62 x 130	8.00	10.00	3.00

Shape No. Unknown, Five-sided Bowl, c.1965

In the mid 1960s, a shallow bowl with a hole on each side and five odd-shaped sides, resembling a spinning Catherine wheel, was added to the Harmony range. It is a larger version of a four-sided bowl produced by Wadeheath in its early-1950s Bramble tableware series.

Photograph not available
at press time

Backstamp: Red printed "Wade England"

No.	Description	Colourways	Size	U.S.$	Can.$	U.K.£
1	Parasols	White; multicoloured parasols	45 x 175	32.00	48.00	25.00

WADE HEATH (cont.)

HARVEST WARE BOWL, SINGLE HANDLE, SHAPE 369, c.1948-c.1952

This Harvest Ware bowl was decorated in the design of the Peony Series of large purple, mauve and dark red peonies.

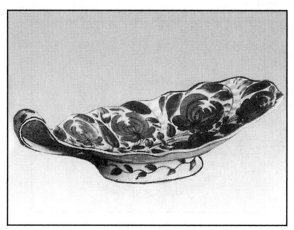

Harvest ware bowl

Backstamp: Black ink stamp "Harvest Ware Wade England" with impressed "369"

No.	Description	Colourways	Size	U.S.$	Can.$	U.K.£
1	Harvest ware	Cream; multicoloured flowers	85 x 220	60.00	80.00	30.00

IMPERIAL BOWL, 1955

Part of the Imperial Series, this bowl was produced in early 1955.

Photograph not available
at press time

Backstamp: Circular print "Wade Made in England Hand Painted"

No.	Description	Colourways	Size	U.S.$	Can.$	U.K.£
1	Imperial	Burgundy; white seed; gold highlights	140	60.00	80.00	30.00

WADE HEATH (cont.)

MILLENNIUM ROSE BOWL, 1999-2000

Produced as part of the Millennium set (see also bells, platters and trinket boxes), this hexagonal rose bowl was produced in two colourways. See also Chintz rose bowl on page 27, and Rose bowl, page 39.

Backstamp: Printed "Wade England" between two lines

No.	Description	Colourways	Size	U.S.$	Can.$	U.K.£
1a	Black/gold	Black; gold decorative prints	85 x 160	35.00	50.00	25.00
1b	Blue/silver	Dark blue; silver decorative prints	85 x 160	35.00	50.00	25.00

NUT BOWLS 1953-c.1968

Produced as nut bowls for card parties, these bowls have different transfer prints in the centre. The bowls are the same shape as the Beacon Bowls and were sold in boxed sets of two. The prices below are for a single bowl.

Georgian man in archway print

Blue flowered print

Backstamp: A. Red transfer print "Wade England"
              B. Green transfer print "Wade England"

No.	Description	Colourways	Size	U.S.$	Can.$	U.K.£
1a	Blue flowers	White; gold rim; blue flowers	115	12.00	18.00	5.00
2a	Georgian lady	Pink; gold rim; gold/pink print	100	10.00	15.00	5.00
2b	Georgian man in archway	Turquoise; gold rim; gold/black print	100	10.00	15.00	5.00
2c	Georgian man by iron gate	Turquoise; gold rim; gold/black print	100	10.00	15.00	5.00
2d	Flower	White; grey/pale blue flower	100	10.00	15.00	5.00
2e	Solid colour	Pale yellow	100	10.00	15.00	5.00

WADE HEATH (cont.)

ORCADIA WARE FRUIT BOWL, 1933-1935

Orcadia Ware was produced in vivid glazes with streaks that occurred during firing when the glaze was liquid.

Backstamp: Black ink stamp "Wadeheath Orcadia Ware British Made"

No.	Description	Colourways	Size	U.S.$	Can.$	U.K.£
1	Orcadia	Orange/green streaks; yellow base and inside	95 x 205	120.00	160.00	60.00

POT-POURRI BOWLS, c.1998-2000

These pot-pourri bowls were part of the contents of the 1998 Wade Goodie box.

Fleur-de-lis print   Red flowers print

Backstamp: Red printed "Wade England" with two lines

No.	Description	Colourways	Size	U.S.$	Can.$	U.K.£
1a	Fleur-de-lis	White; gold fleur-de-lis	90 x 150	10.00	15.00	8.00
1b	Flower spray	White; red flowers	90 x 150	10.00	15.00	8.00

WADE HEATH (cont.)

POWDER BOWL, APPLIED FLOWERS ON LID, SHAPE 126, c.1930-c.1939

These powder bowls with applied handmade earthenware flowers on the lid were part of the flowers series produced by Wade (see section entitled Flowers).

Anemone lid

Backstamp: **A.** Black handwritten "Wade England" with "126"
B. Embossed "Made in England" on base with a handwritten "V Wade England No 120" on the underside of the lid

No.	Description	Colourways	Size	U.S.$	Can.$	U.K.£
1	Anemone lid	Mottled cream/green; pink anemones	60 x 100	80.00	110.00	40.00
2	Rose lid	Mottled cream/green; pink roses	60 x 100	80.00	110.00	40.00

REGENCY BOWL, 1959-1961

The miniature Regency bowl is a scaled-down version of the Empress fruit bowl, see page 26.

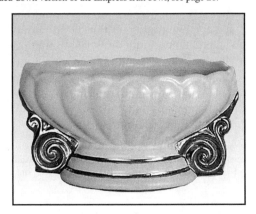

Backstamp: **A.** Red transfer print "Wade England"
B. Black transfer print "Wade England"

No.	Description	Colourways	Size	U.S.$	Can.$	U.K.£
1	Regency	White; gold highlights	52 x 112	30.00	40.00	15.00

ROSE BOWLS, 1999-2000

These hexagonal rose bowls were produced with a variety of designs, and were available from the Wade factory shop. Some of the designs have been used previously on Wade tablewares. See also Chintz rose bowl, page 27 and Millennium rose bowls, page 36.

Photograph not available
at press tim

No.	Description	Colourways	Size	U.S.$	Can.$	U.K.£
1a	Assorted flowers	White, multicoloured print	85 x 160	10.00	15.00	8.00
1b	Daisies and dandelions	White, multicoloured print	85 x 160	10.00	15.00	8.00
1c	Oranges	White, multicoloured print	85 x 160	10.00	15.00	8.00
1d	Pears and plums	White, multicoloured print	85 x 160	10.00	15.00	8.00
1e	Poinsettia	White, multicoloured print	85 x 160	10.00	15.00	8.00
1f	Rosebuds	White, multicoloured print	85 x 160	10.00	15.00	8.00
1g	Strawberries	White, multicoloured print	85 x 160	10.00	15.00	8.00

EXECUTIVE DESK SET
IN HIGH QUALITY CERAMIC BY WADE
MANUFACTURERS SINCE 1810

Available: Desk Tidy, Pencil Holder, Letter Rack, Ink Well, Trinket Box, Ash Tray, Bosuns Decanter, Half Pint Tankard.

BOXES
1935-1993

Most of these boxes were decorated with transfer prints and were produced by Wade England. Wade Heath made hand-painted and copper-lustre boxes from 1936 to the mid 1940s, and Wade Ireland issued boxes in the mid 1950s and again in 1976. The boxes are divided into Wade Heath and Wade Ireland and then listed in alphabetical order in this section under the sub-headings of: Candy Boxes; Cigarette Boxes; Trinket Boxes.

Wade Heath
Wade Ireland

BACKSTAMPS

Ink Stamps

Ink stamps were used on boxes from 1935 to 1953.

Impressed Backstamp

An impressed backstamp was used by Wade Ireland on its Irish Wade boxes in the 1950s.

Transfer Prints

Various transfer prints were used on boxes from 1937 to the mid 1960s.

Embossed Backstamps

In 1960 and 1961, then again from 1983 to 1985, some Wade England boxes were marked with embossed backstamps. Wade Ireland used an embossed backstamp in 1976.

WADE HEATH

CANDY BOXES

COPPER LUSTRE CANDY BOXES, SHAPE 241, c.1945

These boxes stand on four small feet. The springtime design was most often used on Wade Tableware. The Copper lustre boxes were hand-decorated, so no two designs are identical. The original price was 5/-.

Copper candy box

Copper candy box with cream lid

Springtime candy box

Backstamp: **A.** Green ink stamp "Wade Heath England" with impressed "241"
B. Green ink stamp "Wade England" with "Wade Springtime England" in frame and impressed "241"
C. Black ink stamp "Wade England"

No.	Description	Colourways	Size	U.S.$	Can.$	U.K.£
1a	Clover	Copper box, lid; yellow/green/pink clover leaves, flowers	177 x 127	20.00	28.00	12.00
1b	Daisies	Copper box; copper/cream lid; maroon/ yellow flower; green/ brown leaves	177 x 127	20.00	28.00	12.00
1c	Springtime	White box; gold rim; multicoloured flower print	177 x 127	20.00	28.00	12.00

WADE HEATH (cont.)

VETERAN CARS AND HORSE-DRAWN BUSES, CANDY — CIGARETTE BOXES, 1957, 1958-1962

These rectangular boxes have been advertised as both candy and cigarette boxes and could be purchased in gift-box packs. 1a-1c were issued in 1957; 2a-2p from 1958 to 1962. In December 1957, a British car magazine advertised the Veteran Cars Cigarette boxes at 11/9d.

Backstamp: **A.** Black print "A Moko Product by Wade England"
B. Transfer print "Wade England"

No.	Description	Colourways	Size	U.S.$	Can.$	U.K.£
1a	Benz	Black box, print; white lid	55 x 140	40.00	55.00	22.00
1b	Darracq	Black box, print; white lid	55 x 140	40.00	55.00	20.00
1c	Ford	Black box, print; white lid	55 x 140	40.00	55.00	22.00
2a	Baby Peugeot, 1902	Black box, print; white lid	50 x 127	40.00	55.00	22.00
2b	Benz, 1899	Black box, print; white lid	50 x 127	40.00	55.00	22.00
2c	Bugatti, 1927	Black box; multicoloured print; white lid	50 x 127	40.00	55.00	22.00
2d	Cadillac, 1903	Black box, print; white lid	50 x 127	40.00	55.00	22.00
2e	Darracq, 1904	Black box, print; white lid	50 x 127	40.00	55.00	22.00
2f	De Dion Bouton, 1904	Black box, print; white lid	50 x 127	40.00	55.00	22.00
2g	Ford, 1912	Black box, print; white lid	50 x 127	40.00	55.00	22.00
2h	Horse-drawn bus	Black box; multicoloured print; white lid	50 x 127	50.00	65.00	22.00
2i	Itala, 1908	Black box; multicoloured print; white lid	50 x 127	40.00	55.00	22.00
2j	Lanchester, 1903	Black box, print; white lid	50 x 127	40.00	55.00	22.00
2k	Oldsmobile, 1904	Black box, print; white lid	50 x 127	40.00	55.00	22.00
2l	Rolls-Royce, 1907	Black box, print; white lid	50 x 127	40.00	55.00	22.00
2m	Spyker, 1905	Black box, print; white lid	50 x 127	40.00	55.00	22.00
2n	Sunbeam, 1904	Black box, print; white lid	50 x 127	40.00	55.00	22.00
2o	Sunbeam, 1914	Black box; multicoloured print; white lid	50 x 127	40.00	55.00	22.00
2p	White Steam Car, 1903	Black box, print; white lid	50 x 127	40.00	55.00	22.00

WADE HEATH *(cont.)*

CIGARETTE BOXES

CIGARETTE BOXES, SHAPE 242, c.1945

The shape number of these rectangular cigarette boxes is 242. They were advertised as either candy or cigarette boxes. Some were sold gift boxed with a matching ashtray, which was also advertised as a pin tray. The original price was 3/6d.

Clover, copper cigarette box

Daisy, cream cigarette box

Backstamp: **A.** Ink stamp "Wade England"
               B. Green ink stamp "Harvest Ware Wade England" with impressed "242"
               C. Embossed "Wade England" and green ink stamp "Wade Heath England"
               D: Embossed "Made in England Hand Painted"
               E: Gold circular "Royal Victoria Pottery Wade England"

No.	Description	Colourways	Size	U.S.$	Can.$	U.K.£
1a	Aster	Copper box; pink aster flowers; yellow green leaves	88 x 127	45.00	65.00	25.00
1b	Balmoral Castle	Cream box; multi coloured print	88 x 127	40.00	55.00	20.00
1c	Clover	Copper box; pale pink/yellow/green clover and leaves	88 x 127	45.00	65.00	25.00
1d	Copper	Copper box	88 x 127	45.00	65.00	25.00
1e	Cranberry	Cream box; yellow green leaves; red cranberries	88 x 127	45.00	65.00	25.00
1f	Daisies, Version One, heart-shaped petals	Copper box; cream lid with copper band; purple/yellow flower; green leaves; brown streaks	88 x 127	45.00	65.00	25.00
1g	Daisies, Version Two, pointed petals	Cream box; small blue / maroon flowers; brown/green leaves	88 x 127	45.00	65.00	25.00
1h	Georgian	Cream box; copper flower heads/leaves;	88 x 127	45.00	65.00	25.00
1i	Peonies	Copper/cream box, lid; two purple/yellow flowers; green leaves	88 x 127	45.00	65.00	25.00
1j	Tulips	White box, lid; pale blue stylised flowers; grey leaves	88 x 127	42.00	60.00	20.00

WADE HEATH *(cont.)*

CAPT. KIDD CIGARETTE BOX, c.1958

This cigarette box is shaped like a pirate's treasure chest and has "Capt. Kidd 1698" impressed on the lid. The original price was 9/6d.

Backstamp: Red transfer print "Wade England"

No.	Description	Colourways	Size	U.S.$	Can.$	U.K.£
1	Captain Kidd	Amber; copper lustre hinges, lock	80 x 105	40.00	55.00	20.00

TRINKET BOXES

BUTTERFLY AND FLOWERS TRINKET BOXES, SHAPE 104, 1936-c.1945

This hand-decorated, rectangular trinket box could also be used for ladies' handkerchiefs. The Flowers trinket box is the same design as the Butterfly and Flowers box but with the butterfly omitted from the design. There is a rim around the inside of the box, which suggests that originally it had a lid, but to date a box with matching lid has not been seen.

Hand decorated flowered trinket box

Backstamp: Green ink stamp "WadeHeath England"

No.	Description	Colourways	Size	U.S.$	Can.$	U.K.£
1a	Butterfly and flowers	Cream; yellow/brown butterfly; pink/blue/ yellow flowers	80 x 220	70.00	90.00	35.00
1b	Flowers	Cream; pink/blue/yellow flowers	80 x 220	70.00	90.00	35.00

WADE HEATH *(cont.)*

CHRISTMAS TRINKET BOXES, 1997

The small circular trinket boxes were made for the Wade Christmas Extravaganza held at Trentham Park, Stoke-on-Trent, in November 1997. The larger boxes, 2a and 2b, are from a mould originally commissioned by a company named Rooney.

Santa kissing Snowman

Santa and Snowman skating

Santa on roof with sack

Backstamp: **A.** Printed "Wade England" between two lines
B. Printed "Wade England" between two lines with an impressed "Made in England Rooney"
"Wade Made in England"

No.	Description	Colourways	Size	U.S.$	Can.$	U.K.£
1a	Santa kissing snowman	White box; multicoloured print	Small/44 x 70	4.00	6.00	2.00
1b	Santa skating with mistletoe	White box; multicoloured print	Small/44 x 70	4.00	6.00	2.00
1c	Santa with gift list	White box; multicoloured print	Small/44 x 70	4.00	6.00	2.00
1d	Two snowmen in snow	White box; multicoloured print	Small/44 x 70	4.00	6.00	2.00
1e	Three snowmen looking up	White box; multicoloured print	Small/44 x 70	4.00	6.00	2.00
2a	Santa and snowman skating	White box; multicoloured print	Large/45 x 100	5.00	7.00	3.00
2b	Santa on roof with sack	White box; multicoloured print	Large/45 x 100	5.00	7.00	3.00

COPPER-LUSTRE TRINKET BOXES, c.1945

This dainty square-shaped trinket box stands on four small feet. As this box was hand decorated, the design will vary slightly among pieces. A new mould caused a slight variation in sizes. The original price was 3/6d.

Backstamp: **A.** Ink stamp "Wade England"
B. Ink stamp "Harvest Ware Wade England"

No.	Description	Colourways	Size	U.S.$	Can.$	U.K.£
1a	Flower	Copper box; cream lid; copper band; mauve/green flower	76	40.00	55.00	20.00
1b	Flower	Cream box; copper band; purple/yellow flower; brown green leaves	68	40.00	55.00	22.00

WADE HEATH *(cont.)*

COTTAGE AND GARDEN TRINKET BOX

The edges of this box are curved, and it is decorated with a print of a cottage and garden.

Photograph not available
at press time

Backstamp: Unknown

No.	Description	Colourways	Size	U.S.$	Can.$	U.K.£
1	Trinket box	White; gold bands; multicoloured print	88 x 63	40.00	55.00	22.00

EXECUTIVE TRINKET BOX, 1993

This round box was part of an eight-piece executive desk set that Wade sold to companies as presentation sets. It has a stylised lily transfer print in the centre.

Backstamp: Unknown

No.	Description	Colourways	Size	U.S.$	Can.$	U.K.£
1	Trinket box	Black; gold edge, emblem	63	30.00	40.00	15.00

WADE HEATH (cont.)

EXPRESSIONS OF LOVE TRINKET BOXES, 1998

These heart-shaped trinket boxes have a raised heart in the lid. They are decorated with either an English rose print or a multiple red flowered print and are highlighted in 22ct gold. The English rose print was first offered on April 5th, 1998, by *Parade*, a magazine published in the USA. The original cost direct from Wade was £15.00

English rose

Red flowers

Backstamp: Gold printed "Wade England"

No.	Description	Colourways	Size	U.S.$	Can.$	U.K.£
1a	English rose	White; gold highlights; pink roses	55 x 140	45.00	58.00	25.00
1b	Red flowers	White; gold highlights; red flowers	55 x 140	45.00	58.00	25.00

GOTHIC WARE TRINKET BOXES, SHAPE 361, c.1947-c.1952

This large basket-shaped trinket box has a flat lid and is decorated with embossed leaves and tulips and edged with gold lustre. It is shape 361 and is part of a large series of Gothic baskets, bowls, jugs, and vases.

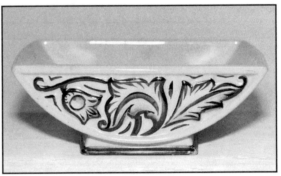

Gothic ware trinket box without cover

Backstamp: Ink stamp "Wade England"

No.	Description	Colourways	Size	U.S.$	Can.$	U.K.£
1a	Gothic ware	Cream; pale pink tulips; pale green/yellow leaves; gold lustre	153 x 101	110.00	135.00	45.00
1b	Gothic ware	Cream; pink/yellow tulips; green/cream leaves; gold lustre	153 x 101	110.00	135.00	45.00

WADE HEATH (cont.)

MILLENNIUM TRINKET BOXES, 1999-2000

Produced as part of a Millennium series these trinket boxes were produced in two colourways.

Millennium trinket box

Backstamp: Printed "Wade England" between two lines

No.	Description	Colourways	Size	U.S.$	Can.$	U.K.£
1a	Black/gold	Black; gold decorative prints	90	32.00	45.00	20.00
1b	Blue/silver	Dark blue; silver decorative prints	90	32.00	45.00	20.00

RABBIT TRINKET BOX, c.1935-1937

This box has a hand painted design of a rabbit wearing large shoes .

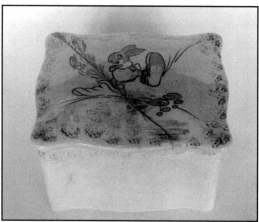

Rabbit trinket box

Backstamp: Ink stamp "Flaxman Ware Hand Made Pottery by Wadeheath England" c.1935-1937

No.	Description	Colourways	Size	U.S.$	Can.$	U.K.£
1	Rabbit	Cream box; brown rabbit; orange flowers; green leaves	65x 130	60.00	75.00	40.00

WADE HEATH *(cont.)*

ROMANCE TRINKET BOXES, 1983-1985

The original price was £1.99 each.

Romance - oval

Romance - rectangular

Backstamp: Raised "Wade Made in England"

No.	Description	Colourways	Shape/Size	U.S.$	Can.$	U.K.£
1a	Oval	Fawn; grey/yellow/white design	Oval/40	25.00	35.00	12.00
1b	Oval	Cream; blue/grey/fawn design	Oval/40	25.00	35.00	12.00
1c	Oval	Pink	Oval/40	30.00	40.00	18.00
2a	Rectangular	Fawn; grey/yellow/white design	Rectangular/46	25.00	35.00	12.00
2b	Rectangular	Cream; blue/grey/fawn design	Rectangular/46	25.00	35.00	12.00

ROUND TRINKET BOXES; 1990-1992, 1999-2000

These trinket boxes / powder bowls were first issued 1990-1992 in the Jacobean and Kawa designs. It was reissued in 1999-2000 with a pink flower design similar to Kawa. The Jacobean design is of red and black enamelled exotic flowers and Kawa is a Japanese design of pastel pink peonies and bamboo stems with gold highlighting. The Kawa decoration was also used on lamps and vases.

Flowered print

Backstamp: **A.** Red transfer print "Wade England" with two red lines and "Jacobean"
B. Gold transfer print "Wade England" with two gold lines and "Kawa"
C. Printed "Wade England" between two lines

No.	Description	Colourways	Size	U.S.$	Can.$	U.K.£
1a	Flowers, leaves	White; gold finial; pink flowers; white daisy;	70	32.00	45.00	20.00
1b	Jacobean	White; red/black enamelled print	70	30.00	40.00	18.00
1c	Kawa	White; pastel pink/green print; gold highlights	70	30.00	40.00	18.00

WADE HEATH (cont.)

TEENAGE POTTERY CASKET, 1960

The official Wade name for these trinket boxes was "Teenage Pottery Heart-shaped Caskets. The original price of these trinket boxes was 7/6d

'Tommy Steele' teenage pottery casket

Backstamp: Embossed "Wade Porcelain Made in England"

No.	Name	Colourways	Size	U.S.$	Can.$	U.K.£
1a	Cliff Richard	Pink; multicoloured print	40 x 85	150.00	200.00	75.00
1b	Tommy Steele	Pink; multicoloured print	40 x 85	150.00	200.00	75.00
1c	Frankie Vaughan	Pink; multicoloured print	40 x 85	150.00	200.00	75.00
1d	Marty Wilde	Pink; multicoloured print	40 x 85	150.00	200.00	75.00

TREASURE CHEST TRINKET BOX, 1961

The original price was 4/11d.

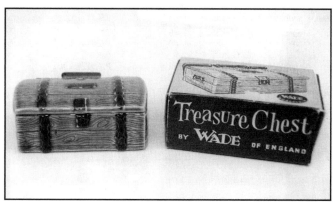

Treasure Chest trinket box

Backstamp: Embossed "Wade Porcelain Made in England"

No.	Description	Colourways	Size	U.S.$	Can.$	U.K.£
1	Trinket box	Honey-brown; red-brown straps, hinges	40 x 90	60.00	80.00	30.00

WADE IRELAND

IRISH PORCELAIN

CANDY / CIGARETTE BOXES, SHAPE I.P.92, c.1955

These boxes have been sold both as candy and cigarette boxes. One gift pack comprised a cigarette box, tankard and ashtray and another included a cigarette box and ashtray. When they were sold as candy boxes, they were sold separately. All had embossed shamrocks around the box and on the lid with a transfer print in the centre.

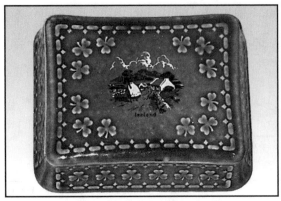

Irish Colleen print   Paddy McGredy, Floribunda roses print

Backstamp: Impressed "Irish Porcelain" over a small shamrock with "Made in Ireland by Wade of Co. Armagh" underneath

No.	Description	Colourways	Size	U.S.$	Can.$	U.K.£
1a	Fox hunter, hat in hand	Grey/blue/green; multicoloured print	I.P.92/127 x 101	60.00	80.00	35.00
1b	Fox hunter, hat on head	Grey/blue/green; multicoloured print	I.P.92/127 x 101	60.00	80.00	35.00
1c	Hunter, firing rifle	Grey/blue/green; multicoloured print	I.P.92/127 x 101	60.00	80.00	35.00
1d	Giant Finn MacCaul	Grey/blue/green; multicoloured print	I.P.92/127 x 101	60.00	80.00	35.00
1e	Irish colleen carrying peat	Grey/blue/green; multicoloured print	I.P.92/127 x 101	60.00	80.00	35.00
1f	Irish kitchen	Grey/blue/green; multicoloured print	I.P.92/127 x 101	60.00	80.00	35.00
1g	Paddy McGredy Floribunda roses	Grey/blue/green; multicoloured print	I.P.92/127 x 101	90.00	125.00	40.00
1h	Stag's head	Grey/blue/green; multicoloured print	I.P.92/127 x 101	60.00	80.00	35.00
1i	Stag's head	Amber; multicoloured print	I.P.92/127 x 101	60.00	80.00	35.00

IRISH PORCELAIN *(cont.)*

CELTIC PORCELAIN TRINKET BOX, SHAPE CK6, 1965

The design of writhing snakes found on this bowl was copied from illustrations made by medieval monks in an Irish manuscript entitled, *The Book of Kells*. The snakes represent those banished from Ireland by Saint Patrick. Only a small quantity of boxes was issued.

Backstamp: Embossed "Celtic Porcelain by Wade Ireland" in an Irish knot wreath

No.	Description	Colourways	Size	U.S.$	Can.$	U.K.£
1	Celtic Porcelain	Mottled blue-green	50	80.00	110.00	40.00

MOURNE SERIES CANDY BOX, SHAPE No. UNKNOWN, 1976

This rectangular candy box was produced as part of the Mourne Series, which also included vases, and is completely different in colour and style from previously produced Wade Ireland products.

Backstamp: Embossed circular "Made in Ireland Irish Porcelain Wade eire tir a dheanta" around a shamrock and crown design

No.	Description	Colourways	Size	U.S.$	Can.$	U.K.£
1	Mourne	Green-brown; orange flower	50 x 127	80.00	110.00	40.00

IRISH PORCELAIN (cont.)

VICTORIAN LADIES CAMEO PORTRAIT TRINKET BOXES, c.1988-1991

These small trinket boxes have Wade Ireland Cameo plaques of Victorian ladies inset in the lids. Only the portrait plaques were produced by Wade Ireland. The boxes were manufactured in Staffordshire, with the portrait plaques added to the lids. It is believed the plaques were produced at the same time as the Wade Ireland Gray's Fine Art plaques.

| Cross and chain necklace, round trinket box | Holding flowers, oval trinket box | Holding flowers, rectangular trinket box |

Backstamp: **A.** Unmarked
B. Incised script "English Porcelain FM"

No.	Description	Colourways	Shape/Size	U.S.$	Can.$	U.K.£
1a	Cross and chain necklace	Dark green; blue-grey lid	Oblong/35 x 80	55.00	85.00	35.00
1b	Pearl necklace	Light grey; blue-grey lid	Oblong/35 x 80	55.00	85.00	35.00
2	Holding flowers	Light green; portrait lid	Oval/unknown	55.00	85.00	35.00
3	Holding flowers	Mottled green/ brown; blue grey portrait	Rect./unknown	55.00	85.00	35.00
4a	Cross and chain	Dark green; blue-grey lid	Round/35 x 80	55.00	85.00	35.00
4b	Holding flowers	Light grey; off-white lid	Round/35 x 80	55.00	85.00	35.00

CANDLES AND CANDLESTICKS

c.1950-1999

Wade England and Wade Ireland produced candles and candlesticks in the 1950s, early 1960s, 1980s, and 1998-1999. The items in this section are listed in alphabetical order.

Wade Heath
Wade Ireland

BACKSTAMPS

Transfer Prints

Embossed Backstamp

Wade began using transfer prints for its backstamps in 1953. From 1953 to 1954 they were used to mark the everlasting candles. In the late 1980s, Wade Ireland used a transfer print.

During the late 1950s, Wade England and Wade Ireland used an embossed backstamp to mark its candlesticks.

WADE HEATH CANDLES AND CANDLESTICKS

DECORATIVE CANDLESTICKS, 1998

These candlesticks were decorated with seasonal flowers for Christmas 1998.

Decorative candlesticks

Backstamp: Red printed "Wade England" between two lines

No.	Description	Colourways	Size	U.S.$	Can.$	U.K.£
1a	Bells and Christmas roses	White; multicoloured print	150	20.00	30.00	14.00
1b	Poinsettia	White; red and white flowers	150	20.00	30.00	14.00

EVERLASTING CANDLES, 1953-1954

This pair of porcelain candles is decorated with flowers. They are hollow with a rubber bung in the base and sit in a candlestick, which consists of six modelled petals. The candles were filled with pink paraffin. The original price was 30/- per boxed pair.

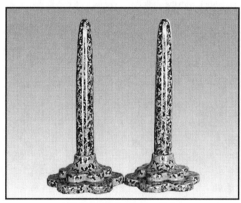

Pair of Everlasting candles

Backstamp: Black transfer print "Wade England"

No.	Description	Colourways	Size	U.S.$	Can.$	U.K.£
1a	Everlasting candle	Pale blue; multicoloured flowers	225	160.00	185.00	65.00
1b	Everlasting candle	Pale green; gold flowers	225	160.00	185.00	65.00
1c	Everlasting candle	White; gold flowers	225	80.00	110.00	40.00
1d	Everlasting candle	White; yellow flowers	225	160.00	185.00	65.00
1e	Everlasting candle	White; multicoloured flowers	225	160.00	185.00	65.00
1f	Everlasting candle	Yellow; orange/blue flowers	225	160.00	185.00	65.00

WADE HEATH (cont.)

HOLLY LEAF CANDLESTICKS, 1961

This pair of candlesticks, modelled in the shape of holly leaves, was sold with two red candy-twist candles in a presentation box marked "Wade Porcelain Candlesticks." They were also found in a presentation box marked "Wade Two Christmas Candlesticks with Candles." The original price was 3/6d.

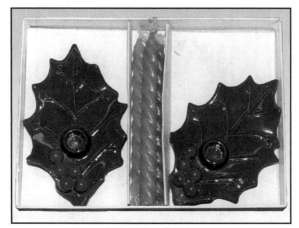

Holly leaf candlesticks

Backstamp: Unmarked

No.	Description	Colourways	Size	U.S.$	Can.$	U.K.£
1	Holly leaf	Dark green leaf; red berries	98	30.00	40.00	15.00

OAK LEAF DISH CANDLESTICKS, 1957-1959

The Leaf dishes were adapted to form a candlestick with the addition of a brass foot, handle and acorn-shaped candle cup. The candle cup can be found either plain or with an embossed design.

Oak leaf candlesticks

Backstamp: Embossed "Wade Porcelain Made in England"

No.	Description	Colourways	Size	U.S.$	Can.$	U.K.£
1a	Oak leaf, embossed candlestick	Beige	45 x 100	25.00	35.00	12.00
1b	Oak leaf, embossed candlestick	Black	45 x 100	25.00	35.00	12.00
1c	Oak leaf, embossed candlestick	Green	45 x 100	25.00	35.00	12.00
1d	Oak leaf, plain candlestick	Green	45 x 100	25.00	35.00	12.00

WADE HEATH (cont.)

RIBBED CANDLESTICKS, 1999

This candlestick was sold through the Wade factory shop during 1999.

Ribbed candlestick

Backstamp: Printed "Wade Made in England"

No.	Description	Colourways	Size	U.S.$	Can.$	U.K.£
1a	Poinsettia	White; multicoloured print	150	20.00	30.00	14.00
1b	Solid colour	Black	150	20.00	30.00	14.00

WADE IRELAND CANDLES AND CANDLESTICKS

IRISH PORCELAIN

CROSSES AND RAISED KNURLS CANDLESTICKS, 1988

A limited number of candlesticks were produced by Wade Ireland. There are three rows of raised knurls and an etched design of crosses on this candlestick.

Pair of crosses and raised knurls candlesticks

Backstamp: Unknown

No.	Description	Colourways	Size	U.S.$	Can.$	U.K.£
1	Crosses and raised dots	Blue/grey	??	40.00	55.00	20.00

DEEP DISH CANDLESTICK, c.1950

Deep dish candlestick

Backstamp: Embossed Circular "Irish Porcelain Made in Ireland Z" around a central shamrock (early 1950s)

No.	Description	Colourways	Size	U.S.$	Can.$	U.K.£
1	Deep dish	Blue/grey	52 x 155	25.00	35.00	12.00

IRISH PORCELAIN (cont.)

HORSE'S HEAD CANDLESTICK, c.1988

A small number of candlesticks with a portrait of a horse's head in the centre was produced by Wade Ireland. There are indentations for four candles, one in each corner. The corners are decorated with shamrock leaves.

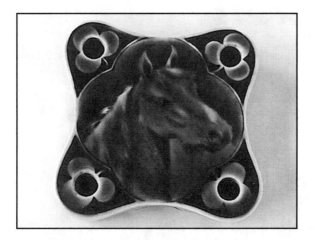

Backstamp: Unmarked

No.	Description	Colourways	Size	U.S.$	Can.$	U.K.£
1	Horse's head	Chestnut brown/beige/grey	23 x 95	40.00	55.00	20.00

SHAMROCK RANGE

CANDLESTICKS, SHAPE S.R.12, c.1987

This Wade Ireland candlestick has a print of shamrocks around the base.

Pair of Shamrock range candlesticks

Backstamp: Circular transfer print "Made in Ireland Porcelain Wade eire tire a dheanta" around a shamrock and "W" crown design

No.	Description	Colourways	Size	U.S.$	Can.$	U.K.£
1	Candlesticks	White; gold rim; green prints	101	20.00	30.00	10.00

Empress

404

402

400

401

403

A range of outstanding ornamental pieces; the classical shapes
are decorated in Regency style with rich underglaze colours and
burnished gold finish.

DISHES

c.1930-1992

The dishes included in this section are considered decorative rather than utilitarian. Some were produced in novelty shapes—such as the aqua dishes, hedgehog tray, pet face dishes and starfish pin tray—and some include a model of a figure attached to the dish—for example, the doggie dishes, the man in a rowboat tray, the swallow dishes and T.T. trays. There is also a wide selection of souvenir dishes.

The dishes are listed in alphabetical order followed by shape number.

Wade Heath
Wade Ireland

BACKSTAMPS

Ink Stamps

Ink stamps were used to mark dishes from the late 1930s to the mid 1950s and from 1963 to 1964.

Transfer Prints

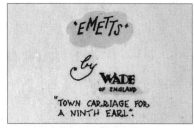

Beginning in 1953 until 1992, most of the dishes produced by Wade were marked with a transfer-print backstamp.

Embossed Backstamps

Like transfer prints, embossed backstamps were commonly used on dishes. They were in use from 1953 to 1984.

Impressed Backstamps

From 1956 to 1986 impressed backstamps were used by Wade on its dishes.

WADE HEATH

"A" DISH, c.1955

This dish has been found with a gold and a black letter A in the centre. There is no information as to why this dish bears the initial.

Backstamp: Red or green transfer print "Wade England"

No.	Description	Colourways	Size	U.S.$	Can.$	U.K.£
1a	"A" dish	White; gold rim, letter	114	6.00	8.00	3.00
1b	"A" dish	White; gold rim; black letter	114	6.00	8.00	3.00

ANIMAL DISHES, 1955-1959

Although Wade called these items butter dishes, they are much more ornamental than utilitarian. The squirrel and rabbit dishes were produced from 1955 to 1959; the koala dish was issued in 1959 only.

Koala animal dish

Squirrel animal dish

Backstamp: Embossed "Wade England"

No.	Description	Colourways	Size	U.S.$	Can.$	U.K.£
1a	Koala	Green; beige/white koala	80	85.00	125.00	38.00
1b	Koala	Brown; beige/white koala	80	85.00	125.00	38.00
2a	Rabbit	Beige	80	30.00	45.00	22.00
2b	Rabbit	Green	80	30.00	45.00	22.00
3a	Squirrel	Beige	80	30.00	45.00	22.00
3b	Squirrel	Green	80	30.00	45.00	22.00

WADE HEATH Cont.)

AQUA DISHES, 1958-1961, 1973

These bloater and goldfish-shaped dishes were produced in Wade's high-gloss Scintillite finish with an embossed scale design. Packaged as a boxed pair, the original price was 3/11d per box. The goldfish dish was first issued in January 1958 and withdrawn in January 1960. It was reissued by Wade Ireland in 1973 in lighter colours and priced at 4/6d per boxed pair. The bloater dish was first issued in January 1960.

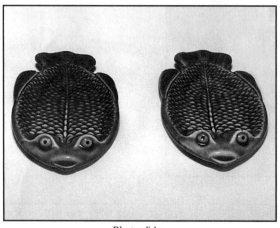

Bloater dishes

Goldfish dishes

Backstamp: A. Embossed "Wade Porcelain Made In England"
B. Embossed "Wade Porcelain Made In Ireland"

No.	Description	Colourways	Size	U.S.$	Can.$	U.K.£
1a	Bloater	Brown/dark blue	65 x 98	25.00	35.00	15.00
1b	Goldfish	Brown/dark blue	100 x 80	20.00	30.00	12.00
1c	Goldfish	Beige/light blue	100 x 80	20.00	30.00	12.00

WADE HEATH (cont.)

BALLET SERIES DISHES, 1957-1958

The Ballet Series comprises dishes and vases in white with black silhouette transfer prints of ballerinas in dance poses. The dishes were originally sold either individually boxed, as a set of four dishes or one dish with two miniature vases.

Backstamp: Black and red transfer print "Ballet Wade of England"

No.	Description	Colourways	Size	U.S.$	Can.$	U.K.£
1	Ballerina, hands forward	White; red/yellow/black print	112	10.00	15.00	5.00
2	Ballerina, head turned back	White; red/yellow/black print	112	10.00	15.00	5.00
3	Ballerina on one toe	White; red/yellow/black print	112	10.00	15.00	5.00
4	Ballerina on points	White; red/yellow/black print	112	10.00	15.00	5.00

WADE HEATH (cont.)

BALMORAL AND WINDSOR CASTLE PIN TRAYS, c.1952-c.1955

Windsor Castle

Backstamp: Gold transfer print "Royal Victoria Pottery - Wade England"

No.	Description	Colourways	Size	U.S.$	Can.$	U.K.£
1a	Balmoral Castle	Off white; gold rim; multicoloured print	105	20.00	30.00	10.00
1b	Balmoral Castle	White; silver rim; multicoloured print	105	20.00	30.00	10.00
1c	Windsor Castle	Off white; gold rim; multicoloured print	105	20.00	30.00	10.00

B.O.A.C. AIRCRAFT DISHES, 1960

This series of square dishes has a transfer print of a Boeing aeroplane in the centre.

Boeing 707   Bristol Britannia 312

Backstamp: **A.** Black transfer print "Boeing 707 Engines: Rolls Royce Conway Pure Jet. Length: 152 ft 11 ins.
Span: 142 ft 5 ins. All up Weight: 295,000 lbs. Average Cruising Speed: 530 m.p.h.
Maximum Range: 6,650 miles. Reproduction by Wade of England in collaboration with B.O.A.C."
B. Black transfer print "Bristol Britannia 312 Engine: Bristol Proteus 755 Turbo Prop Length: 124 ft 3 ins.
Span: 142 ft 3 ins. All up Weight: 180,000 lbs. Average Cruising Speed: 360 m.p.h. Maximum Range: 4,400 miles.
Reproduction by Wade of England in collaboration with B.O.A.C."

No.	Description	Colourways	Size	U.S.$	Can.$	U.K.£
1a	Boeing	White; blue/black/silver print	107	20.00	30.00	10.00
1b	Boeing Bristol Britannia 312	White; blue/black/silver print	107	20.00	30.00	10.00
1c	Boeing 707	White; blue/black/silver print	107	20.00	30.00	10.00
1d	Douglas DC7C	White; blue/black/silver print	107	20.00	30.00	10.00
1e	4 D.H. Comet 4	White; blue/black/silver print	107	20.00	30.00	10.00

WADE HEATH *(cont.)*

BRITISH FORD DISHES, 1959-1960

This set of square dishes depicts modern British Ford cars of the time. A different well-known London scene is in the background of each dish.

Ford Consul

Ford Zodiac

Backstamp: **A.** Black transfer print "Ford Consul Saloon. 4-Cyl Reproduced by Wade England"
B. Black transfer print "Ford Zodiac Saloon. G Cyl 2553 C.C. Reproduced by Wade England"

No.	Description	Colourways	Size	U.S.$	Can.$	U.K.£
1a	Ford Consul saloon car	White; red car; black Tower Bridge	110	10.00	15.00	5.00
1b	Ford Zephyr saloon car	White; yellow car; black Big Ben	110	10.00	15.00	5.00
1c	Ford Zodiac	White; blue car; black St. Paul's Cathedral	110	10.00	15.00	5.00

WADE HEATH (cont.)

CAMEO DISHES

This series of oval dishes has an embossed design of an animal or roses in the centre. The first variation dishes are a two-tone colourway with a dark blue or green rim. The original price was 5/11d each. The second variation is a solid colourway.

First variation, 1965

Cairn Cameo dish, First variation   Fawn Cameo dish, First variation   Kitten Cameo dish, First variation

Backstamp: Embossed "Wade England"

No.	Description	Colourways	Shape/Size	U.S.$	Can.$	U.K.£
1a	Cairn	Brown/dark blue rim	Round corners/110	20.00	28.00	10.00
1b	Cairn	Green/dark green rim	Round corners/110	20.00	28.00	10.00
2a	Chicks	Brown/dark blue rim	Round/100	20.00	28.00	10.00
2b	Chicks	Green/dark green rim	Round/100	20.00	28.00	10.00
3a	Fawn	Brown/dark blue rim	Oval/110	20.00	28.00	10.00
3b	Fawn	Brown/dark green rim	Oval/110	20.00	28.00	10.00
4a	Horse	Brown/dark blue rim	Round corners/110	20.00	28.00	10.00
4b	Horse	Green/dark green rim	Round corners/110	20.00	28.00	10.00
5a	Kitten	Brown/dark blue rim	Oval/110	20.00	28.00	10.00
5b	Kitten	Green/dark green rim	Oval/110	20.00	28.00	10.00
6a	Roses	Brown/darak blue rim	Round/100	20.00	28.00	10.00
6b	Roses	Green/dark green rim	Round/100	20.00	28.00	10.00

WADE HEATH (cont.)

CAMEO DISHES (cont.)
Second Variation, 1979-1982

The Cameo dishes were reissued in 1979 in a solid colour. They were renamed Pet dishes.

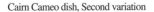

Cairn Cameo dish, Second variation   Horse Cameo dish, Second variation   Kitten Cameo dish, Second variation

Backstamp: Embossed "Wade England"

No.	Description	Colourways	Shape/Size	U.S.$	Can.$	U.K.£
1a	Cairn	Brown	Round corners/110	15.00	22.00	7.00
1b	Cairn	Green	Round corners/110	15.00	22.00	7.00
2a	Chicks	Brown	Round/100	15.00	22.00	7.00
2b	Chicks	Green	Round/100	15.00	22.00	7.00
3a	Fawn	Brown	Oval/110	15.00	22.00	7.00
3b	Fawn	Green	Oval/110	15.00	22.00	7.00
4a	Horse	Brown	Round corners/110	15.00	22.00	7.00
4b	Horse	Green	Round corners/110	15.00	22.00	7.00
5a	Kitten	Brown	Oval/110	15.00	22.00	7.00
5b	Kitten	Green	Oval/110	15.00	22.00	7.00
6a	Roses	Brown	Round/100	15.00	22.00	7.00
6b	Roses	Green	Round/100	15.00	22.00	7.00

WADE HEATH, (cont.)

CANDY DISH, ROUND, SHAPE S.25/38, 1953

This candy dish is from the same mould as the 1953 coronation dish, but with all the animals and inscriptions removed. The original selling price was 2/11d.

Backstamp: Embossed "Wade England"

No.	Description	Colourways	Size	U.S.$	Can.$	U.K.£
1a	Candy dish	Pale ming green	120	25.00	35.00	10.00
1b	Candy dish	Dark blue	120	25.00	35.00	10.00
1c	Royal Victoria hospital crest	Pale blue; gold coat of arms and lettering	120	25.00	35.00	10.00

WADE HEATH *(cont.)*

CHARLES DICKENS DISHES, 1959-1960

The transfer prints on this set of octagonal dishes portray characters from Dickens's novels. They were sold singly or as a boxed pair.

Miss Nipper	Mrs. Gamp	Uriah Heep

Backstamp: Red transfer print "Wade England" and a black print of Dickens's portrait

No.	Description	Colourways	Size	U.S.$	Can.$	U.K.£
1a	Little Nell	White; silver band; multicoloured print	110	10.00	15.00	5.00
1b	Miss Nipper	White; silver band; multicoloured print	110	10.00	15.00	5.00
1c	Mr. Micawber	White; silver band; multicoloured print	110	10.00	15.00	5.00
1d	Mr. Pickwick	White; silver band; multicoloured print	110	10.00	15.00	5.00
1e	Mrs. Gamp	White; silver band; multicoloured print	110	10.00	15.00	5.00
1f	Uriah Heep	White; silver band; multicoloured print	110	10.00	15.00	5.00

WADE HEATH (cont.)

CHRISTMAS GREETINGS DISHES, 1959-c.1962

Sold in boxes marked Christmas Greetings, these four dishes have a Christmas theme. Three of the dishes Cottage, Deer and Shepherd have been found in two colourways.

Cottage in snow

Santa on scooter in snow

Shepherd and Star of Bethlehem

Backstamp: Red transfer print "Wade England"

No.	Description	Colourways	Shape/Size	U.S.$	Can.$	U.K.£
1a	Cottage in snow	White; gold line; black/blue print	Octagonal/110	10.00	15.00	5.00
1b	Cottage in snow	White; gold line; multicoloured print	Octagonal/110	10.00	15.00	5.00
1c	Deer and rabbits in snow	White; gold line; black/blue print	Octagonal/110	10.00	15.00	5.00
1d	Deer and rabbits in snow	White; gold line; multicoloured print	Octagonal/110	10.00	15.00	5.00
1e	Santa on Scooter in snow	White; gold line; multicoloured print	Octagonal/110	10.00	15.00	5.00
1f	Shepherd and Star of Bethlehem	White; gold line; black/blue print	Octagonal/110	10.00	15.00	5.00
1g	Shepherd and Star of Bethlehem	White; gold line; multicoloured print	Octagonal/110	10.00	15.00	5.00

COBNUTS AND FLOWERS, SHAPE 373, c.1938

This pretty nut tray has an embossed design of cobnuts and flowers.

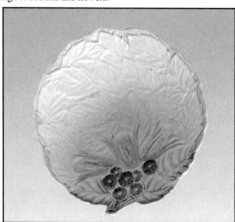

Backstamp: A. Green ink stamp "Wade Heath England"
B. Green ink stamp "Harvest Ware Wade England"

No.	Description	Colourways	Size	U.S.$	Can.$	U.K.£
1	Cobnuts and flowers	Cream; yellow cobnuts; mauve/maroon flowers	180	40.00	55.00	22.00

WADE HEATH (cont.)

COUNTRYMEN 'DOG AND HORSE HEAD' DISHES, 1959-c.1963

These round dishes have a wide brown band around the rim and a transfer print of an animal head or heads in the centre. The design was known as 'Countrymen' and was also used on the Countrymen pint traditional tankards (See *The Charlton Standard Catalogue of Wade, Volume One, General Issues*) and on the cube ashtrays (see page 3).

Photograph not available
at press time

Backstamp: Red transfer print "Wade England"

No.	Description	Colourways	Size	U.S.$	Can.$	U.K.£
1a	Horse's head	White; brown band; multicoloured print	108	10.00	15.00	5.00
1b	Horses' heads	White; brown band; multicoloured print	108	10.00	15.00	5.00
1c	Poodle, black	White; brown band; multicoloured print	108	10.00	15.00	5.00
1d	Poodle, grey	White; brown band; multicoloured print	108	10.00	15.00	5.00
1e	Spaniel, black	White; brown band; multicoloured print	108	10.00	15.00	5.00
1f	Spaniel, brown	White; brown band; multicoloured print	108	10.00	15.00	5.00

COUNTRYMEN 'HUNT' DISHES, 1959-c.1963

These round dishes have a wide brown band around the rim and a transfer print of fox hunters and hounds in the centre. Similar prints were used on the 'Countrymen' pint traditional tankards (See *The Charlton Standard Catalogue of Wade, Volume One, General Issues*).

Backstamp: Red transfer print "Wade England"

No.	Description	Colourways	Size	U.S.$	Can.$	U.K.£
1a	Four horsemen	White; brown band; multicoloured print	108	10.00	15.00	5.00
1b	Horsemen; black, white horses	White; brown band; multicoloured print	108	10.00	15.00	5.00
1c	Horsemen, jumping gate	White; brown band; multicoloured print	108	10.00	15.00	5.00
1d	Horsemen; white, brown horses	White; brown band; multicoloured print	108	10.00	15.00	5.00

WADE HEATH (cont.)

DISH FOR FLOWER CENTRE, c.1930-c.1935

These earthenware dishes were made to hold the flower centres produced by Wade (see Flowers section). It was part of the first series of flowers.

Backstamp: A. Raised "British Made" with an impressed code letter and sometimes a black handwritten
"Wade England" or "Made in England"
B. Raised "British" with an impressed code letter and sometimes a black handwritten
"Wade England" or "Made in England"

No.	Description	Colourways	Size	U.S.$	Can.$	U.K.£
1	Dish	Black	25 x 60	10.00	15.00	5.00
2	Dish	Black	25 x 115	10.00	15.00	5.00

DOGGIE DISHES, 1956-1958

These kidney-shaped dishes have a model of a fox terrier or a spaniel on the back rim. The dish with the fox terrier was issued in January 1956 and was withdrawn in January 1958. The spaniel dish was introduced in February 1957 and was discontinued in January 1958. Their original price was 3/11d. This dish shape was reused for the Lesney gift trays in 1961 (see *The Charlton Standard Catalogue of Wade, Volume One, General Issues*).

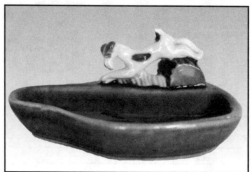

Backstamp: Impressed "Wade Made In England"

No.	Description	Colourways	Size	U.S.$	Can.$	U.K.£
1a	Fox terrier	Beige; white/brown dog	100	50.00	70.00	25.00
1b	Fox terrier	Green; white/brown dog	100	50.00	70.00	25.00
1c	Fox terrier	Light grey; white/brown dog	100	50.00	70.00	25.00
1d	Fox terrier	Dark grey; white/brown dog	100	50.00	70.00	25.00
2a	Spaniel	Beige; white/brown dog	100	50.00	70.00	25.00
2b	Spaniel	Green; white/brown dog	100	50.00	70.00	25.00
2c	Spaniel	Light grey; white/brown dog	100	50.00	70.00	25.00
2d	Spaniel	Dark grey; white/brown dog	100	50.00	70.00	25.00

WADE HEATH *(cont.)*

EMETTS DISHES, c.1958

These dishes are decorated in the centre with a cartoon by British cartoonist Rowland Emetts. They were sold individually and in a boxed set of four dishes.

Backstamp: **A.** Black transfer print "Emetts by Wade of England Town Carriage for a Ninth Earl"
B. Black transfer print "Emetts by Wade of England Pastoral Interlude"
C. Black transfer print "Emetts by Wade of England Dog and Dogstar"
D. Black transfer print "Emetts by Wade of England Chivalry"

No.	Description	Colourways	Size	U.S.$	Can.$	U.K.£
1a	Chivalry	White; yellow/blue/pink print	106	15.00	18.00	9.00
1b	Dog and dogstar	White; yellow/blue/pink print	106	15.00	18.00	9.00
1c	Pastoral interlude	White; yellow/blue/pink print	106	15.00	18.00	9.00
1d	Town carriage for a Ninth Earl	White; yellow/blue/pink print	106	15.00	18.00	9.00

ENGLISH COACHING INNS DISHES, 1959-c1962

Two shapes of dishes have been found with the English Coaching Inns theme, a round and an oval dish.

Oval - Old Coach House, Stratford   Round - Old Coach House, York

Backstamp: Red transfer print "Wade England"

No.	Description	Colourways	Size	U.S.$	Can.$	U.K.£
1a	Old Coach House, Bristol	White; multicoloured print	Oval/110	10.00	15.00	5.00
1b	Old Coach House, Stratford	White; multicoloured print	Oval/110	10.00	15.00	5.00
1c	Old Coach House, York	White; multicoloured print	Oval/110	10.00	15.00	5.00
2a	Old Coach House, Bristol	White; brown rim; multicoloured print	Round/110	10.00	15.00	5.00
2b	Old Coach House, Stratford	White; brown rim; multicoloured print	Round/110	10.00	15.00	5.00
2c	Old Coach House, York	White; brown rim; multicoloured print	Round/110	10.00	15.00	5.00

WADE HEATH *(cont.)*

FAMOUS SHIPS TYRE DISHES, 1958

This set of three white tyre dishes is decorated with transfer prints of famous sailing ships in the centre. The same prints were originally used on the 1956 Snippets sailing ships set (see *The Charlton Standard Catalogue of Wade Whimsical Collectables*).

Mayflower

Santa Maria

Backstamp: **A.** Red transfer print "Wade England"
B. Printed "Mayflower Carried 102 Pilgrims to North America 1620 Wade England"
C. Printed "Santa Maria Flagship of Columbus 1492 Wade England"

No.	Description	Colourways	Size	U.S.$	Can.$	U.K.£
1a	Mayflower	White; multicoloured print	105	10.00	15.00	5.00
1b	The Revenge	White; multicoloured print	105	10.00	15.00	5.00
1c	Santa Maria	White; multicoloured print	105	10.00	15.00	5.00

FANTASIA WARE, 1957-1962

The transfer prints used on this set of decorative ware were based on scenes from the 1940 Walt Disney film, *Fantasia*. This series utilizes the same shapes as the Harmony Ware series.

Kidney Shape, Three-footed, Shape 455

Photograph not available
at press time

Backstamp: Black transfer print "Fantasia by Wade of England—copyright Walt Disney Productions," impressed "England 455"

No.	Description	Colourways	Size	U.S.$	Can.$	U.K.£
1a	Fantasia	Grey outside/pink inside; black/white/pink print	55	85.00	120.00	45.00
1b	Fantasia	Pink outside/grey inside; black/white/pink print	55	85.00	120.00	45.00

WADE HEATH *(cont.)*

FAWN TRAY, 1961

This tray or butter dish was produced in the shape of a sliced log with a model of a fawn lying on the back rim. It was modelled by William Harper, and was first issued in September 1961. The original price was 4/11d.

Backstamp: Embossed "Wade Porcelain Made in England"

No.	Description	Colourways	Size	U.S.$	Can.$	U.K.£
1	Fawn	Honey/dark brown; beige/orange-brown fawn	95	52.00	75.00	28.00

GOLF CARTOON DISHES, 1960s

This was probably a set of four dishes, but only three have been reported to date. 1a reads *Many Happy Returns!*; 1b reads *Isn't it Wonderful, No Bunkers!*, and 1c reads *I've had dozens of lessons and read books but no-one told me that golf involved walking!*.

Many Happy Returns!   No Bunkers!   Walking!

Backstamp: Red or black printed "Wade England"

No.	Description	Colourways	Size	U.S.$	Can.$	U.K.£
1a	Many Happy Returns!	White; black print	105	10.00	15.00	5.00
1b	No Bunkers!	White; black print	105	10.00	15.00	5.00
1c	Walking!	White; black print	105	10.00	15.00	5.00

WADE HEATH (cont.)

HARLEQUIN DISHES, 1957-1958

This set of four curved-edge, nesting dishes has a starburst design in the centre. They were issued in February 1957 and withdrawn in January 1958. The original price for a boxed set was 6/11d.

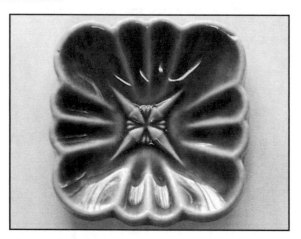

Backstamp: Embossed "Wade Porcelain Made in England"

No.	Description	Colourways	Size	U.S.$	Can.$	U.K.£
1a	Harlequin	Blue	70	10.00	15.00	5.00
1b	Harlequin	Dark grey	70	10.00	15.00	5.00
1c	Harlequin	Pink	70	10.00	15.00	5.00
1d	Harlequin	Yellow	70	10.00	15.00	5.00

WADE HEATH (cont.)

HARMONY WARE, 1957-c.1962
Kidney Shape, Three-footed, Shape 438

Wade produced 13 assorted shapes of bowls, jugs and vases called Harmony Ware, which were decorated in five different patterns. The Parasols three-footed dish, No. 1d, has the name 'Kilmarnock,' a Scottish town, added to the rim. These dishes are kidney-shaped and have three small feet.

Kidney shape, solid colour

Backstamp: **A.** Red transfer print "Wade England" with impressed "England" and "438"
B. Red transfer print "Wade England Fern" with impressed "England" and "438"
C. Black transfer print "Wade England Parasol" with impressed "England" and "438"
D. Black transfer print "A Dee Cee Souvenir by Wade England" with impressed "England" and "438"
E. Black "Wade England" and green shooting stars with impressed "England" and "438"
F. Impressed "Wade England" and "438"

No.	Description	Colourways	Size	U.S.$	Can.$	U.K.£
1a	Carnival	White; yellow/red/green flowers	98 x 300	50.00	70.00	25.00
1b	Fern	White; black/red fern	98 x 300	50.00	70.00	25.00
1c	Parasols	White; multicoloured parasols	98 x 300	50.00	70.00	25.00
1d	Parasols and 'Kilmarnock'	White; multicoloured parasols	98 x 300	50.00	70.00	25.00
1e	Shooting Stars	White; multicoloured stars	98 x 300	50.00	70.00	25.00
1f	Solid colour	Black	98 x 300	40.00	55.00	20.00
1g	Solid colour	Green	98 x 300	40.00	55.00	20.00
1h	Solid colour	White	98 x 300	40.00	55.00	20.00
1i	Solid colour	Yellow	98 x 300	40.00	55.00	20.00
1j	Two-tone	Green/peach	98 x 300	40.00	55.00	20.00
1k	Two-tone	Grey/pink	98 x 300	40.00	55.00	20.00

WADE HEATH (cont.)

HARMONY WARE (cont.)
Kidney Shape, Three-footed, Shape 455

Photograph not available
at press time

Backstamp:
A. Red transfer print "Wade England" with impressed "England" and "455"
B. Red transfer print "Wade England Fern" with impressed "England" and "455"
C. Black transfer print "Wade England Parasol" with impressed "England" and "455"
D. Black "Wade England" and green shooting stars with impressed "England" and "455"
E. Impressed "Wade England" and "455"

No.	Description	Colourways	Size	U.S.$	Can.$	U.K.£
1a	Carnival	White; yellow/red/green flowers	50 x 275	40.00	55.00	20.00
1b	Fern	White; black/red fern	50 x 275	40.00	55.00	20.00
1c	Parasols	White; multicoloured parasols	50 x 275	40.00	55.00	20.00
1d	Shooting stars	White; multicoloured stars	50 x 275	40.00	55.00	20.00
1e	Solid colour	Black	50 x 275	30.00	40.00	15.00
1f	Solid colour	Green	50 x 275	30.00	40.00	15.00
1g	Solid colour	White	50 x 275	30.00	40.00	15.00
1h	Solid colour	Yellow	50 x 275	30.00	40.00	15.00
1i	Two-tone	Green/peach	50 x 275	30.00	40.00	15.00
1j	Two-tone	Grey/pink	50 x 275	30.00	40.00	15.00

HEDGEHOG TRAY, 1961

Modelled in the shape of a hedgehog, the spiny back of the animal forms a detachable blue-grey lid. The original price was 6/6d.

Hedgehog tray

Backstamp: Embossed "Wade Porcelain Made in England"

No.	Description	Colourways	Size	U.S.$	Can.$	U.K.£
1	Hedgehog	Honey/red-brown; blue-grey design, lid	100	80.00	110.00	45.00

WADE HEATH (cont.)

HOLLYHOCKS AND LUPINS, SHAPE 372, c.1938

This pretty nut tray has an embossed design of hollyhocks and lupins. A tray has been found decorated in the 'gold blush' colours as used on Bramble Ware (see *The Charlton Standard Catalogue of Wade, Volume Three, Tableware*.)

Backstamp: Green ink stamp "Wade Heath England"

No.	Description	Colourways	Size	U.S.$	Can.$	U.K.£
1a	Hollyhocks and lupins	Cream; maroon/gold blush flowers	173	40.00	55.00	20.00
1b	Hollyhocks and lupins	Cream; multicoloured flowers	173	40.00	55.00	22.00

INDIAN CHIEF DISH, 1954
Round Irregular, Shape S.25/37

Issued in January 1954, the Indian chief dish portrays the embossed head of an Indian chief wearing a feather war bonnet. The original price was 11d.

Backstamp: Embossed "Wade England"

No.	Description	Colourways	Size	U.S.$	Can.$	U.K.£
1	Indian chief	Honey brown	85 x 90	100.00	150.00	60.00

WADE HEATH (cont.)

JACOBEAN AND KAWA PEDESTAL DISHES, 1990-1992

The Jacobean design is of red and black enamelled exotic flowers. Kawa is a Japanese design of peonies and bamboo stems.

Jacobean dish

Backstamp: **A.** Red print "Wade England" with two red lines and "Jacobean"
B. Gold print "Wade England" with two gold lines and "Kawa"

No.	Description	Colourways	Size	U.S.$	Can.$	U.K.£
1a	Jacobean	White; red/black print	153	30.00	40.00	15.00
1b	Kawa	White; pastel pink/green print; gold highlights	153	30.00	40.00	15.0

LADIES' TRAYS, c.1985

Backstamp: Green transfer print "Wade England"

No.	Description	Colourways	Size	U.S.$	Can.$	U.K.£
1a	Man's head	White; gold rim, silhouette; turquoise band, centre	125	15.00	20.00	8.00
1b	Regency couple	White; gold rim, decorations; multicoloured print	125	15.00	20.00	8.00

WADE HEATH (cont.)

LADY AND THE TRAMP SWEET TRAY, 1955

A scene from Walt Disney's *Lady and The Tramp* is shown on this dish, the backstamp indicates that this may have been intended as a set of dishes depicting scenes from *Lady and the Tramp*, but only the one dish has been found.

Backstamp: Blue transfer print "Scenes from Walt Disney's 'Lady & the Tramp' Sweet Tray by Wade England" in a scroll and "Copyright Walt Disney Productions. Made in England"

No.	Description	Colourways	Size	U.S.$	Can.$	U.K.£
1	Lady and the Tramp	White; yellow rim; multicoloured print	112	45.00	60.00	32.00

LADY CLARE DISHES, 1996

Although these dishes do not carry a Wade backstamp they were sold in the Wade shop during September 1996. They were produced in two colours

Lady Clare - Burgundy

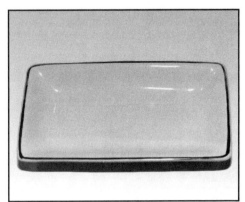

Lady Clare - White

Backstamp: Printed "Lady Clare"

No.	Description	Colourways	Size	U.S.$	Can.$	U.K.£
1a	Burgundy	White; gold rim	90	5.00	8.00	3.00
1b	White	Burgundy; gold rim	90	5.00	8.00	3.00

WADE HEATH (cont.)

LEAF DISHES, 1957-1959, 1980-1986

Three types of leaf-shaped dishes were produced between 1957 and 1959. The oak leaf dishes were issued from January 1957 to January 1958, the horse chestnut leaf dishes were issued from August 1957 to January 1958, and the ash-leaf dishes were issued from August 1958 to January 1959. They were originally sold in a boxed set of two for 3/6d. The beige and green horse chestnut dishes were re-issued by Wade Ireland from 1980-1986 in the same colours as the originals, the only difference being the backstamp.

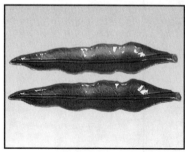  

| Ash leaf dishes | Horse chestsnut leaf dishes | Oak leaf dish |

Backstamp: **A:** Embossed "Wade Porcelain Made in England"
B: Impressed "Made in Ireland—Irish Porcelain—Eire tir a dheanta" with a shamrock and crown design

No.	Description	Colourways	Size	U.S.$	Can.$	U.K.£
1a	Ash	Beige	190	42.00	58.00	20.00
1b	Ash	Green	190	42.00	58.00	20.00
2a	Horse chestnut	Beige	80	8.00	10.00	4.00
2b	Horse chestnut	Green	80	8.00	10.00	4.00
2c	Horse chestnut	Yellow	80	14.00	20.00	10.00
3a	Oak	Beige	100	8.00	10.00	4.00
3b	Oak	Green	100	8.00	10.00	4.00

WADE HEATH (cont.)

MAMBO/ZAMBA, 1957
Oval dish, Shape 462

The Mambo design was first advertised in January 1957, a later advertisement shows a name change to Zamba. The name Mambo appears in the backstamp. Only one item has been found with the Mambo name. The larger Mambo dish has black transfer prints around the front edge, whereas the Zamba dish does not.

Mambo, large oval, two dancers

Backstamp: A. Red transfer print "Wade England Mambo"
B. Red transfer print "Wade England"

No.	Description	Colourways	Size	U.S.$	Can.$	U.K.£
1	Mambo	White; black prints	240	50.00	70.00	35.00
2	Zamba	White; black prints	125	40.00	55.00	25.00

Round, irregular dish, Shape 474

Zamba, round, irregular, two dancers

Backstamp: Black transfer print "Wade England"

No.	Description	Colourways	Size	U.S.$	Can.$	U.K.£
1	Zamba	White; black prints	125	40.00	55.00	24.00

WADE HEATH (cont.)

MAMBO/ZAMBA (cont.)
Square, Shape No. Unknown

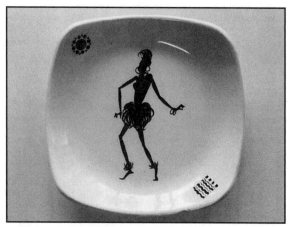

Zamba, square, dancer (1e)

Backstamp: Red transfer print "Wade England"

No.	Description	Colourways	Size	U.S.$	Can.$	U.K.£
1a	Dancer, both hands raised	White; black print	107	10.00	15.00	5.00
1b	Dancer, leaning forward, hands out	White; black print	107	10.00	15.00	5.00
1c	Dancer, left hand on skirt, right hand out	White; black print	107	10.00	15.00	5.00
1d	Dancer, right hand and leg raised	White; black print	107	10.00	15.00	5.00
1e	Dancer, right hand on skirt, left hand out	White; black print	107	10.00	15.00	5.00
1f	Two dancers	White; black print	107	10.00	15.00	5.00

WADE HEATH (cont.)

MAN IN A ROWBOAT TRAY, 1978-1984

The original tool for the 1961 seagull and boat tray was used for this model. A sleeping, bearded fisherman was added to the boat and the seagull was omitted, however the plinth on which it stood still appeared on some early models. The later style of boat does not have the plinth, and the width of the planks and the boat have been altered slightly.

The position of the man varies in some examples, The man has been placed slightly higher in some rowboats than others, the position difference is illustrated below.

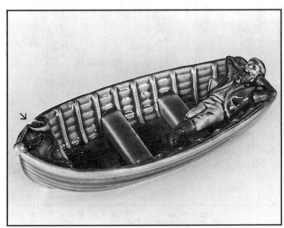

Rowboat with plinth

First position   Second position

Backstamp: Embossed "Wade Porcelain Made in England"

No.	Description	Colourways	Size	U.S.$	Can.$	U.K.£
1	With plinth	Honey-brown boat; blue/green/brown man	50 x 155	135.00	180.00	48.00
2	Without plinth	Honey-brown boat; blue/green/brown man	45 x 155	135.00	180.00	48.00

WADE HEATH *(cont.)*

MISCELLANEOUS DISHES, 1959-c.1962

A number of octagonal, round and square dishes were produced by Wade with different multicoloured transfer prints on them. The name of the set or the theme is unknown.

Baby Pegasus and Pan

Baby Pegasus and Pegasus

Horse-drawn passenger coach

Backstamp: Red transfer print "Wade England"

No.	Description	Colourways	Shape/Size	U.S.$	Can.$	U.K.£
1a	Baby Pegasus and Pan	White; multicoloured print	Square/106	20.00	30.00	10.00
1b	Baby Pegasus and Pegasus	White; multicoloured print	Square/106	20.00	30.00	10.00
2	Riviera woman with black cat	White; multicoloured print	Square/106	20.00	30.00	10.00
3	Shooting star	White; multicoloured print	Square/115	10.00	15.00	6.00
4a	Crinoline girl dancing	White; gold line; blue dress	Octagonal/110	10.00	15.00	5.00
4b	Crinoline girl dancing	White; gold line; green dress	Octagonal/110	10.00	15.00	5.00
4c	Crinoline girl dancing	White; gold line; grey dress	Octagonal/110	10.00	15.00	5.00
5	Horse-drawn passenger coach	White; gold line; multicoloured	Octagonal/110	10.00	15.00	5.00
6	Kitten in hat	Blue; brown hat; white kitten	Octagonal/110	10.00	15.00	5.00
7	Lady with parasol	White; gold line; blue dress	Octagonal/110	10.00	15.00	5.00
8	Mountain and lake	White; brown mountain; blue lake	Octagonal/110	10.00	15.00	5.00
9	Polish lady	White; gold line; white fur jacket; red dress	Octagonal/110	10.00	15.00	5.00
10	Public house	White; gold line; black print	Octagonal/110	10.00	15.00	5.00
11a	Roses, pink	White; gold line; pink roses	Octagonal/110	10.00	15.00	5.00
11b	Roses, yellow	White; gold line; yellow roses	Octagonal/110	10.00	15.00	5.00
12	Prince Festiniog railway	White; green train	Round/112	15.00	20.00	8.00
13a	Roses, blue	White; gold rim; blue roses	Round/108	14.00	18.00	5.00
13c	Rose, red	Pink; gold rim; red rose	Round/108	14.00	18.00	5.00

WADE HEATH (cont.)

MY FAIR LADY DISHES, 1958

These square dishes are decorated with transfer prints of characters from George Bernard Shaw's play, *Pygmalion*, which was produced in 1956 as the musical, *My Fair Lady*.

Eliza Dolittle, flower seller

Eliza and Professor Higgins

Backstamp: Red transfer print "Wade England"

No.	Description	Colourways	Size	U.S.$	Can.$	U.K.£
1a	Eliza Dolittle, flower girl	White; blue/black print	112	8.00	10.00	4.00
1b	Eliza Dolittle at Ascot	White; blue/black print	112	8.00	10.00	4.00
1c	Professor Henry Higgins	White; blue/black print	112	8.00	10.00	4.00
1d	Eliza Dolittle and Professor Higgins	White; blue/black print	112	8.00	10.00	4.00
1e	Eliza Dolittle, flower girl	Grey; multicoloured print	112	8.00	12.00	5.00
1f	Eliza Dolittle at Ascot	Grey; multicoloured print	112	8.00	12.00	5.00
1g	Professor Henry Higgins	Grey; multicoloured print	112	8.00	12.00	5.00
1h	Eliza Dolittle and Professor Higgins	Grey; multicoloured print	112	8.00	12.00	5.00

WADE HEATH *(cont.)*

NEST-O-TRAYS, 1960-1961

First issued in August 1960, the original price of the Nest-o-trays was 7/11d for a set of four.

Impressed buttercups

Backstamp: Embossed "Wade Porcelain Made in England"

No.	Description	Colourways	Size	U.S.$	Can.$	U.K.£
1a	Nest-o-trays	Beige/grey	96	8.00	10.00	4.00
1b	Nest-o-trays	Black	96	8.00	10.00	4.00
1c	Nest-o-trays	Grey-blue	96	8.00	10.00	4.00
1d	Nest-o-trays	Honey	96	8.00	10.00	4.00
1e	Nest-o-trays	Rose	96	8.00	10.00	4.00
1f	Nest-o-trays	Straw yellow	96	8.00	10.00	4.00
1g	Nest-o-trays	White	96	8.00	10.00	4.00

NEW ZEALAND DISHES, EARLY 1960s

Backstamp: **A.** Red transfer print "Wade England"
B. White printed "A Wade Product" inside a black diamond

No.	Description	Colourways	Size	U.S.$	Can.$	U.K.£
1a	Kiwi	White; multicoloured print	112	10.00	15.00	5.00
1b	Tiki	White; multicoloured print	112	10.00	15.00	5.00
1c	Maori house	White; multicoloured print	112	10.00	15.00	5.00
1d	Maori chief	White; multicoloured print	112	10.00	15.00	5.00

WADE HEATH (cont.)

ORCHARD FRUITS AND BERRIES DISHES, 1960

The Apple and Grapes dish has been found in two shapes, octagonal and square.

Apple and grapes

Backstamp: Red transfer print "Wade England"

No.	Description	Colourways	Size	U.S.$	Can.$	U.K.£
1a	Apple and grapes	White; multicoloured print	Octagonal/122	10.00	15.00	5.00
2a	Apple and grapes	White; multicoloured print	Square/105	10.00	15.00	5.00
2b	Apple and strawberries	White; multicoloured print	Square/105	10.00	15.00	5.00
2c	Pears and grapes	White; multicoloured print	Square/105	10.00	15.00	5.00
2d	Plums and grapes	White; multicoloured print	Square/105	10.00	15.00	5.00

PET FACES DISHES, 1959-1960

The original price of the Pet Faces dishes was 4/6d.

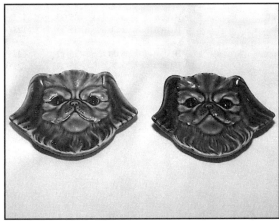

Pekinese pet faces dishes

Siamese pet faces dishes

Backstamp: Impressed "Wade Porcelain Made in England"

No.	Description	Colourways	Size	U.S.$	Can.$	U.K.£
1	Pekinese	Beige; blue markings	75	25.00	35.00	15.00
	Boxed pair			50.00	70.00	25.00
2	Siamese cat	Beige; blue markings	80	25.00	35.00	15.00
	Boxed pair			50.00	70.00	25.00

WADE HEATH (cont.)

RECTANGULAR TRAYS, c.1945

Some of these trays were sold packaged with a matching box, which could be used for cigarettes or candy. Because they were all hand decorated, the decoration varies somewhat from piece to piece. The original price was 1/6d each.

 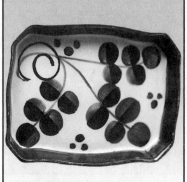 

| Rectangular Aster tray | Rectangular Cranberry tray | Rectangular Shamrock tray |

Backstamp: **A.** Green ink stamp "Harvest Ware Wade England"
B. Black ink stamp "Wade England," 1940s-early 1950s

No.	Description	Colourways	Size	U.S.$	Can.$	U.K.£
1a	Aster	Copper; pink/yellow flower; green leaves;	105	25.00	35.00	12.00
1b	Aster	Cream; pink/yellow flower; green leaves; brown streaks	105	25.00	35.00	12.00
1c	Blue Tulip	White; pale blue stylised flower; grey leaves	105	25.00	35.00	12.00
1d	Clover	Copper outside; cream inside; copper/ purple lustre clover leaves	105	25.00	35.00	12.00
1e	Cranberry	Copper outside; white inside; red berries; brown streaks; green leaves	105	25.00	35.00	12.00
1f	Daisy	Cream; purple daisy; green/brown leaves	105	25.00	35.00	12.00
1g	Fruit	White/maroon; copper lustre; maroon leaves; black berries	105	25.00	35.00	12.00
1h	Peony	Copper outside; cream inside; mauve/	105	25.00	35.00	12.00
		yellow flower; green leaves; brown lines green leaves; brown streaks	105	25.00	35.00	12.00
1i	Shamrock	Cream; green leaves	105	25.00	35.00	12.00

WADE HEATH (cont.

SCALLOPED DISHES, S25/11, 1954

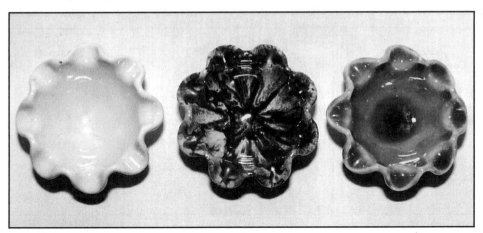

Original Issue, 1954

Backstamp: Embossed "Wade England" in the hollow of the base

No.	Description	Colourways	Size	U.S.$	Can.$	U.K.£
1a	Scalloped dish	Dark green	85	13.00	18.00	5.00
1b	Scalloped dish	Beige	85	13.00	18.00	5.00
1c	Scalloped dish	Mint green	85	13.00	18.00	5.00
1d	Scalloped dish	Light grey	85	13.00	18.00	5.00
1e	Scalloped dish	Pale blue	85	13.00	18.00	5.00
1f	Scalloped dish	Pale yellow	85	13.00	18.00	5.00
1g	Scalloped dish	Turquoise	85	13.00	18.00	5.00

Reissued as Crackle Ashtrays, 1962

Reissued in 1962 and renamed crackle ashtrays. They were coloured in marbled glazes and were sold in a boxed set of four for 7/11d.

Backstamp: Embossed "Wade England"

No.	Description	Colourways	Size	U.S.$	Can.$	U.K.£
1a	Crackle ashtray	Dark blue/light blue	85	15.00	20.00	8.00
1b	Crackle ashtray	Dark blue/light green	85	15.00	20.00	8.00
1c	Crackle ashtray	Dark brown/grey	85	15.00	20.00	8.00
1d	Crackle ashtray	Dark red/light red	85	15.00	20.00	8.00
1e	Crackle ashtray	Maroon/cream	85	15.00	20.00	8.00
1f	Crackle ashtray	Purple/blue	85	15.00	20.00	8.00
1g	Crackle ashtray	Turquoise/green	85	15.00	20.00	8.00
1h	Crackle ashtray	Yellow/brown	85	15.00	20.00	8.00

Reissued as Crackle Dishes, 1971

Now named crackle dishes, they were glazed in darker colours than the original 1950s dishes. The dark green glaze was re-used. Each was individually boxed.

Backstamp: Embossed "Wade England"

No.	Description	Colourways	Size	U.S.$	Can.$	U.K.£
1a	Crackle dish	Dark blue	85	13.00	18.00	5.00
1b	Crackle dish	Dark green	85	13.00	18.00	5.00
1c	Crackle dish	Dark grey	85	13.00	18.00	5.00
1d	Crackle dish	Honey brown	85	13.00	18.00	5.00
1e	Crackle dish	Maroon	85	13.00	18.00	5.00

WADE HEATH (cont.)

SCOTLAND DISHES, 1959-c.1962

These dishes can be found in boxes marked "Frae Bonnie Scotland" and are decorated with prints of Scotsmen and Scottish scenes.

Forth Bridge, Firth of Forth, Scotland

Scots piper

Scots dancer

Backstamp: Red transfer print "Wade England"

No.	Description	Colourways	Shape/Size	U.S.$	Can.$	U.K.£
1a	Scots piper/busby	White; silver bands; red/yellow/blue tartan	Round/108	10.00	15.00	5.00
1b	Scots piper/glengarry	White; silver bands; blue/red tartan	Round/108	10.00	15.00	5.00
1c	Scots dancer	White; silver bands; red/yellow tartan	Round/108	10.00	15.00	5.00
2a	Forth Bridge	White; gold band; black/blue print	Octagonal/110	10.00	15.00	5.00
2b	Scots piper/busby	White; red/yellow/blue tartan	Octagonal/110	10.00	15.00	5.00
2c	Scots piper/glengarry	White; blue/red tartan	Octagonal/110	10.00	15.00	5.00
2d	Scots dancer	White; red/yellow tartan	Octagonal/110	10.00	15.00	5.00

SEAGULL BOAT TRAY, 1961

This tray comprises a rowboat with an open-winged seagull perched on a small plinth in the prow. First issued in January 1961, it sold for 6/11d.

Backstamp: Embossed "Wade Porcelain Made in England"

No.	Description	Colourways	Size	U.S.$	Can.$	U.K.£
1	Seagull boat tray	Honey-brown boat; white seagull; black wing tips	155	80.00	110.00	40.00

WADE HEATH (cont.)

SHELL DISHES, 1953-1956

The base of the shell on version one is plain; version two is decorated with a curling rib on each side of the base. For Shell Dishes with hand written slogans 'Turn Right,' 'Keep Left,' etc, see *The Charlton Standard Catalogue of Wade, Volume One, General Issuue,* Commissioned section.

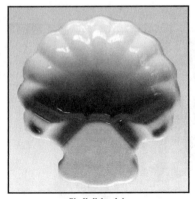  

Shell dish, plain   Shell dish, curl, gold edging   Shell dish, gold edging, rose print

Backstamp: **A.** Gold transfer print "Wade England A" with embossed "BCM/OWL"
             B. Embossed "BCM/OWL"

No.	Description	Colourways	Size	U.S.$	Can.$	U.K.£
1a	Shell/plain	Beige	85	20.00	30.00	10.00
1b	Shell/plain	Pale blue	85	20.00	30.00	10.00
1c	Shell/plain	Pale green	85	20.00	30.00	10.00
1d	Shell/plain	Pink	85	20.00	30.00	10.00
1e	Shell/plain	Yellow	85	20.00	30.00	10.00
2a	Shell/curl	Pale blue; gold edging	85	20.00	30.00	10.00
2b	Shell/curl	Pale green; gold edging; rose print	85	20.00	30.00	10.00
2c	Shell/curl	Pink; gold edging	85	20.00	30.00	10.00
2d	Shell/curl	Violet; gold edging	85	20.00	30.00	10.00
2e	Shell/curl	Yellow; gold edging	85	20.00	30.00	10.00

SHORE CRAB DISH, 1960-1961

This crab-shaped dish has an embossed lift-off lid. First issued in January 1960, the original price was 4/6.

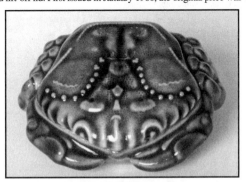

Crab dish

Backstamp: Embossed "Wade Porcelain Made in England"

No.	Description	Colourways	Size	U.S.$	Can.$	U.K.£
1	Shore crab	Brown; blue/grey design	75	38.00	60.00	25.00

WADE HEATH (cont.)

SILHOUETTE SERIES TRAYS, 1961-1962

These trays were modelled in the shape of a parallelogram with animals embossed on them. The giraffe and zebra trays were first issued in September 1961, their original price was 3/11d. In the spring of 1962 a Viking ship tray, with an original price of 4/6d, was added to the series. During the summer of 1962, a lion tray was also added to the series.

Silhouette series trays

Backstamp: Embossed "Wade Porcelain made in England"

No.	Description	Colourways	Size	U.S.$	Can.$	U.K.£
1a	Giraffe	Pale blue/black; blue giraffe	130	25.00	35.00	12.00
1b	Giraffe	Pale blue/black; white giraffe	130	25.00	35.00	12.00
2a	Lion	Pale blue/black; blue lion	120	25.00	35.00	15.00
2b	Lion	Pale blue/black; white lion	120	25.00	35.00	15.00
3a	Viking ship	Pale blue/black; blue ship	135	25.00	35.00	15.00
3b	Viking ship	Pale blue/black; white ship	135	25.00	35.00	15.00
3c	Viking ship	Pale blue/black; yellow/lilac ship	135	25.00	35.00	15.00
3d	Viking ship	White; black/blue/yellow ship	135	25.00	35.00	15.00
4a	Zebra	Blue	130	25.00	35.00	15.00
4b	Zebra	Pale blue/black; blue zebra	130	25.00	35.00	15.00
4c	Zebra	Pale blue/black; white zebra	130	25.00	35.00	15.00

WADE HEATH *(cont.)*

SOLDIERS OF THE QUEEN DISHES, 1959

These transfer prints were also used on tankards, see *The Charlton Standard Catalogue of Wade, Volume One, General Issues.*

Scots Guards, Life Guards, Drum Horse on round dish   Trumpeter on square dish

Backstamp: **A.** Black transfer print "Drum Horse - drums were formerly used for giving orders to a regiment. Their combined weight is 116lbs. Pompey is probably the most illustrious Drum Horse of recent years. He was on duty at the Coronation of Queen Elizabeth II. By Wade of England"

B. Black transfer print "The Life Guards - Formed in 1660 from a body of gentlemen who went into exile with Charles Stuart. The scarlet cloak was worn by the regiment in the eighteenth century. Sleeves were added in 1796. By Wade of England"

C. Black transfer print "The Scots Guards - Formed in 1642 by the 8th Earl of Argyll. Officers wear 'Orders of the Thistle' as Badges of rank. The Guards fought at the battle of Dettengen in 1764 under George II. The last British Sovereign to lead his army in the field. By Wade of England"

D. Black transfer print "Trumpeters - Were originally chosen as having an acceptable manner to act as special orderlies to Generals, & to parley with the enemy. Their swords had broken off blades, to symbolise these non-combatant roles. By Wade of England"

E. Black transfer print "The Royal Horse Guards - the only old regiment which has always worn blue. At the battle of Warburg 1760 their commander. The Marquess of Granby lost his wig while leading a charge. giving rise to the expression 'going for it baldheaded', by Wade of England"

No.	Description	Colourways	Shape/Size	U.S.$	Can.$	U.K.£
1a	Drum horse	White; gold rim; multicoloured print	Round/105-110	10.00	15.00	5.00
1b	Life Guards	White; gold rim; multicoloured print	Round/105-110	10.00	15.00	5.00
1c	Life Guards trooper	White; gold rim; multicoloured print	Round/105-110	10.00	15.00	5.00
1d	The Royal Horse Guards	White; gold rim; multicoloured print	Round/105-110	10.00	15.00	5.00
1e	Scots Guards	White; gold rim; multicoloured print	Round/105-110	10.00	15.00	5.00
1f	Trumpeter	White; gold rim; multicoloured print	Round/105-110	10.00	15.00	5.00
2a	Drum horse	White; multicoloured print	Square/110	10.00	15.00	5.00
2b	Life Guards	White; multicoloured print	Square/110	10.00	15.00	5.00
2c	Life Guards trooper	White; multicoloured print	Square/110	10.00	15.00	5.00
2d	The Royal Horse Guards	White; multicoloured print	Square/110	10.00	15.00	5.00
2e	Scots Guards	White; multicoloured print	Square/110	10.00	15.00	5.00
2f	Trumpeter	White; multicoloured print	Square/110	10.00	15.00	5.00

WADE HEATH *(cont.)*

SOUTH AFRICA DISHES, c.1962

These dishes, decorated with coloured transfer prints of African animals, were originally sold as a boxed set. Only one dish, the Giraffe, has been reported in the round shape.

Set of four - Rhino, Giraffe, Zebra and Lion

Backstamp: Red transfer print "Wade England"

No.	Description	Colourways	Size	U.S.$	Can.$	U.K.£
1a	Giraffe	White; multicoloured print	Square/112	10.00	15.00	5.00
1b	Lion	White; multicoloured print	Square/112	10.00	15.00	5.00
1c	Rhino	White; multicoloured print	Square/112	10.00	15.00	5.00
1d	Zebra	White; multicoloured print	Square/112	10.00	15.00	5.00
2	Giraffe	White; gold rim; multicoloured print	Round/112	10.00	15.00	5.00

WADE HEATH (cont.)

SOUVENIR DISHES
Bahamas Dishes, c.1952-c.1962

Three different shapes of dishes, round, square and tyre, can be found carrying transfer prints of various Bahamian scenes. The tyre dishes types 3a and 3b, are from the same mould as the Veteran Car tyre dishes.

Nassau, horse and landau, tyre dish

Straw market, Nassau, tyre dish

Backstamp: Red transfer print "Wade England"

No.	Description	Colourways	Shape/Size	U.S.$	Can.$	U.K.£
1a	Bahamian constable	White; red band; multicoloured print	Round/110	8.00	12.00	4.00
1b	Nassau, Bahamas	White; red band; multicoloured print	Round/110	8.00	12.00	4.00
2	Paradise Beach, Nassau	White; multicoloured print	Square/130	8.00	12.00	4.00
3a	Nassau, Bahamas	White; grey rim; multicoloured print	Tyre/105	10.00	12.00	5.00
3b	Straw Market, Nassau, Bahamas	White; grey rim; multicoloured print	Tyre/105	10.00	12.00	5.00

Bermuda Dish, c.1962

This dish has a transfer printed 'Coat of Arms' of the Lions Club of Bermuda in the centre.

Photograph not available
at press time

Backstamp: Black transfer print "Wade England"

No.	Description	Colourways	Shape/Size	U.S.$	Can.$	U.K.£
1	Lions Club Bermuda	White; blue band; multicoloured print blue and black lettering	Round/110	8.00	12.00	4.00

WADE HEATH (cont.)

SOUVENIR DISHES (cont.)
British Columbia, c.1952-c.1962

Backstamp: Black transfer print "British Columbia Canada's evergreen playground on the Pacific Coast has for its official emblem the flower of the Dogwood tree - by Wade of England"

No.	Description	Colourways	Shape/Size	U.S.$	Can.$	U.K.£
1	Victoria, dogwood	White; multicoloured print	Round/110	8.00	12.00	4.00

WADE HEATH (cont.)

SOUVENIR DISHES (cont.)
British Isles Dishes, 1957-c.1962

Bexhill-on-Sea

Great Britain

Channel Islands

Guernsey, Coat of Arms

Ilfracombe bikini girl

Backstamp: **A.** Red transfer print "Wade England"
B. Black transfer print "A Dee Cee Souvenir by Wade"
C. Black transfer print "Dee-Cee a Souvenir by Wade England"

No.	Description	Colourways	Shape/Size	U.S.$	Can.$	U.K.£
1a	Bexhill-on-Sea, Pixie	White; yellow band; red/green pixie; black lettering	Round/110	10.00	15.00	5.00
1b	Bognor, Jersey	White; red band/pennant; black lettering	Round/110	10.00	15.00	5.00
1c	Brighton, Jersey	White; red band/pennant; black lettering	Round/110	10.00	15.00	5.00
1d	Corbiere Lighthouse, Jersey	White; yellow band; multicoloured print	Round/110	10.00	15.00	5.00
1e	Prince Festiniog Railway Train	White; gold band; multicoloured print	Round/110	10.00	15.00	5.00
1f	Stockport, gypsy caravan	White; yellow band; multicoloured print	Round/110	10.00	15.00	5.00
1g	Warkworth Castle	White; yellow band; multicoloured print	Round/110	10.00	15.00	5.00
2a	Channel Islands	White; multicoloured maps	Square/108	10.00	15.00	5.00
2b	Great Britain	White; multicoloured flags	Square/108	10.00	15.00	5.00
2c	Guernsey, Coat of Arms	White; red shield; green laurel wreath	Square/108	10.00	15.00	5.00
2d	Guernsey, cow	White; multicoloured print	Square/108	10.00	15.00	5.00
2e	Ilfracombe Bikini Girl	White; multi coloured print	Square/108	10.00	15.00	5.00
2f	Polperro, Pixie	White; red/green pixie; black lettering	Square/108	10.00	15.00	5.00
2g	Woolcombe, Pixie	White; red/green pixie; black lettering	Square/108	10.00	15.00	5.00

WADE HEATH (cont.)

SOUVENIR DISHES (cont.)
British Seaside Tyre Dishes, c.1955-c.1962

These white tyre dishes can be found with transfer prints of galleons or sail boats. Each dish has the name of a different British seaside town beneath the transfer print. The galleon tyre dish No. 1a has been found without the town name, see page 115.

Beccles, galleon

Felixstowe, galleon

Guernsey, sailboat

Backstamp A. Red transfer print "Wade England"
B. Printed "A Dee Cee Souvenir by Wade"

No.	Description	Colourways	Size	U.S.$	Can.$	U.K.£
1a	Beccles	White; blue line, galleon	Tyre/105	10.00	15.00	5.00
1b	Brightlingsea	White; red line, sail boat	Tyre/105	10.00	15.00	5.00
1c	Felixstowe	White; green line, galleon	Tyre/105	10.00	15.00	5.00
1d	Guernsey	White; red line, sail boat	Tyre/105	10.00	15.00	5.00
1e	Isle of Wight	White; red line, sail boat	Tyre/105	10.00	15.00	5.00
1f	Oulton Broad	White; red line, sail boat	Tyre/105	10.00	15.00	5.00
1g	Whitby	White; red line, sail boat	Tyre/105	10.00	15.00	5.00

WADE HEATH (cont.)

SOUVENIR DISHES (cont.)
Canadian Dishes, c.1952-c.1962

Lobster, from Canada's East Coast

Royal Canadian Mounted Police

Backstamp: Red transfer print "Wade England"

No.	Description	Colourways	Shape/Size	U.S.$	Can.$	U.K.£
1a	Lobster and miniature trap	White; pale blue band; multicoloured print	Round/110	10.00	15.00	8.00
1b	Lobster and miniature trap	White; red band; multicoloured print	Round/110	10.00	15.00	8.00
1c	Lobster and miniature trap	White; yellow band; multicoloured print	Round/110	10.00	15.00	8.00
1d	Lobster, from Canada's East Coast	White; red band; multicoloured print	Round/110	10.00	15.00	8.00
1e	Royal Canadian Mounted Police	White; black band; multicoloured print	Round/110	10.00	15.00	8.00

Characters of London Dishes, c.1955-c.1962

Although only one dish has been reported to date, the backstamp implies there should be a set of dishes with this theme.

Backstamp: Blue transfer print "Characters of London by Wade England"

No.	Description	Colourways	Shape/Size	U.S.$	Can.$	U.K.£
1	Beefeater	White; multicoloured print	Square/115	10.00	15.00	5.00

WADE HEATH *(cont.)*

SOUVENIR DISHES *(cont.)*
London Souvenir Dishes, c.1955-c.1962

| Houses of Parliament | Nelson's Column | Tower Bridge | St. Paul's Cathedral |

Backstamp: A. Red transfer print "Wade England" **B.** Small transfer print of a lamppost and wrought-iron fence

No.	Description	Colourways	Shape/Size	U.S.$	Can.$	U.K.£
1a	Big Ben	White; blue band; black/blue print	Round/110	12.00	18.00	6.00
1b	Big Ben	White; green band; black/blue print	Round/110	12.00	18.00	6.00
1c	Big Ben	White; red band; black/blue print	Round/110	12.00	18.00	6.00
1d	Big Ben	White; yellow band; black/blue print	Round/110	12.00	18.00	6.00
1e	City of London Arms	White; gold line; multicoloured print	Round/110	12.00	18.00	6.00
1f	Eros, Piccadilly Circus	White; black band; black/blue print	Round/110	12.00	18.00	6.00
1g	Eros, Piccadilly Circus	White; blue band; black/blue print	Round/110	12.00	18.00	6.00
1h	Eros, Piccadilly Circus	White; green band; black/blue print	Round/110	12.00	18.00	6.00
1i	Eros, Piccadilly Circus	White; red band; black/blue print	Round/110	12.00	18.00	6.00
1j	Eros, Piccadilly Circus	White; yellow band; black/blue print	Round/110	12.00	18.00	6.00
1k	St Paul's Cathedral	White; blue band; black/blue print	Round/110	12.00	18.00	6.00
1l	Tower Bridge	Black; gold line; white print	Round/110	12.00	18.00	6.00
1m	Tower Bridge	White; blue band; black/blue print	Round/110	12.00	18.00	6.00
1n	Tower Bridge	White; green band; black/blue print	Round/110	12.00	18.00	6.00
1o	Tower Bridge	White; red band; black/blue print	Round/110	12.00	18.00	6.00
1p	Tower Bridge	White; red band; multicoloured print	Round/110	12.00	18.00	6.00
1q	Tower Bridge	White; yellow band; black/blue print	Round/110	12.00	18.00	6.00
1r	Trafalgar Square	White; blue band; black/blue print	Round/110	12.00	18.00	6.00
1s	Trafalgar Square	White; green band; black/blue print	Round/110	12.00	18.00	6.00
1t	Trafalgar Square	White; red band; black/blue print	Round/110	12.00	18.00	6.00
1u	Trafalgar Square	White; yellow band; black/blue print	Round/110	12.00	18.00	6.00
2	Tower Bridge	White; blue band; black/blue print	Round/135	12.00	18.00	6.00
3a	Big Ben	White; multicoloured print	Square/108	12.00	18.00	6.00
3b	Buckingham Palace	White; gold rim; multicoloured print	Square/108	12.00	18.00	6.00
3c	Houses of Parliament	White; gold rim; multicoloured print	Square/108	12.00	18.00	6.00
3d	Houses of Parliament and Big Ben	White; multicoloured print	Square/108	12.00	18.00	6.00
3e	London Coat of Arms	White; multicoloured print	Square/108	12.00	18.00	6.00
3f	London Palladium	White; multicoloured print	Square/108	12.00	18.00	6.00
3g	Nelson's Column Trafalgar Square	White; gold rim; multicoloured print	Square/108	12.00	18.00	6.00
3h	Piccadilly Circus	White; gold rim; multicoloured print	Square/108	12.00	18.00	6.00
3i	Piccadilly Circus	White; multicoloured print	Square/108	12.00	18.00	6.00
3j	St. Paul's Cathedral	White; multicoloured print	Square/108	12.00	18.00	6.00
3k	Tower Bridge	White; gold rim; multicoloured print	Square/108	12.00	18.00	6.00
3l	Tower Bridge	White; multicoloured print	Square/108	12.00	18.00	6.00
3m	Trafalgar Square	White; gold rim; multicoloured print	Square/108	12.00	18.00	6.00
4	St. Paul's Cathedral	White; gold rim; multicoloured print	Square, ribbed/108	12.00	18.00	6.00

WADE HEATH *(cont.)*

SOUVENIR DISHES *(cont.)*
New Brunswick, c.1952-c.1962

Backstamp: Red transfer print "Wade England"

No.	Description	Colourways	Shape/Size	U.S.$	Can.$	U.K.£
1a	Covered bridge	White; red band; multicoloured print	Round/110	10.00	15.00	8.00
1b	Map	White; pale green band; multicoloured print	Round/110	10.00	15.00	8.00
1c	Map	White; red band; multicoloured print	Round/110	10.00	15.00	8.00
1d	Map	White; yellow band; multicoloured print	Round/110	10.00	15.00	8.00
1e	Reversing Falls	White; red band; multicoloured print	Round/110	10.00	15.00	8.00
1f	Reversing Falls	White; yellow band; multicoloured print	Round/108	10.00	15.00	8.00
2a	Map and emblems	White; multicoloured print	Square/108	10.00	15.00	8.00
2b	Alexander Graham Bell Museum	White; multicoloured print	Square/108	10.00	15.00	8.00

WADE HEATH *(cont.)*

SOUVENIR DISHES *(cont.)*
Nova Scotia, c.1952-c.1962

Nova Scotia, The Gateway to Canada

Welcome to Nova Scotia

Replica of "H.M.S. Bounty"

Backstamp: Red transfer print "Wade England"

No.	Description	Colourways	Shape/Size	U.S.$	Can.$	U.K.£
1a	Bluenose Ferry	White; black band; multicoloured print; "Bar Harbour Maine to Yarmouth Nova Scotia"	Round/110	10.00	15.00	8.00
1b	Bluenose Ferry	White; blue band; multicoloured print; "Bar Harbour Maine to Yarmouth Nova Scotia"	Round/110	10.00	15.00	8.00
1c	Bluenose Ferry	White; yellow band; multicoloured print; "Bar Harbour Maine to Yarmouth Nova Scotia"	Round/110	10.00	15.00	8.00
1d	Canso Causeway	White; red band; multicoloured print;	Round/110	10.00	15.00	8.00
1e	Cape Breton Island	White; green band; multi coloured print	Round/110	10.00	15.00	8.00
1f	Nova Scotia, Piper	White; red band; multicoloured print; "The Gateway to Canada"	Round/110	10.00	15.00	8.00
1g	Nova Scotia, Piper	White; blue band; multicoloured print; "Welcome to Canada"	Round/110	10.00	15.00	8.00
1h	Nova Scotia, Piper	White; yellow band; multicoloured print; "Welcome to Nova Scotia"	Round/110	10.00	15.00	8.00
1i	Nova Scotia, Piper	White; black band; multicoloured print; "Welcome to Nova Scotia"	Round/110	10.00	15.00	8.00
1j	Replica of "HMS Bounty	White; blue band; multicoloured print "Replica of H.M.S Bounty built at Lunenburg, Nova Scotia. 1960"	Round/110	10.00	15.00	8.00
2a	Map and emblems	White; multicoloured print	Square/108	10.00	15.00	8.00
2b	Nova Scotia	White; multicoloured print; "The Gateway to Canada"	Square/108	10.00	15.00	8.00
2c	Replica of "H.M.S. Bounty"	White; multicoloured print; "Replica of H.M.S. Bounty Built at Lunenburg, Nova Scotia. 1960"	Square/108	10.00	15.00	8.00

WADE HEATH (cont.)

SOUVENIR DISHES (cont.)
Prince Edward Island, c.1952-c.1962

Photograph not available
at press time

Backstamp: Red transfer print "Wade England"

No.	Description	Colourways	Shape/Size	U.S.$	Can.$	U.K.£
1a	Anne of Green Gables' home	White; yellow band; multicoloured print	Round/110	10.00	15.00	8.00
1b	Anne of Green Gables' home	White; pale blue band; multicoloured print	Round/110	10.00	15.00	8.00
1c	Map	White; pale blue band; multicoloured print	Round/110	10.00	15.00	8.00
1d	Map	White; yellow; multicoloured print	Round/110	10.00	15.00	8.00

Province Quebec, c.1952-c.1962

Percé Rock, Percé, P.Q.

Backstamp: Red transfer print "Wade England"

No.	Description	Colourways	Shape/Size	U.S.$	Can.$	U.K.£
1	Percé Rock, Percé, P.Q.	White; red band; multicoloured print	Round/110	10.00	15.00	8.00

WADE HEATH (cont.)

SOUVENIR DISHES (cont.)
Remember? Dishes, 1957-c.1960

These dishes all have the same multicoloured print of a very tired baggage porter in the centre, but with different names of towns.

Remember? Broadway

Backstamp: **A.** Red transfer print "Wade England"
B. Black transfer print "Wade England"
C. Blue transfer print "A Desmond Cooper Souvenir by Wade"

No.	Description	Colourways	Shape/Size	U.S.$	Can.$	U.K.£
1a	Remember? Aberdovey	White; red band; multicoloured print	Round/110	10.00	15.00	5.00
1b	Remember? Broadway	White; yellow band; multicoloured print	Round/110	10.00	15.00	5.00
1c	Remember? Cleveleys	White; yellow band; multicoloured print	Round/110	10.00	15.00	5.00
1d	Remember? London	White; blue band; multicoloured print	Round/110	10.00	15.00	5.00
1e	Remember? London	White; red band; multicoloured print	Round/110	10.00	15.00	5.00
2	Remember? Broadway	White; multicoloured print	Square/108	10.00	15.00	5.00
2	Remember? Great Yarmouth	White; multicoloured print	Square/108	10.00	15.00	5.00

SHAPE INDEX

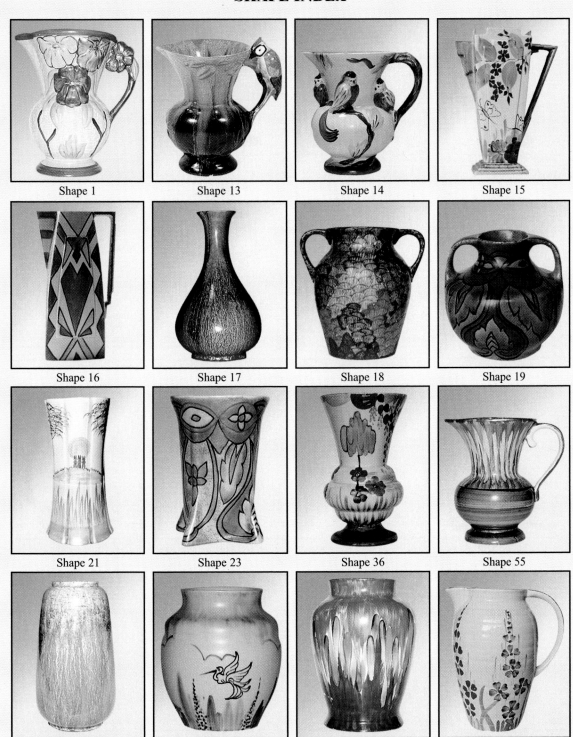

Shape 1

Shape 13

Shape 14

Shape 15

Shape 16

Shape 17

Shape 18

Shape 19

Shape 21

Shape 23

Shape 36

Shape 55

Shape 60

Shape 61

Shape 69

Shape 76

Shape 88

Shape 90

Shape 92

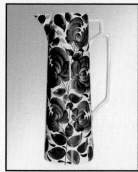

Shape 93

Shape 94

Shape 98/2

Shape 99

Shape 100

Shape104

Shape106

Shape 107

Shape 110

Shape 112

Shape 113

Shape 114

Shape 119

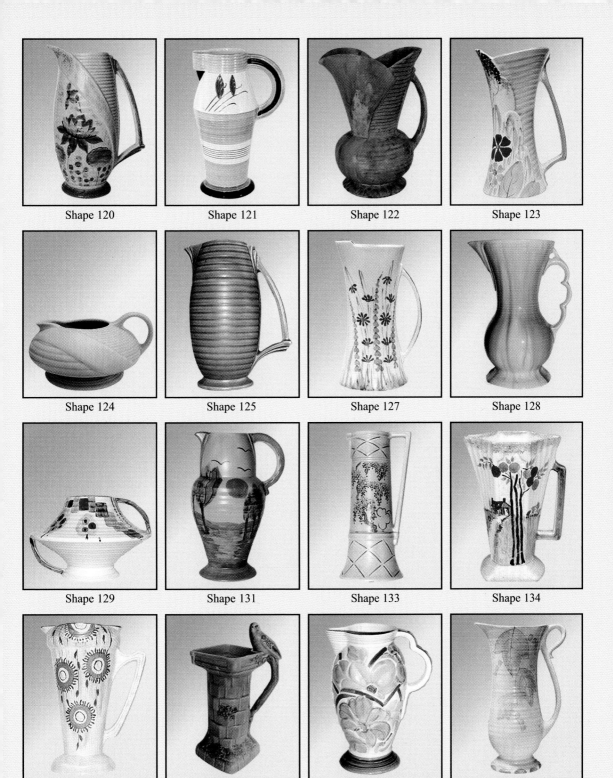

Shape 120

Shape 121

Shape 122

Shape 123

Shape 124

Shape 125

Shape 127

Shape 128

Shape 129

Shape 131

Shape 133

Shape 134

Shape 135

Shape 143

Shape 144

Shape 145

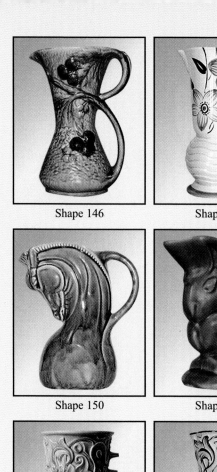

Shape 146

Shape 147

Shape 148

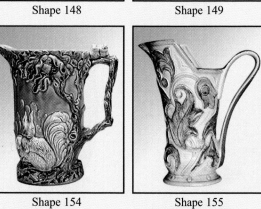

Shape 149

Shape 150

Shape 152

Shape 154

Shape 155

Shape 156

Shape 157

Shape 158

Shape 159

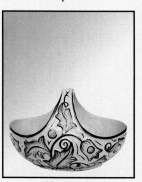

Shape 161

Shape 164

Shape 168

Shape 169

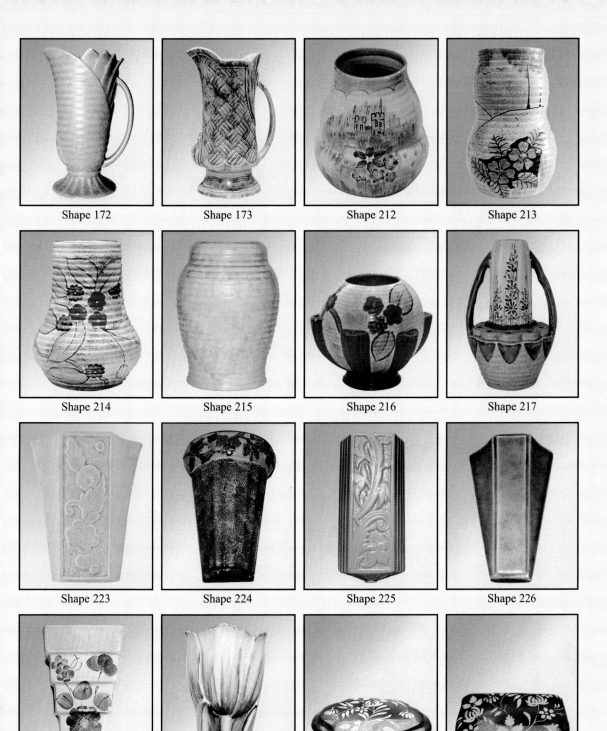

Shape 172

Shape 173

Shape 212

Shape 213

Shape 214

Shape 215

Shape 216

Shape 217

Shape 223

Shape 224

Shape 225

Shape 226

Shape 228

Shape 229

Shape 241

Shape 242

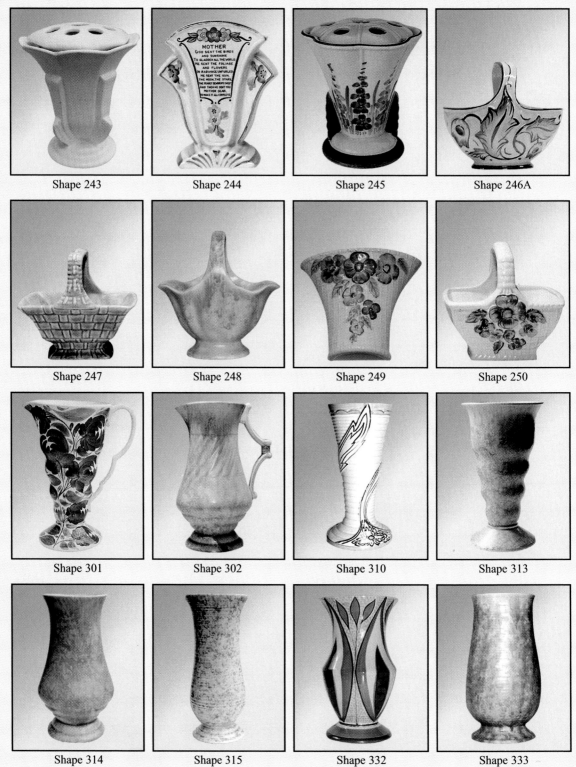

Shape 243

Shape 244

Shape 245

Shape 246A

Shape 247

Shape 248

Shape 249

Shape 250

Shape 301

Shape 302

Shape 310

Shape 313

Shape 314

Shape 315

Shape 332

Shape 333

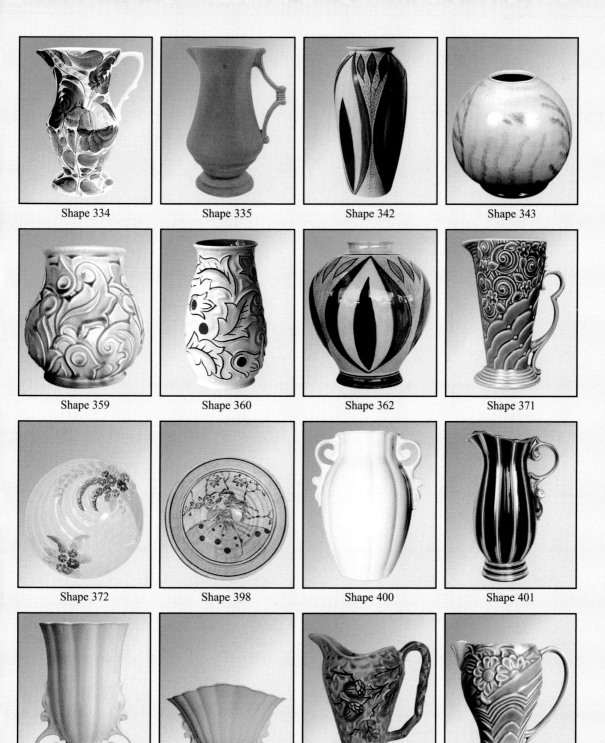

Shape 334

Shape 335

Shape 342

Shape 343

Shape 359

Shape 360

Shape 362

Shape 371

Shape 372

Shape 398

Shape 400

Shape 401

Shape 402

Shape 403

Shape 405

Shape 406

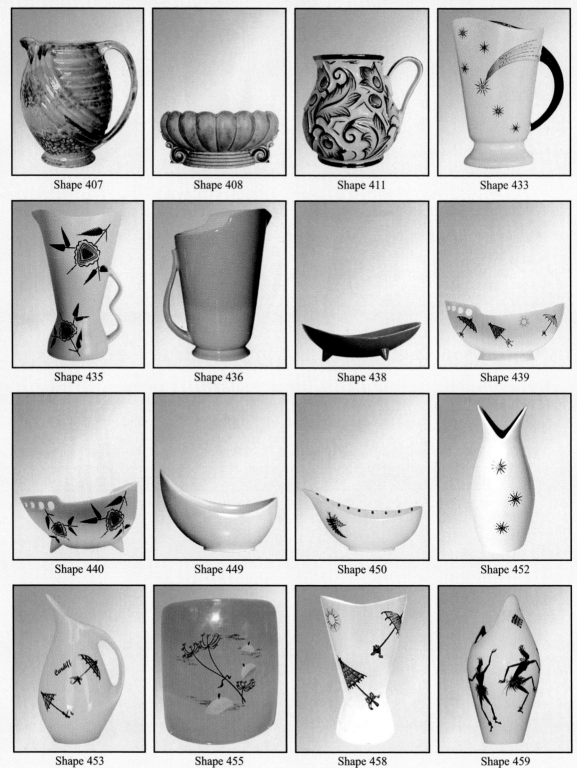

Shape 407

Shape 408

Shape 411

Shape 433

Shape 435

Shape 436

Shape 438

Shape 439

Shape 440

Shape 449

Shape 450

Shape 452

Shape 453

Shape 455

Shape 458

Shape 459

WADE HEATH (cont.)

STARFISH PIN TRAY, 1959-1961, 1973

First issued in December 1959, this embossed dish (1a) was intended to be used as a pin tray or as an ashtray. The original price was 3/6d. In 1973 the starfish pin tray (1b) was re-issued by Wade Ireland in a slightly lighter glaze colour, and also sold for 3/6d.

Backstamp: **A.** Impressed "Wade Made in England"
             B. Impressed "Made in Ireland-Irish Porcelain-Eire tir a dheanta" with a shamrock and crown design

No.	Description	Colourways	Size	U.S.$	Can.$	U.K.£
1a	Starfish	Brown; dark blue design	115	20.00	30.00	14.00
1b	Starfish	Beige; light blue design	115	20.00	30.00	14.00

SWALLOW DISHES, 1958-1961

First issued in August 1958, these oval-shaped dishes have an open-winged bird on the rear edge of the dish. The bird is the Wade Blue Bird, though it was advertised as the 'Swallow' dish. The original price was 3/3d. This dish shape was reused for the Lesney gift trays in 1961 (see *The Charlton Standard Catalogue of Wade*, *Volume One*).

Backstamp: Embossed "Wade Porcelain Made in England"

No.	Description	Colourways	Size	U.S.$	Can.$	U.K.£
1a	Swallow	Beige; beige/blue bird	145	26.00	38.00	18.00
1b	Swallow	Lime green; grey/green bird	145	40.00	55.00	22.00

WADE HEATH (cont.)

TRINKET TRAYS, 1998-2000

These rectangular trays were available from the Wade Factory Shop in a wide variety of designs. Some of the designs 'Butterflies' and 'Flowers' type one are parts of a larger design that was used on Wade Table Lamps.

Backstamp: None

No.	Description	Colourways	Size	U.S.$	Can.$	U.K.£
1a	Butterflies	White; multicoloured print	80 x 125	8.00	10.00	5.00
1b	Doberman	White; gold rim; multicoloured print	80 x 125	8.00	10.00	5.00
1c	Flowers, type one	White; multicoloured print	80 x 125	8.00	10.00	5.00
1d	Flowers, type two	White; blue circle; multicoloured print	80 x 125	8.00	10.00	5.00
1e	Poinsettia	White; gold rim; multicoloured print	80 x 125	8.00	10.00	5.00
1f	Roses	White; pink roses; green leaves	80 x 125	8.00	10.00	5.00
1g	Yorkshire Terrier	White; gold rim; multicoloured print	80 x 125	8.00	10.00	5.00

TYRE DISHES, MOTOR VEHICLES, c.1962

Although these dishes are very similar to the Veteran Car dishes, they do not have the "Design Authenticated by the Veteran Car Club of Great Britain" on the back. However, they do have a short history of the vehicle included in the backstamp.

Backstamp: **A.** Black transfer print "By Wade of England 30 CWT. Guy Lorry, Built in 1914. The first product of Guy Motors Ltd. Incorporated an overdrive gear & independent 3 point engine mounting"
B. Black transfer print "1909 The Little Britain - 2Cyl 4 x 4.5 - 10. H.P. Wade England"

No.	Description	Colourways	Size	U.S.$	Can.$	U.K.£
1a	Guy Lorry, 1914	White; grey rim; black print	125	30.00	40.00	15.00
1b	The Little Britain, 1909	White; grey rim; black print	125	30.00	40.00	15.00

WADE HEATH *(cont.)*

TYRE DISH, GALLEON, c.1962

This white tyre dish has a transfer print of a galleon in the centre. For tyre dishes with a galleon and a town name see page 106.

Galleon

Backstamp: Red transfer print "Wade England"

No.	Description	Colourways	Size	U.S.$	Can.$	U.K.£
1	Galleon	White; blue line, brown galleon; two yellow pennants	105	10.00	15.00	8.00

TOPLINE DISHES, 1963

The Topline dishes are from a series of contemporary shapes and decorations by freelance designer Michael Caddy. They were produced for only a short time in 1963. Two designs of these dishes have been found. Versions 1a - 1d, 1f are decorated with green, pink and yellow transfer prints of early 19th century transport with drivers and passengers. Version 1e has a stylized medallion of a leaf in the centre with black and gold bands around it. The dishes were sold as a pair in black presentation boxes. For other Topline items and decorations see Jars and Vases sections.

Stanhope Phaeton   Governess Cart   Breaking Cart

Backstamp: Red transfer print "Wade England"

No.	Description	Colourways	Size	U.S.$	Can.$	U.K.£
1a	Breaking cart - 1895	White; gold band; multicoloured print	111	15.00	20.00	8.00
1b	Duryea phaeton - 1904	White; gold band; multicoloured print	111	15.00	20.00	8.00
1c	Governess cart - 1900	White; gold band; multicoloured print	111	15.00	20.00	8.00
1d	Leaf medallion	Off white; gold/black bands; black/silver-grey medallion	111	25.00	35.00	12.00
1e	Stanhope phaeton 1900	White; gold band; multicoloured print	111	15.00	20.00	8.00

WADE HEATH *(cont.)*

TROPICAL FRUIT GATHERERS DISHES, 1961

The Tropical Fruit Gatherers dishes were sold singly or as a boxed set of two.

| Pineapple gatherer | Prickly pear gatherer | Sugar cane cutter |

Backstamp: Red transfer print "Wade England"

No.	Description	Colourways	Size	U.S.$	Can.$	U.K.£
1a	Banana gatherer	White; multicoloured print	105	10.00	15.00	5.00
1b	Coconut gatherer	White; multicoloured print	105	10.00	15.00	5.00
1c	Date gatherer	White; multicoloured print	105	10.00	15.00	5.00
1d	Pineapple gatherer	White; multicoloured print	105	10.00	15.00	5.00
1e	Prickly pear gatherer	White; multicoloured print	105	10.00	15.00	5.00
1f	Sugar cane cutter	White; multicoloured print	105	10.00	15.00	5.00

TRUMPS DISHES, 1961

Designed as nut dishes for card parties, these dishes have a cartoon transfer print of a king, queen or knave in the centre. They were sold in a boxed set of four.

Backstamp: Red transfer print "Wade England"

No.	Description	Colourways	Size	U.S.$	Can.$	U.K.£
1a	King of Diamonds	White; black rim; multicoloured print	112	15.00	20.00	8.00
1b	Knave of Spades	White; red rim; multicoloured print	112	15.00	20.00	8.00
1c	Queen of Clubs	White; red rim; multicoloured print	112	15.00	20.00	8.00
1d	Queen of Hearts	White; black rim; multicoloured print	112	15.00	20.00	8.00

WADE HEATH (cont.)

T (ourist) T (rophy) TRAYS, 1959-1960

These rarely seen trays have a sloping ramp at the back edge, on top of which is a motorcycle (number 7) with a rider. They were produced as a souvenir of the Tourist Trophy Motorcycle Races held on the Isle of Man. They were sold in boxes decorated with a chequered flag design. The original price was 5/6d.

Backstamp: Black transfer print "Wade England"

No.	Description	Colourways	Size	U.S.$	Can.$	U.K.£
1a	T.T. tray	Grey tray; beige rider; white/dark red bike; grey helmet	74 x 90	180.00	240.00	90.00
1b	T.T. tray	Grey tray; beige rider; white/dark red bike; white helmet	74 x 90	180.00	240.00	90.00
1c	T.T. tray	Grey tray/rider; white/dark red bike; blue helmet	74 x 90	180.00	240.00	90.00
1d	T.T. tray	Grey tray; white rider; white/dark red bike; blue helmet	74 x 90	180.00	240.00	90.00

WADE HEATH *(cont.)*

VETERAN CAR DISHES

Variations 1b, 1c, and 1d of these round dishes can be found with and without a full Backstamp (ie: Backstamp C). The other dishes do not have a series number or car information on the backs. There are two types of Bugatti car illustrated on these dishes, one is a family car type and the other a racing car type.

| Italia | Bugatti | Alfa Romeo |

Backstamp: **A.** Gold transfer print "A Moko Product by Wade England Design authenticated by the Vintage Sports Car Club of Great Britain"
B. Red transfer print "Wade England"
C. Black transfer print "Veteran Cars Series 5 (No 13) Competition Cars 1908 Itala (Italy) 60HP 4CYL 12 LITRES Tourer Body (1910 Brooklands Lap Speed 101.8 m.p.h.) An R.K. product by Wade of England Design Authenticated by the Veteran Car Club of Great Britain"

No.	Description	Colourways	Size	U.S.$	Can.$	U.K.£
1a	Alfa Romeo	White; gold rim; multicoloured print	110	10.00	15.00	5.00
1b	Benz, 1898	White; gold rim; multicoloured print	111	10.00	15.00	5.00
1c	Benz, 1899	Black; gold rim, white print	110	10.00	15.00	5.00
1d	Bugatti	White; black family car; gold rim; multicoloured print	110	10.00	15.00	5.00
1e	Bugatti	White; blue race car; gold rim; multicoloured print	110	10.00	15.00	5.00
1f	Itala	White; gold rim; multicoloured print	110	10.00	15.00	5.00
1g	Vauxhall	White; gold rim; multicoloured print	110	10.00	15.00	5.00

VETERAN CAR PEANUT DISHES, c1958

These dishes vary slightly from the Veteran Car tyre dishes in that they are deeper and have a smooth rim instead of a ribbed design. They were issued in a box as a pair.

Photograph not available
at press time

Backstamp: "A Moko Product by Wade England"

No.	Description	Colourways	Size	U.S.$	Can.$	U.K.£
1a	Bugatti 1913	White; grey rim; black/grey/yellow print	105	10.00	15.00	5.00
1b	Itala 1908	White; grey rim; red/black/yellow print	105	10.00	15.00	5.00

WADE HEATH (cont.)

VETERAN CAR TYRE DISHES, 1956-c.1965

All these dishes have "Design Authenticated by the Veteran Car Club of Great Britain" on the back along with the series number and car history. In December 1957, a British car magazine advertised the Tyre Dishes at 3/9d.

Backstamp: **A.** "A Moko Product by Wade England"
B. "A Moko Line by Wade England"
C. "An RK Product by Wade of England"

Set 1 — Black Transfer Print

No.	Description	Colourways	Size	U.S.$	Can.$	U.K.£
1a	Benz 1899	White; grey rim; black print	125	12.00	18.00	9.00
1b	Darracq 1904	White; grey rim; black print	125	12.00	18.00	9.00
1c	Ford 1912	White; grey rim; black print	125	12.00	18.00	9.00

Set 2 — Black Transfer Print

No.	Description	Colourways	Size	U.S.$	Can.$	U.K.£
2a	Baby Peugeot 1902	White; grey rim; black print	125	12.00	18.00	9.00
2b	Rolls-Royce 1907	White; grey rim; black print	125	12.00	18.00	9.00
2c	Sunbeam 1904	White; grey rim; black print	125	12.00	18.00	9.00

Set 3 — Black Transfer Print

No.	Description	Colourways	Size	U.S.$	Can.$	U.K.£
3a	De Dion Bouton 1904	White; grey rim; black print	125	12.00	18.00	9.00
3b	Lanchester 1903	White; grey rim; black print	125	12.00	18.00	9.00
3c	Spyker 1905	White; grey rim; black print	125	12.00	18.00	9.00

Set 4 — Black Transfer Print

No.	Description	Colourways	Size	U.S.$	Can.$	U.K.£
4a	Cadillac 1903	White; grey rim; black print	125	12.00	18.00	9.00
4b	Oldsmobile 1904	White; grey rim; black print	125	12.00	18.00	9.00
4c	White Steam Car 1903	White; grey rim; black print	125	12.00	18.00	9.00

Set 5 — Multicoloured Transfer Print

No.	Description	Colourways	Size	U.S.$	Can.$	U.K.£
5a	Bugatti, 1913	White; grey rim; black/grey/yellow print	125	12.00	18.00	9.00
5b	Itala, 1908	White; grey rim; red/black/yellow print	125	12.00	18.00	9.00
5c	Sunbeam 1914	White; grey rim; green/black/brown print	125	12.00	18.00	9.00

WADE HEATH (cont.)

WAGON TRAIN DISHES, 1960-1961

First issued in August 1960, the original price for each dish was 6/6d.

Flint McCullogh   Major Seth Adams

Backstamp: Impressed "Wade Porcelain made in England © 1960 by Revue Studios"

No.	Description	Colourways	Size	U.S.$	Can.$	U.K.£
1	Flint McCullogh	Brown/honey	140	75.00	120.00	42.00
2	Major Seth Adams	Brown/honey	140	75.00	120.00	42.00

WADE IRELAND

IRISH PORCELAIN

CELTIC DISH, SHAPE CK2, 1965

The embossed design of writhing snakes was copied from illustrations made by medieval monks in an Irish manuscript entitled, *The Book of Kells*. The snakes represent those banished from Ireland by Saint Patrick.

Backstamp: Embossed "Celtic Porcelain by Wade Ireland" in an Irish knot wreath

No.	Description	Colourways	Size	U.S.$	Can.$	U.K.£
1	Celtic dish	Mottled blue-green	114	85.00	125.00	40.00

MOURNE SERIES OF DISHES, SHAPE C349, C354, and C360, 1967

These three dishes are completely different in colour and style from previously produced Irish Wade. Shape C349 is a rectangular footed bowl, shape C354 is a square bowl, and shape C360 is an oval bowl. They have an impressed design of orange or red flowers.

Rectangualr, footed, C349

Square, C354

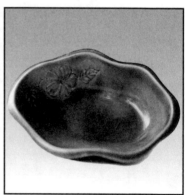

Oval, C360

Backstamp: **A.** Black print "Made in Ireland Porcelain Wade eire tira dheanta"
B. Black print "Made in Ireland Porcelain Wade eire tira dheanta" and red transfer print "Wade"

No.	Description	Colourways	Shape/Size	U.S.$	Can.$	U.K.£
1	Mourne, C349	Browny green; range flowers	Rectangular, footed/185	50.00	70.00	25.00
2	Mourne, C354	Grey/green; red rose	Square/135	50.00	70.00	25.00
3	Mourne, C360	Grey/green; orange rose	Oval/130	50.00	70.00	25.00

IRISH PORCELAIN (cont.)

PEARLSTONE GEODE DISH, SHAPE No. UNKNOWN, 1963-1964

These dishes resembling a cut and polished geode were produced at the same time as the Pearlstone wall plaques (see Wall Plaques section). They can be found in two sizes and with a different number of white 'crystals' in the centre, some have four to six crystals, others have none.

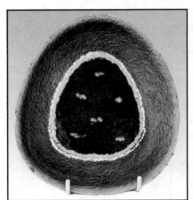

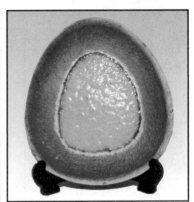

| Pearlstone, six white crystals | Pearlstone, four white crystals | Pearlstone, no crystals |

Backstamp: Black ink stamp "Made in Ireland by Wade County Armagh"

No.	Description	Colourways	Size	U.S.$	Can.$	U.K.£
1a	Pearlstone	Stone rim; white/yellow bands; shiny brown centre; six white crystals	150	35.00	45.00	18.00
1b	Pearlstone	Stone rim; white/yellow bands; shiny brown centre; four white crystals	150	35.00	45.00	18.00
2	Pearlstone	Stone rim; white/brown bands; bright yellow centre; no crystals	137	35.00	45.00	18.00

IRISH PORCELAIN (cont.)

ROUND PIN TRAYS, SHAPE I.P. 619, c.1950s-1976

This small round pin tray was also produced as a butter pat without the print (see *The Charlton Standard Catalogue of Wade Table Ware*) and with one of the Lucky Leprechauns fixed in the middle and named Leprechaun Pin tray (see *The Charlton Standard Catalogue of Wade Whimsical Collectables*).

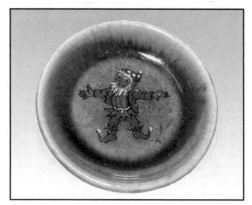

Leprechaun

Backstamp: A. Embossed circular 'Irish Porcelain Made in Ireland' around a central shamrock (early 1950s)
B. Impressed 'Made in Ireland- Irish Porcelain Wade - Eire tir a dheanta' with shamrock and crown design

No.	Description	Colourways	Size	U.S.$	Can.$	U.K.£
1a	Colleen carrying peat to a cottage	Greenish brown; multicoloured print	73mm	5.00	8.00	4.00
1b	Leprechaun	Greenish brown; multicoloured print	73mm	5.00	8.00	4.00
1c	The Giant Finn MacCaul	Greenish brown; multicoloured print	73mm	5.00	8.00	4.00

SHAMROCK DISH, SHAPE No. UNKNOWN, c.1955-c.1958

This unusual three-section dish has a raised shamrock inside each section.

Shamrocks

Backstamp: Embossed "Irish Porcelain" over a shamrock leaf that has "Wade" in the centre and "Co. Armagh" underneath

No.	Description	Colourways	Size	U.S.$	Can.$	U.K.£
1	Shamrock dish	Blue-grey	120	25.00	35.00	12.00

IRISH PORCELAIN (cont.)

SHAMROCK PIN TRAY, SHAPE I.P.609, c.1965

An embossed design of shamrocks decorates the inside of this dish. It was reissued with the addition of a pixie and tree stump as the baby pixie pin tray (see *The Charlton Standard Catalogue of Wade Whimsical Collectables*). It was also catalogued by Wade Ireland as an ashtray.

Backstamp: Embossed circular "Irish Porcelain Made in Ireland" with a shamrock in the centre

No.	Description	Colourways	Size	U.S.$	Can.$	U.K.£
1	Shamrock pin tray	Grey-blue	90	8.00	10.00	4.00

TUDOR ROSE DISH, SHAPE I.P. 625, c.1955-c.1958

This unusual shaped dish, resembling a Tudor rose, can be found with and without the embossed shape number 625 on the base.

Backstamp: **A.** Embossed "Irish Porcelain" over a shamrock leaf "By Wade County Armagh" with embossed "625"
B. Embossed "Irish Porcelain" over a shamrock leaf "By Wade County Armagh"

No.	Description	Colourways	Size	U.S.$	Can.$	U.K.£
1	Tudor Rose dish	Blue-grey	135	35.00	45.00	22.00

FLOWERS
c.1930-1939

At the same time they were producing the Jessie Van Hallen lady figures (see *The Charlton Standard Catalogue of Wade, Volume One, General Issues*), the George Wade and Wade Heath potteries issued a series of handmade earthenware and china flowers in bowls, pots, vases, baskets, miniature jugs and other containers. Jessie, who had a staff of approximately forty people working under her supervision, made the original moulds which were cast and decorated by her staff. Included in this range are flowers that were produced without containers. At least a hundred and thirty variations of flowers, pots and bowls are thought to exist as a Posy Ring with the number 130 has been found. Catalogue names are not known for items number 65 to 80 and from number 109. Prices for the flower posies ranged from 1/- to 25/-. As the flowers were all handmade, they can vary in height, and width from 5mm-20mm.

EARTHENWARE FLOWERS, c.1930-c.1935

The first series of flowers was made of earthenware. Ninety percent of the bowls, baskets, vases and pots, etc., that contain the flowers are black, but a few examples were also produced in mottled greens and yellows and plain yellow. The earthenware flower colours can be easily recognised, as they were all hand painted in dark blue, dark red, dark pink, maroon, purple, mauve and deep yellow with bright green leaves.

CHINA FLOWERS, c.1935-1939

The second series was produced in china and includes a variety of spring flowers. These flowers were produced in natural pastel shades of blues, pinks, mauves and yellows.

Unfortunately these flowers are rarely found undamaged. With so many edges to chip and snap off, it is the fortunate collector who finds a perfect example. The price given is for flowers in mint or near-mint condition; damaged models are worth 50 to 75 percent less. In 1939 the original price for the china flowers ranged from 1/- to 25/-.

When an item is described as miniature, small, medium, large or extra large, the reference is to the container only not the size of the flowers, as all flowers are handmade their sizes will vary.

This section is divided into two parts—flower centres and holders with flowers—and the items are listed alphabetically within each part.

BACKSTAMPS

Handwritten Backstamps

Handwritten marks can be found on both series of flowers. They all say "Wade England."

Ink Stamps

Flaxman Ware ink stamps, as well as "Wade Made in England" and "Wade England," can be found on series one and series two flowers.

Embossed Backstamps

Almost all the embossed backstamps found on series one and two flowers include the words, "British Made."

Some flowers have two handwritten numbers and a handwritten letter on them. One of the numbers corresponds to the Wade catalogue number, the other number is the code for the variety of flower, some numbers have been seen that do not correspond with the known catalogue or flower code numbers and are thought to be the identifying number of the decorator. Different flowers have been found with a woman's name included in the backstamp i.e.: Camelia, Elsa, Gay, Gwen and Nini these names are believed to be some of the artists/modellers who worked under Jessie Van Hallen. A letter refers to the size and type of container.

FLOWER CODE NUMBERS

1.	Primula	10.	Pansy
2.	Poppy	11.	Rosebud
3.	Tulip	12.	Oleander
4.	Primrose	13.	Unknown
5.	Narcissus	14.	Stock
6.	Forget-me-not or Tulip	15.	Unknown
7.	Unknown	16.	Violet
8.	Anemone or daffodil	17.	Wild rose
9.	Rose	18.	Carnation

Some of the flowers are hard to distinguish from one another because of their similarity and the colours used. For example, it is difficult to tell a tulip and rosebud apart, but on close inspection you will see that the central petals of the tulip come to a point, while the rosebud petals have a swirl with a small central hole. The difference between the anemone and the wild rose is that the anemone has long black or yellow stamens.

To date 26 flower types are known, but the code numbers for the buttercup, campanula, dahlia, daisy, delphinium, hibiscus, shamrock and water lily have not yet been identified. We would welcome any further information on this. The anemone and daffodil have been found with the number 8 on the base and forget me not and tulip have been found with a number 6 on the base. The reason for this number conflict is unknown.

CONTAINER CODE LETTERS

D.	Medium	J.	Large
E.	Small	K.	Extra large
G.	Miniature	SB.	Small basket
H.	Flower centre, long stem, no container		

EARTHENWARE FLOWERS

Two types of flower centres were produced:

1. Flowers on long stems with no container

Miniature—three flowers
Small—four flowers
Medium—six flowers
Large—eight or more flowers, approximately 130 x 100 mm
Extra large—eight or more flowers, approximately 175 x 150 mm

2. Flowers on short stems with no container

Large—eight or more flowers, approximately 110 x 110mm
Extra large—12 or more flowers, approximately 135 x 155 mm

Wade produced two types of containers for the flower centres, low bowls and dishes in small, medium and large sizes, which could be purchased separately from the flowers. Apparently there were 79 models in the earthenware set, although information is not available for numbers 66 to 79 of the earthenware series, or for numbers 109 - 130 of the china series.

FLOWER CENTRES

FLOWER CENTRES (EARTHENWARE), c.1930-c.1935

Catalogue numbers for earthenware flower centres are 21-25, 29-30, 36-37 and 45-49.

Delphiniums, long stemmed   Anemones, long stemmed   Wild roses, short stemmed

Backstamp:
A. Raised "British Made"
B. Raised "British Made" and black handwritten "Wade England"
C. Raised "British Made" and black handwritten "Made in England"
D. Black handwritten "Wade England"
E. Black handwritten "No 29 Wade England"
F. Black handwritten "Wade England No 47 Dell (E)"

LONG STEM:

No.	Description	Colourways	Size	U.S.$	Can.$	U.K.£
1	Tulips/long stem	Blue/dark pink/yellow flowers	Miniature/60 x 50	40.00	55.00	20.00
2	Wild roses/long stem	Purple/pink/yellow/blue flowers	Small/70 x 60	40.00	55.00	20.00
3	Delphiniums/wild roses/ long stem	Blue/pink flowers	Medium/100 x 60	45.00	65.00	35.00
4	Rose bud/long stem	Yellow/blue/dark pink flowers	Medium/95 x 50	30.00	40.00	15.00
5	Anemones/long stem	Maroon/mauve/yellow/pink flowers	Large/146 x 170	70.00	95.00	35.00
6	Delphiniums/long stem	Blue/pink flowers	Large/150 x 120	45.00	65.00	35.00
7	Delphiniums/wild roses/ long stem	Blue/pink flowers	Large/150 x 120	65.00	85.00	45.00
8	Pansies/ long stem	Blue/maroon/yellow flowers	Large/145 x 120	45.00	65.00	35.00
9	Poppies/long stem	Blue/maroon/yellow flowers	Large/140 x 120	30.00	40.00	20.00
10	Tulips/long stem	Yellow/blue/dark pink flowers	Large/146 x 78	40.00	55.00	22.00
11	Wild rose/long stem	Yellow/blue/dark pink flowers	Large/146 x 78	40.00	55.00	22.00

SHORT STEM: Catalogue numbers for short stem earthenware flower centres are 38, 42 and 50.

No.	Description	Colourways	Size	U.S.$	Can.$	U.K.£
1	Anemone/pansy/poppy/ short stem	Pink/yellow/blue flowers	Large/145 x 140	70.00	95.00	35.00
2	Anemone/rose/wild rose/ short stem	Pink/yellow/blue flowers	Large/145 x 140	70.00	95.00	35.00
3	Roses/wild roses/ short stem	Pink/yellow/blue flowers	Large/105 x 120	70.00	95.00	35.00
4	Wild roses/short stem	Pink/yellow/blue flowers	Large/145 x 140	70.00	95.00	35.00

FLOWER CENTRES (CHINA), c.1935-1939

Catalogue numbers for china flower centres are: 81-82, 96-98, and 101-102.

Tulips, long stemmed

Anemones, pansies and poppies, short stemmed

Backstamp: **A.** Handwritten "Wade England"
                B. Black ink stamp "Wade Made in England"

No.	Description	Colourways	Size	U.S.$	Can.$	U.K.£
1	Tulips/long stem	Pale blue/pale pink/pale yellow flowers	Miniature/60 x 50	40.00	55.00	20.00
2	Anemones/long stem	Mauve/white flowers	Small/60 x 60	70.00	95.00	35.00
3	Daffodils/long stem	Pale yellow/orange flowers	Small/60 x 50	40.00	55.00	25.00
4	Anemones/pansies/ poppies/short stem	Orange/pink/mauve/yellow flowers	Large/130 x 220	70.00	95.00	35.00

HOLDERS WITH FLOWERS

ARCHES (EARTHENWARE), c.1930-c.1935

Catalogue numbers for the arches are 56 and 57.

| Pansies, roses, wild roses | Violets | Roses |

Backstamp: **A.** Black handwritten "Wade England"
B. Black ink stamp "Wade England"
C. Black handwritten "Wade England No. 57 Stock"
D. Black handwritten "Wade England No. 57 Violet"

No.	Name	Colourways	Size	U.S.$	Can.$	U.K.£
1a	Assorted flowers	Red/blue/yellow flowers; dark green arch	Small/130 x 145	65.00	95.00	45.00
1b	Pansies	Yellow/maroon/mauve/blue flowers; pale green arch	Small/130 x 145	65.00	95.00	45.00
1c	Stock	Yellow/maroon/mauve/blue flowers; yellow arch	Small/130 x 145	65.00	95.00	45.00
1d	Violets	Yellow/maroon/mauve/blue flowers; yellow arch	Small/130 x 145	65.00	95.00	45.00
1e	Wild roses	Yellow/maroon/mauve/blue flowers; yellow arch	Small/130 x 145	65.00	95.00	45.00
2a	Anemones	Blue/maroon/red/pink/yellow flowers; cream/pale green arch	Large/170 x 190	85.00	110.00	50.00
2b	Anemones	Blue/maroon/red, pink/yellow flowers; yellow arch	Large/170 x 190	85.00	110.00	50.00
2c	Pansies/roses/stock	Pink/yellow flowers; yellow arch	Large/170 x 190	85.00	110.00	50.00
2d	Roses	Pink/yellow flowers; pale green arch	Large/170 x 190	85.00	110.00	50.00

BASKETS WITH HANDLES (EARTHENWARE), c.1930-c.1935

Catalogue number for the basket with handle is 54.

Wild roses

Stock flowers

Backstamp: **A.** Black ink stamp "Wade England"
B. Black ink stamp "Wade England No.54 Stock"

No.	Description	Colourways	Size	U.S.$	Can.$	U.K.£
1a	Pansies	Yellow/pink flowers; yellow basket	75 x 86	40.00	55.00	20.00
1b	Stock	Yellow/pink flowers; yellow basket	75 x 86	40.00	55.00	22.00
1c	Wild roses	Blue/yellow/pink/maroon flowers; black basket	75 x 86	40.00	55.00	22.00
1d	Wild roses	Blue/yellow/pink/maroon flowers; yellow basket	75 x 86	40.00	55.00	22.00

OVAL WICKER BASKETS, WITHOUT HANDLES, c.1930-c.1935

Catalogue numbers for the large oval wicker baskets are 4, 5 and 6, but catalogue numbers for the small baskets have not been found.

Unknown flower

Earthenware, c. 1930c.1935

Backstamp: **A.** Black handwritten "Wade England"
B. Black handwritten "Wade England No.6 Tulip"

No.	Description	Colourways	Size	U.S.$	Can.$	U.K.£
1a	Primroses	Yellow flowers; black basket	Small/40 x 70	45.00	55.00	30.00
1b	Rosebuds	Yellow/pink/blue flowers; black basket	Small/40 x 70	45.00	55.00	30.00
1c	Roses	Yellow/pink/blue flowers; black basket	Small/40 x 70	45.00	55.00	30.00
1d	Roses/rosebuds	Yellow/pink flowers; yellow basket	Small/40 x 70	45.00	55.00	30.00
1e	Wild roses	Yellow/pink/blue flowers; black basket	Small/37 x 70	45.00	55.00	30.00
1f	Wild roses	Yellow/pink/blue flowers; yellow basket	Small/37 x 70	45.00	55.00	30.00
2a	Pansies	Yellow/blue/maroon flowers; black basket	Large/70 x 105	48.00	58.00	32.00
2b	Pansies	Yellow/blue/dark pink flowers; yellow basket	Large/70 x 105	48.00	58.00	32.00
2c	Tulips	Yellow/blue/maroon flowers; black basket	Large/70 x 105	48.00	58.00	32.00
2d	Unknown flower	Yellow/pink/blue flowers; black basket	Large/65 x 105	48.00	58.00	32.00
2e	Wild roses	Yellow/pink/maroon/blue flowers; black basket	Large/65 x 105	48.00	58.00	32.00

Primroses

China, c.1935-c.1939

Backstamp: Black ink stamp "Wade Made in England"

No.	Description	Colourways	Size	U.S.$	Can.$	U.K.£
1a	Primroses	Pale yellow flowers; black basket	Small/37 x 70	35.00	45.00	22.00
1b	Primrose/pansy/rose	Pale yellow/pink/mauve flowers; black basket	Small/37 x 70	35.00	45.00	22.00
1c	Roses	Pale yellow/pink flowers; black basket	Small/37 x 70	35.00	45.00	22.00

ROUND BASKETS WITHOUT HANDLES (EARTHENWARE), C.1930-c.1935

These round baskets have a hollow base. The catalogue numbers are 20, 26, and 27.

Assorted flowers

Backstamp: **A.** Raised "British Made" and black handwritten "Wade England"
B. Raised "British Made"
C. Black handwritten "Wade England"
D. Raised "Made in England" and model number
E. Black handwritten "Wade England No.20 W. Rose"

No.	Description	Colourways	Size	U.S.$	Can.$	U.K.£
1a	Assorted flowers	Yellow/blue/pink/maroon flowers; black basket	66 x 50	40.00	55.00	25.00
1b	Oleanders	Yellow/maroon/mauve flowers; black basket	66 x 50	45.00	58.00	28.00
1c	Roses ·	Yellow/blue/red/pink flowers; black basket	66 x 50	40.00	55.00	25.00
1d	Tulips	Yellow/pink/maroon flowers; black basket	66 x 50	40.00	55.00	25.00
1e	Wild roses	Blue/yellow/pink/maroon flowers; black basket	66 x 50	40.00	55.00	25.00
1f	Wild roses	Blue/yellow/pink/maroon flowers; yellow basket	66 x 50	40.00	55.00	25.00

BOWLS, POTS AND MENU HOLDERS

AJAX BOWL (EARTHENWARE), c.1930-c.1935

Catalogue numbers for the Ajax bowls are 39-41.

Backstamp: A. Black handwritten "Wade England"
B. Black handwritten "Wade England Camelia E" with embossed "British"

No.	Description	Colourways	Size	U.S.$	Can.$	U.K.£
1a	Roses	Purple/pink/yellow/blue flowers; black bowl	130 x 115	40.00	55.00	20.00
1b	Tulips	Purple/pink/yellow/blue flowers; black bowl	130 x 110	40.00	55.00	20.00
1c	Wild roses	Purple/pink/yellow/blue flowers; black bowl	130 x 115	40.00	55.00	20.00
1d	Wild roses	Purple/pink/yellow/blue flowers; yellow bowl	130 x 110	40.00	55.00	20.00

BASKET-WEAVE FOOTED BOWL (EARTHENWARE), c.1930-c.1935

The catalogue number for the Basket-weave bowl is unknown.

Wild roses

Pansies, roses, wild roses

Backstamp: A. Black ink stamp "Wade England GAY"
B. Black ink stamp "Wade England GWEN Mixed"

No.	Description	Colourways	Size	U.S.$	Can.$	U.K.£
1a	Anemones	Blue/red/maroon/yellow flowers; black bowl	Small/116 x 60	50.00	55.00	25.00
1b	Assorted	Blue/red/maroon/yellow flowers; green/brown speckled bowl	Small/116 x 60	50.00	55.00	25.00
1c	Pansies	Blue/red/maroon/yellow flowers; black bowl	Small/110 x 75	40.00	55.00	25.00
1d	Poppies/roses	Blue/pink/yellow flowers; yellow bowl	Small/116 x 60	50.00	55.00	25.00
1e	Wild roses	Blue/red/maroon/yellow flowers; black bowl	Small/116 x 60	40.00	55.00	25.00
2	Pansies/rose/wild rose	Blue/red/maroon/yellow flowers; green bowl	Large/210 x 120	60.00	80.00	40.00

134

FOOTED BOWL (EARTHENWARE), c.1930-c.1935

This footed bowl has a catalogue number 115 on the base, no information has been found as to the Wade catalogue name for this item.

Backstamp: Black handwritten "L Wade England No. 115"

No.	Description	Colourways	Size	U.S.$	Can.$	U.K.£
1	Anemone/carnation/ dahlia	Maroon/purple/yellow flowers; creamy yellow bowl	140 x 150	65.00	80.00	38.00

MEDIUM BOWLS (EARTHENWARE), c.1930-c.1935

Photograph not available
at press time

Backstamp: **A.** Black handwritten "Wade England"
B. Raised "British Made"
C. Raised "British Made" and black handwritten "Wade England"
D. Raised "British Made," black handwritten "Wade England" and " Made in England"

No.	Description	Colourways	Size	U.S.$	Can.$	U.K.£
1a	Assorted flowers	Blue/yellow/pink/maroon flowers; black bowl	65 x 57	30.00	40.00	22.00
1b	Tulips	Pink/yellow/blue flowers; black bowl	58 x 45	30.00	40.00	15.00
2	Wild rose	Blue/yellow/pink/maroon flowers; black bowl	65 x 57	30.00	40.00	22.00

OCTAGONAL BOWLS

Pansies, roses, wild roses

Poppies

Earthenware, c.1930-c.1935

Backstamp: **A.** Raised "British Made" and "Wade England Made in England"
B. Raised "British Made" and black handwritten "Wade England"
C. Raised "British Made"
D. Black handwritten "Wade England"
E. Black ink stamp "Wade England"
F. Black ink stamp "14 Wade England No. 55" with impressed England

No.	Description	Colourways	Size	U.S.$	Can.$	U.K.£
1a	Pansies/roses/wildroses	Yellow/mauve/purple flowers; black bowl	70 x 60	60.00	80.00	34.00
1b	Poppies	Yellow/mauve/purple flowers; yellow bowl	70 x 60	60.00	80.00	34.00
1c	Stock	Yellow/mauve/purple flowers; yellow bowl	70 x 60	60.00	80.00	34.00

Forget-me-nots

Narcissus

China, c.1935-1939

No.	Description	Colourways	Size	U.S.$	Can.$	U.K.£
1	Forget-me-nots	Pale blue /pink flowers; black bowl	Miniature/60 x 60	60.00	80.00	30.00
2	Narcissus	White/yellow flowers; black bowl	Large/60 x 75	60.00	80.00	30.00
3	Primula	Blue/yellow/pink flowers; black bowl	Extra large/75 x 90	60.00	80.00	30.00

OVAL BOWLS (EARTHENWARE), c.1930-c.1935

Although this bowl has the number 14 on the base it does not correspond with the Wade catalogue number or flower type.

Pansies, roses, wild roses   Anemones, wild roses

Backstamp: Raised "New Oval Bowl 14 Wade England"

No.	Description	Colourways	Size	U.S.$	Can.$	U.K.£
1a	Anemones/wild roses	Yellow/mauve/purple flowers; mottled cream/green bowl	140 x 160	85.00	120.00	55.00
1b	Pansies/roses/wild roses	Yellow/mauve/purple flowers; green bowl	140 x 160	85.00	120.00	55.00

POWDER BOWL (CHINA), c.1935-c.1939

This bowl has been produced from the base of one of the Wadeheath powder bowls and has been filled with china roses.

Backstamp: Black handwritten "Wade Made in England"

No.	Description	Colourways	Size	U.S.$	Can.$	U.K.£
1	Roses	Pink/yellow/white flowers; brown bowl	140 x 160	65.00	90.00	45.00

SHALLOW BOWLS / POSY POTS

Listed as Posy Pots in the Wade sales catalogues these shallow bowls have been found in three sizes: miniature, catalogue numbers 1, 2 and 9; small, numbers 8, 10 and 47; and medium, numbers 18, 19 and 28.

Earthenware flowers - Anemone and rosebuds   China flowers - Primroses   China flowers - Roses, rosebuds

Backstamp: **A.** Raised "British Made" with an impressed code letter (sometimes includes a black handwritten "Wade England" or "Made in England")
B. Raised "British Made" and "Wade England"
C. Raised "British Made" and "Made in England"
D. Handwritten "Wade England"
E. Ink stamped "Wade Made in England E"
F. Ink stamped "Made in England Wade"

Earthenware Bowls, c.1930-c.1935

No.	Description	Colourways	Size	U.S.$	Can.$	U.K.£
1a	Anemone/rosebuds	Mauve/pale yellow/pale pink flowers	Miniature/32 x 35	25.00	38.00	22.00
1b	Assorted flowers	Pink/maroon/yellow/blue flowers	Miniature/30 x 35	25.00	34.00	18.00
1c	Rosebuds	Pink/maroon/yellow/blue flowers	Miniature/35 x 35	25.00	34.00	18.00
1d	Roses	Pink/maroon/yellow/blue flowers	Miniature/35 x 35	25.00	34.00	18.00
1e	Roses/rosebuds	Mauve/pale yellow/pink flowers	Miniature/32 x 35	25.00	34.00	18.00
1f	Tulips	Yellow/pink/maroon/blue flowers	Miniature/35 x 35	25.00	34.00	18.00
1g	Wild roses	Yellow/pink/maroon/blue flowers	Miniature/32 x 35	25.00	34.00	18.00
2a	Assorted flowers	Blue/yellow/maroon flowers	Small/42 x 45	25.00	34.00	18.00
2b	Pansies	Pink/maroon/yellow/blue flowers	Small/40 x 35	25.00	34.00	18.00
2c	Primroses	Pink/maroon/yellow/blue flowers	Small/40 x 35	25.00	34.00	18.00
2d	Roses	Pink/maroon/yellow/blue flowers	Small/40 x 45	25.00	34.00	18.00
2e	Stock	Pink/maroon/yellow/blue flowers	Small/40 x 35	25.00	34.00	18.00
2f	Tulips	Pink/maroon/yellow/blue flowers	Small/40 x 35	25.00	34.00	18.00
2g	Wild roses	Purple/yellow/pink/blue flowers	Small/45 x 57	25.00	34.00	18.00
2h	Wild roses	Yellow/blue/pink flowers	Small/42 x 45	25.00	34.00	18.00
3a	Assorted Flowers	Pink/yellow/blue flowers	Medium/58 x 45	28.00	38.00	20.00
3b	Rosebuds	Pink/yellow/blue flowers	Medium/58 x 45	28.00	38.00	20.00
3c	Tulips	Pink/yellow/blue flowers	Medium/58 x 47	28.00	38.00	20.00
3d	Wild rose	Pink/yellow/blue flowers	Medium/58 x 45	28.00	38.00	20.00

China Bowls, c.1935-1939

No.	Description	Colourways	Size	U.S.$	Can.$	U.K.£
1a	Pansies/primrose/rose	Pink/mauve/yellow flowers	Small/45 x 35	40.00	50.00	26.00
1b	Primroses	Pink/maroon/yellow/blue flowers	Small/45 x 35	40.00	50.00	26.00
1c	Roses/rosebuds	Pale yellow/pale pink flowers	Small/45 x 60	40.00	50.00	26.00
2	Roses/rosebuds	Pale yellow flowers	Medium/58 x 45	40.00	50.00	26.00

SPHERICAL BOWLS (EARTHENWARE), c.1930-c.1935

No Wade sales catalogue number has been found for this shaped bowl.

Stock

Wild roses

Wild roses (damaged flowers in this image)

Backstamp: A. Black handwritten "Wade England Stock Elsa"
B. Black handwritten "Wade England"

No.	Description	Colourways	Size	U.S.$	Can.$	U.K.£
1a	Assorted	Bright yellow/pink/blue/maroon flowers; black bowl	90 x 70	40.00	55.00	25.00
1b	Stock	Bright yellow/pink/blue/maroon flowers; black bowl	90 x 70	40.00	55.00	25.00
1c	Stock	Bright yellow/pink/blue/maroon flowers; yellow bowl	90 x 70	40.00	55.00	25.00
1d	Wild roses	Bright yellow/pink/blue/maroon flowers; yellow bowl	90 x 70	40.00	55.00	25.00
1e	Wild roses	Bright yellow/pink/blue/maroon flowers; black bowl	90 x 70	40.00	55.00	25.00

STEPPED BOWL (EARTHENWARE), c.1930-c.1935

This unusual shaped bowl which at first glance resembles a teapot lid has a hollowed base with embossed Wade England No. 506. No Wade sales catalogue number has been found for this shaped bowl.

Photograph not available
at press time

Backstamp: Embossed "Wade England No. 506" with a black handwritten "Wild Rose J"

No.	Description	Colourways	Size	U.S.$	Can.$	U.K.£
1	Wild rose	Yellow/pink/blue/mauve flowers; black bowl	55 x 60	40.00	55.00	25.00

BINNIE POTS (EARTHENWARE), c.1930-c.1935

The Binnie Pots are Wade catalogue number 64.

| Pansies | Pansies, rose, wild rose | Wild rose |

Backstamp: **A.** Black ink stamp "Wade England"
  B. Black ink stamp "L Wade England No. 64 Mixed"

No.	Description	Colourways	Size	U.S.$	Can.$	U.K.£
1a	Pansies	Purple/blue/yellow flowers; black pot	145 x 77	40.00	55.00	25.00
1b	Pansy/rose/wild rose	Purple/blue/yellow flowers; black pot	155 x 77	40.00	55.00	25.00
1c	Wild roses	Purple/blue /yellow flowers; yellow pot	145 x 77	40.00	55.00	25.00

MOSS COVERED POTS (EARTHENWARE), c.1930-c.1935

These flowers are in a moss covered flowerpot, with a round base. The Wade sales catalogue number is 104.

Poppies, large and medium sizes

Backstamp: Black handwritten "M Wade England No. 104"

No.	Name	Description	Size	U.S.$	Can.$	U.K.£
1	Unknown flower	White/mauve/dark pink flowers; green pot	Small/60 x 60	40.00	55.00	28.00
2a	Poppies	Purple/blue/yellow flowers; green pot	Medium/90 x 110	45.00	60.00	33.00
2b	Poppies	Purple/blue/yellow flowers; green pot	Large/125 x 130	50.00	65.00	38.00

VULCAN POTS (EARTHENWARE), c.1930-c.1935

Wild roses

Backstamp: Black handwritten "Wade England"

No.	Name	Description	Size	U.S.$	Can.$	U.K.£
1a	Pansies	Purple/blue/yellow flowers; black pot	110 x 75	45.00	58.00	25.00
1b	Poppies	Red/purple/yellow flowers; black pot	110 x 75	45.00	58.00	25.00
1c	Tulips	Red/blue/yellow flowers; black pot	110 x 75	45.00	58.00	25.00
1d	Wild roses	Purple/blue/yellow flowers; yellow pot	110 x 75	45.00	58.00	25.00

MENU HOLDERS (EARTHENWARE), c.1930-c.1935

Although listed in the Wade sales catalogue as menu holders, there is no slot or fixture on these flowers in which to stand a menu. Produced in two sizes the catalogue numbers are as follows: roses, large-12, small-11; water lilies, large-15, small-16.

Rose

Water lily

Backstamp: **A.** Black handwritten "Wade England N.12" on roses
B. Black handwritten "Wade England No.15" on waterlily

No.	Description	Colourways	Size	U.S.$	Can.$	U.K.£
1	Water lily	Pink flower; green leaves	Small/Unknown	28.00	38.00	18.00
2a	Roses	Deep red flowers; green leaves	Large/55 x 100	28.00	38.00	18.00
2b	Water lily	Pink flower; green leaves	Large/50 x 90	28.00	38.00	18.00
2c	Water lily	Yellow flower; green leaves	Large/50 x 90	28.00	38.00	18.00

MISCELLANEOUS SHAPES

ANGLE (EARTHENWARE), c.1930-c.1935

The Angle has been found with the number 65 included in the backstamp, which is the number used for the 'square.'

Wild roses

Backstamp: Black ink stamp "Wade England"

No.	Description	Colourways	Size	U.S.$	Can.$	U.K.£
1a	Pansies	Yellow/maroon/blue flowers; black angle	Unknown	60.00	80.00	35.00
1b	Wild roses	Yellow/maroon/pink flowers; brown angle	Unknown	60.00	80.00	35.00

BRICK (EARTHENWARE), c.1930-c.1935

The Wade sales catalogue number for the Brick is 52.

Photograph not available
at press time

Backstamp: Black handwritten "Wade England"

No.	Description	Colourways	Size	U.S.$	Can.$	U.K.£
1	Assorted flowers	Yellow/blue/maroon flowers; light green brick	150 x 175	80.00	110.00	45.00

GLOBE, 1936-1937

This globe-shaped flower bowl is from the Wadeheath Flaxman range of ornamental ware. For an example of the bowl shape please see page 289. The Wade sales catalogue number for the globe flower bowl is 53.

Photograph not available
at press time

Backstamp: Black ink stamp "Flaxman Ware Hand Made Pottery By Wadeheath England"

No.	Description	Colourways	Size	U.S.$	Can.$	U.K.£
1	Assorted flowers	Maroon/blue/red/yellow flowers; mottled green/brown globe	Large/225 x 175	150.00	200.00	75.00

HORSESHOE WINDOW BOX (EARTHENWARE), c. 1930-c. 1935

The Wade sales catalogue number for the Window box is unknown. "May Window Box" is handwritten on the bottom of the horseshoe.

Roses

Roses, wild roses

Roses, wild roses, speckled window box

Backstamp: Black handwritten "Wade England May Window Box"

No.	Description	Colourways	Size	U.S.$	Can.$	U.K.£
1a	Roses	Pink/yellow flowers; green/maroon window box	55 x 130	70.00	95.00	45.00
1b	Roses/wild roses	Yellow/pink/blue flowers; grey and green speckled window box	95 x 140	80.00	110.00	45.00
1c	Roses/wild roses	Yellow/pink/blue flowers; green window box	95 x 140	80.00	110.00	45.00

POSY RINGS, c.1930-c.1935

Wild roses

Earthenware, Catalogue No. 59, c.1930-c.1935

Backstamp: **A.** Raised "British Made, Wade England" and "Made in England"
B. Black handwritten "Wade England"
C. Black handwritten "Wade England" with impressed "British"

No.	Description	Colourways	Size	U.S.$	Can.$	U.K.£
1a	Pansies	Yellow/maroon/blue flowers	60 x 130	80.00	110.00	45.00
1b	Wild rose	Yellow/blue/maroon flowers;	50 x 140	80.00	110.00	40.00

China, Catalogue No. 130, c.1930-c.1935

Backstamp: Black handwritten "4 Wade England May 130 Mixed"

No.	Description	Colourways	Size	U.S.$	Can.$	U.K.£
1	Anemone/carnation/ dahlia/pansy/poppy	Blue/pink/purple/yellow flowers	65 x 180 diam	80.00	110.00	48.00

ROCK GARDEN WITH GNOME (EARTHENWARE), c.1930-c.1935

Produced in two sizes the Gnome rock garden catalogue numbers are: large-3 and small-7. Although not listed as menu holders in the Wade sales catalogue, the Gnome rock garden does a have a slot to one side in which a menu / name card could be placed.

Rock garden

Backstamp: Black ink stamp "Wade 3 England No.3"

No.	Description	Colourways	Size	U.S.$	Can.$	U.K.£
1	Garden/gnome	Red hat; grey jacket; black shoes; pink trousers; multicoloured flowers	Small/45 x 65	95.00	130.00	55.00
2	Garden/gnome	Red hat; grey jacket; black shoes; pink trousers; multicoloured flowers	Large/70 x 100	105.00	145.00	65.00

SQUARE (EARTHENWARE), c.1930-c.1935

The Wade sales catalogue number for the Square is 65, this number has also been seen on the Angle.

Photograph not available
at press time

Backstamp: Unknown

No.	Description	Colourways	Size	U.S.$	Can.$	U.K.£
1	Assorted flowers	Multicoloured flowers; black square	Unknown	70.00	90.00	45.00

FLOWERS WITH CONTAINERS

c.1930-1935

JUGS

LARGE-SPOUT MINIATURE JUGS

The Wade catalogue number for the large-spout miniature jug is unknown.

Poppies   Roses

Backstamp: A. Black handwritten "Wade England"
             B. Black handwritten "Wade Made in England A. Jug"

No.	Description	Colourways	Size	U.S.$	Can.$	U.K.£
1a	Pansies	Maroon/yellow flowers; yellow jug; green handle	66 x 68	35.00	40.00	20.00
1b	Poppies	Maroon/yellow flowers; yellow jug; green handle	66 x 68	35.00	40.00	20.00
1c	Rosebuds	Pink/yellow flowers; black jug; yellow handle	60 x 68	35.00	40.00	20.00
1d	Roses	Pink/yellow flowers; black jug	66 x 68	35.00	40.00	20.00

LONG-NECK MINIATURE JUGS

The Wade sales catalogue number for the long-neck miniature jug is 35.

Photograph not available
at press time

Backstamp: Unknown

No.	Description	Colourways	Size	U.S.$	Can.$	U.K.£
1	Wild roses	Dark pink/yellow/blue flowers; black jug	110 X 40	35.00	40.00	20.00

REGENCY MINIATURE JUG

This miniature jug has a ribbed body similar to the Wade Regency and Empress design items. The Wade sales catalogue number for this jug is unknown.

Backstamp: Black handwritten "Wade England 9 G. Jug"

No.	Description	Colourways	Size	U.S.$	Can.$	U.K.£
1	Roses	Dark pink/yellow flowers; yellow jug; green handle	80 x 35	35.00	45.00	22.00

ROMAN JUG

The Wade sales catalogue number for this jug is 63.

Backstamp: Black handwritten "Wade 9 England No 63"

No.	Description	Colourways	Size	U.S.$	Can.$	U.K.£
1a	Roses	Dark pink/yellow flowers; green/brown speckled jug	240 x 195	80.00	110.00	55.00
1b	Roses	Dark pink/yellow flowers; green jug	240 x 195	80.00	110.00	55.00

SHORT-NECKED MINIATURE JUG

The Wade sales catalogue number for this jug is 31.

Backstamp: **A.** Black handwritten "Wade 2 England"
                 B. Black handwritten "Wade England No. 31 Wild Rose"

No.	Description	Colourways	Size	U.S.$	Can.$	U.K.£
1a	Poppies	Dark pink/blue flowers; black jug	60 X 35	35.00	40.00	20.00
1b	Tulips	Dark pink/yellow flowers; black jug	60 X 35	35.00	40.00	20.00
1c	Wild roses	Dark pink/yellow/blue flowers; black jug	60 X 35	35.00	40.00	20.00

SLOPING-NECK MINIATURE JUGS

Backstamp: Black handwritten "Wade England"

No.	Description	Colourways	Size	U.S.$	Can.$	U.K.£
1a	Pansies	Blue/yellow/maroon flowers; black jug; pale yellow handle	65 x 21	35.00	40.00	20.00
1b	Wild roses	Blue/yellow/maroon flowers; black jug; pale yellow handle	80 x 22	35.00	40.00	20.00

STRAIGHT-BACKED MINIATURE JUGS

Backstamp: Black handwritten "Wade England"

No.	Description	Colourways	Size	U.S.$	Can.$	U.K.£
1a	Roses	Pink/yellow flowers; yellow jug; black handle	85 x 25	35.00	40.00	20.00
1b	Roses	Pink/yellow flowers; yellow jug; pale green handle	85 x 25	35.00	40.00	20.00

WIDE-MOUTH MINIATURE JUG

Backstamp: Raised "British Made" and black handwritten "Wade England"

No.	Description	Colourways	Size	U.S.$	Can.$	U.K.£
1	Wild roses	Pink/yellow flowers; black jug; yellow handle	75 x 50	35.00	40.00	20.00

VASES

ART DECO FLOWER VASE (EARTHENWARE), c.1930-c.1935

The Wade sales catalogue number for the Art Deco vase is 51. Impressed on the base is the shape number 105, which would suggest that it was originally produced as a vase and later the flowers were added to produce a new item.

Assorted flowers

Assorted flowers

Backstamp: **A.** Black handwritten "Wade England"
B. Black handwritten "Wade England No 51" with impressed "105"

No.	Description	Colourways	Size	U.S.$	Can.$	U.K.£
1a	Assorted flowers	Red/pink/blue/yellow flowers; light grey/ blue speckled vase	305 x 250	200.00	300.00	145.00
1b	Assorted flowers	Red/pink/blue/yellow flowers; light grey/ pale green vase	325 x 245	200.00	300.00	145.00

MINIATURE VASE WITH HANDLES (EARTHENWARE), c.1930-c.1935

Pansies

Backstamp: Black handwritten "Wade England"

No.	Description	Colourways	Size	U.S.$	Can.$	U.K.£
1	Roses/pansies	Purple/yellow/blue flowers; black vase; green handles	80 x 50	35.00	40.00	20.00

MINIATURE VASE WITH HANDLES (CHINA), c.1935-1939

Photograph not available
at press time

Backstamp: Black handwritten "Wade England Nina 4"

No.	Description	Colourways	Size	U.S.$	Can.$	U.K.£
1	Primula	Purple/yellow/blue flowers; yellow vase; black handles	80 x 50	35.00	40.00	22.00

SATURN VASES (EARTHENWARE), c.1930-c.1935

The Wade sales catalogue numbers for these vases are 60, 61 and 62.

Saturn vases

Backstamp: **A.** Embossed "Regd 827224" and black handwritten "Wade England No. 60"
B. Black handwritten "Wade England Saturn"
C. Black ink stamp "Wade England"

No.	Name	Description	Size	U.S.$	Can.$	U.K.£
1a	Primroses	Yellow flowers; pale green ring	Small/130 x 110	65.00	80.00	40.00
1b	Roses	Yellow/pink/blue flowers; cream/green speckled ring	Small/130 x 110	65.00	80.00	40.00
1c	Wild roses	Yellow/maroon/pink/blue flowers; bright yellow ring	Small/130 x 110	65.00	80.00	40.00
2a	Roses	Yellow/maroon/pink/blue flowers; cream and green ring	Medium/145 x 135	70.00	90.00	45.00
2b	Roses/wild roses	Yellow/maroon/pink/blue flowers; cream and green ring	Medium/145 x 135	70.00	90.00	45.00
3a	Roses	Yellow/maroon/blue flowers; green ring	Large/157 x 145	80.00	110.00	45.00
3b	Roses	Yellow/maroon/blue flowers; yellow ring	Large/157 x 145	80.00	110.00	45.00

SMALL-WAISTED VASES (CHINA), c.1935-1939

The Wade sales catalogue numbers for the small waisted vases are 83, 84, 85 and 100.

Backstamp: A. Black handwritten "Wade England"
B. Black ink stamp "Wade Made in England"

No.	Description	Colourways	Size	U.S.$	Can.$	U.K.£
1a	Campanula/ primroses/roses	Blue/yellow/pink flowers; white vase; green base; gold band	80 x 40	50.00	70.00	28.00
1b	Carnations/tulips	Pink/yellow/red flowers; black vase	80 x 40	50.00	70.00	28.00
1c	Carnations/tulips	Pink/yellow/red flowers; white vase; gold band	80 x 40	50.00	70.00	28.00
1d	Daisies/violets/tulips	White/violet/red flowers; black vase	80 x 40	50.00	70.00	28.00
1e	Roses/primroses	Yellow/pink/maroon flowers; black vase	80 x 40	50.00	70.00	28.00
2a	Hibiscus	White/yellow flowers; black vase	95 x 80	40.00	55.00	28.00
2b	Oleanders	Dark pink/yellow flowers; black vase	95 x 80	50.00	70.00	28.00
2c	Oleanders	Dark pink/yellow flowers; light green vase	95 x 80	50.00	70.00	28.00
2d	Pansies	Yellow/mauve/dark pink flowers; white/green vase; gold band	85 x 80	40.00	55.00	28.00

TEMPLE VASE (EARTHENWARE), c.1930-c.1935

The Wade Catalogue number for the Temple vase is 58.

Backstamp: A. Handwritten "Wild Rose No. 58 by Wade England" with embossed "Made in England"
B. Black ink stamp "Wade England No. 58"

No.	Description	Colourways	Size	U.S.$	Can.$	U.K.£
1a	Pansies/roses/ wild roses	Red/yellow/blue flowers; yellow vase	110 x 95	40.00	55.00	30.00
1b	Wild rose	Red/yellow/blue flowers; black vase	120 x 100	40.00	55.00	30.00
1c	Wild rose	Red/yellow/blue flowers; mottled green/yellow vase	120 x 95	40.00	55.00	30.00

TRIANGULAR VASE, STEPPED BASE, c.1930-c.1935

The Wade sales catalogue number for this triangular vase with a stepped base is unknown.

China vase

Earthenware, c. 1930-1935

Backstamp: **A.** Black handwritten "Wade England"
B. Black handwritten "Wade England NINI 4"

No.	Description	Colourways	Size	U.S.$	Can.$	U.K.£
1	Assorted flowers	Red/blue/yellow flowers; green vase	130 x 185	80.00	120.00	60.00

China, c. 1935-1939

Backstamp:

No.	Description	Colourways	Size	U.S.$	Can.$	U.K.£
1	Carnations/roses	Pink/mauve/yellow flowers; pale green vase	Large/125 x 170	95.00	135.00	75.00

Jacobean Ginger Jar

JARS
1963-1992

The majority of the jars listed are part of a series that contain matching vases, dishes or bowls. The jars in this section are divided into two sections and then listed in alphabetical order with the shape number second if known.

Wade Heath
Wade Ireland

BACKSTAMPS

Transfer Prints

From 1963 through to 1992, Wade used transfer prints on its jars. Wade Ireland used a transfer print on its Celtic Porcelain jars in 1965

Embossed Backstamp

Wade Ireland used an embossed backstamp on its Celtic Porcelain jars in 1965.

WADE HEATH

JACOBEAN AND KAWA GINGER JARS, 1990-1992

The Jacobean design consists of enamelled exotic flowers, and Kawa is a Japanese design of peonies and bamboo stems.

Small size Jacobean jar

Medium size Jacobean jar

Backstamp: **A.** Red print "Wade England" with two red lines and "Jacobean"
B. Gold print "Wade England" with two gold lines and "Kawa"

No.	Name	Colourways	Size	U.S.$	Can.$	U.K.£
1a	Jacobean	White; red/black print	Small/Unknown	30.00	40.00	15.00
1b	Kawa	White; pastel pink/green print; gold highlights	Small/Unknown	30.00	40.00	15.00
2a	Jacobean	White; red/black print	Medium/210	40.00	55.00	20.00
2b	Kawa	White; pastel pink/green print; gold highlights	Medium/210	40.00	55.00	20.00

LIDDED JAR, 1927

This brightly coloured splash design looks almost like crocus flowers.

Backstamp: **A.** Red ink stamp "Wadeheath England" with lion

No.	Name	Colourways	Size	U.S.$	Can.$	U.K.£
1	Lidded jar	Orange/brown lid; blue/green/mauve splashes	110	30.00	45.00	28.00

WADE HEATH (cont.)

TOPLINE JARS, 1963

Topline is a series of contemporary shapes and decoration by freelance designer Michael Caddy and produced for only a short time in 1963. The jars are cylindrical, and can be found in several sizes and all have lids. The abstract panels are purple or gold, the leaf medallion can be white, black or silver grey. The multicoloured prints are of horse-drawn carriages or a vintage car. There has been some confusion as to which are Topline vintage cars and which are Wade veteran cars, all Topline vintage vehicles whether horse driven or motor driven cars, have drivers and passengers, the veteran cars series did not have people included in the design. Three types of lid were used, a concave lid, a domed lid, and a pointed finial lid. A pierced concave lid was produced for Topline flower vases. The pierced concave lid has also been found on the Black Frost series vases. For other Topline items see Dishes, Vases and Urns section.

Concave Lids

Backstamp: Red print "Wade England"

No.	Description	Colourways	Size	U.S.$	Can.$	U.K.£
1a	Abstract	White; gold abstract panels; black/white lid	76	70.00	95.00	35.00
1b	Abstract	White; purple abstract panels; black/white lid	76	70.00	95.00	35.00
1c	Abstract	White; purple and gold abstract panels; black/white lid	76	70.00	95.00	35.00
2	Feather	Black; white feather medallion; gold band on lid	125	60.00	80.00	30.00

Domed Lid

No.	Description	Colourways	Size	U.S.$	Can.$	U.K.£
1	Feather	Black; gold bands and feather medallion	140	60.00	80.00	30.00

Duryea Phaeton 1904

Finial Lids

No.	Description	Colourways	Size	U.S.$	Can.$	U.K.£
1	Abstract	White; gold abstract panels, finial	114	60.00	80.00	30.00
2	Abstract	White; black bands; gold abstract panels, finial	148	70.00	95.00	35.00
3	Duryea Phaeton 1904	White; multicoloured print; gold finial	175	60.00	80.00	30.00

WADE IRELAND

CELTIC JARS, 1965

IRISH PORCELAIN, SHAPE CK1 and CK4

The designs of writhing snakes and men with long beards were copied from illustrations made by medieval monks in an Irish manuscript called, *The Book of Kells*. The snakes represent those banished from Ireland by Saint Patrick. The beard-pullers jar has an embossed design of old men with entwined arms, legs, hair, and long beards. These men are said to represent the merchants and moneychangers who were cast out of the temple by Jesus.

Beard-pullers jar

Backstamp: **A.** Embossed "Celtic Porcelain by Wade Ireland" in an Irish knot wreath
B. Black transfer print "Celtic Porcelain made in Ireland by Wade Co. Armagh"
Shape No.: CK1 Serpent jar
CK4 Beard-pullers jar

No.	Description	Colourways	Size	U.S.$	Can.$	U.K.£
1	Serpents jar	Mottled blue-green	114	95.00	125.00	55.00
2	Beard-pullers jar	Blue/green	114	95.00	125.00	55.00

JUGS

c.1928-1995

The jugs in this section are more decorative than utilitarian. They come in a large range of shapes with embossed or impressed designs, with hand-painted decorations, transfer prints or in plain or mottled colours, sometimes with several of these components combined on one item.

Flaxman Ware jugs are usually produced with a mottled glaze, although at times they were issued in solid colours. Transfer prints began to be used as decoration on jugs in the 1950s.

The jugs are listed first in shape-number order, then those without shape numbers follow in alphabetical order.

Wade Heath

160

BACKSTAMPS

Impressed Backstamp

The first jug produced by Wade, shape 98/2, which was issued in the late 1920s, has an impressed backstamp. Except for this jug, Wade used impressed backstamps from 1957 to the early 1960s, and they appeared on some of its Harmony Ware jugs.

Hand-painted Backstamp

Only one jug has a hand-painted backstamp, the Big Bad Wolf jug, produced from 1937 to 1939.

Ink Stamps

From 1933 to the 1940s, Wade Heath marked its jugs with ink stamps in a variety of colours — black, red, grey, green, brown and orange. Many of these backstamps included a lion and either an impressed or embossed shape number.

For Gothic Ware jugs, produced during 1940, black and gold ink stamps were used. Black ink stamps can be found on Harvest Ware jugs from the late 1940s to the early 1950s.

Standard Wade England ink stamps were used on jugs from 1934 to 1961, in either black, red or grey. They often included either an impressed or embossed shape number.

Transfer Prints

Beginning with a Gothic Ware jug of 1953, Wade used a variety of transfer-printed backstamps on its jugs until 1995. They can be found in gold, red, black, white and in black and orange.

WADE HEATH

SHAPE 1, FLOWER HANDLE, 1934-1935

These jugs have a large embossed seven-petal flower on the top of the handle and three large flowers on the neck. There are embossed leaves and a pebble design in the background.

Flower handle and flowers

Backstamp: Black ink stamp "Wadeheath England" with a black lion and a small impressed triangle

No.	Description	Colourways	Size	U.S.$	Can.$	U.K.£
1a	Flower handle	Cream; yellow, brown/orange flowers; green stems	240	110.00	145.00	60.00
1b	Flower handle	Pale yellow; pale green flowers; pale orange stems	240	110.00	145.00	60.00
1c	Flower handle	Yellow; dark blue/pale blue flowers; brown stems	240	110.00	145.00	60.00
1d	Flower handle	Yellow; yellow/blue/orange flowers; brown stems	240	110.00	145.00	60.00

WADE HEATH (cont.)

SHAPE 13, WOODPECKER HANDLE, 1933-c.1945

These waisted jugs are decorated with swirling tree branches around the bowl. A woodpecker forms the handle.

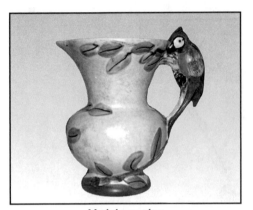

Mottled green glaze

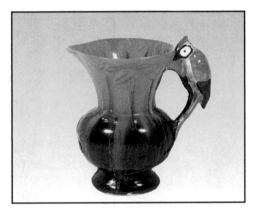

Orange and black glaze

Backstamp: **A.** Red ink stamp "Wadeheath England" with a lion
B. Black ink stamp "Wadeheath England" with a lion
C. Black ink stamp "Wade Heath England"
D. Black ink stamp "Wadeheath Orcadia Ware British Made"

No.	Description	Colourways	Size	U.S.$	Can.$	U.K.£
1a	Woodpecker	Yellow jug; brown leaves; yellow/orange/brown bird	Small/180	150.00	200.00	75.00
1b	Woodpecker	Yellow jug; brown/orange leaves; green /yellow/ orange/blue bird	Small/180	150.00	200.00	75.00
2a	Woodpecker	Amber/brown jug, bird	Medium/190	150.00	200.00	75.00
2b	Woodpecker	Mottled green jug; brown/dark blue bird	Medium/190	150.00	200.00	75.00
2c	Woodpecker	Orange/black streaked jug; orange/green/ dark blue bird	Medium/190	150.00	200.00	75.00
2d	Woodpecker	Orange/black streaked jug; orange/blue/ green/yellow bird	Medium/190	150.00	200.00	75.00
2e	Woodpecker	Yellow/orange/black jug; blue/orange bird	Medium/190	150.00	200.00	75.00
2f	Woodpecker	Yellow/orange/brown jug; green/orange bird	Medium/190	150.00	200.00	75.00

WADE HEATH (cont.)

SHAPE 14, LOVEBIRDS, 1934-1935

Lovebirds

Backstamp: Black ink stamp "Wadeheath England" with a lion

No.	Description	Colourways	Size	U.S.$	Can.$	U.K.£
1	Lovebirds	Yellow; brown handle; green/orange birds	Small/165	180.00	240.00	90.00
2	Lovebirds	Yellow; brown handle; green/orange birds	Large/ 193	180.00	240.00	90.00

SHAPE 15, CASTILE, 1934-1935

Butterfly and flower   Imari   Orcadia

Backstamp: **A.** Black ink stamp "Wadeheath England" with a lion and impressed "Castile 15"
             B. Orange ink stamp "Wadeheath Orcadia Ware"

No.	Description	Colourways	Size	U.S.$	Can.$	U.K.£
1a	Butterfly and Flowers	Off white; brown handle, butterfly; green leaves; blue/orange/yellow flowers	220	170.00	225.00	85.00
1b	Butterfly and Flowers	Off white; green handle, leaves; pink flowers; yellow butterfly	220	170.00	225.00	85.00
1c	Imari	White; blue handle, spout; blue/gold/orange design	220	170.00	225.00	85.00
1d	Flying Bird	Off white; brown handle, bird; orange flowers	220	170.00	225.00	85.00
1e	Orcadia	Turquoise; orange handle, spout; orange/yellow streaks	220	170.00	225.00	85.00

WADE HEATH (cont.)

SHAPE 16 and 24, PYRAMID, 1933-1935

These jugs have been reported with both 16 and 24 as the shape number. The long, straight handle steps in at the bottom of the jug. The hand-painted 'Imari' decoration was a popular 1930s design used many times by Wade on decorative and tableware products.

Abstract, shape 16

Abstract and flower, shape 16

Imari, shape 16

Backstamp: **A.** Black ink stamp "Wadeheath England" with a lion and impressed "16" (1934-1935)
B. Black ink stamp "Flaxman Ware Hand Made Pottery by Wadeheath" (1935-1937)

No.	Description	Colourways	Size	U.S.$	Can.$	U.K.£
1a	Imari	White; cobalt blue spout, handle, panels; white/orange/ gold decoration	185	170.00	225.00	85.00
2a	Abstract	Brown handle; brown/orange/yellow abstract design	215	170.00	225.00	85.00
2b	Abstract/Flower	Orange handle; black/orange/yellow design; black/orange flower	215	170.00	225.00	85.00
2c	Imari	White; blue handle, spout; blue/gold/orange design	215	170.00	225.00	85.00
2d	Rose	Green; orange spout, handle; pink rose; cream centre panel	215	170.00	225.00	85.00

WADE HEATH (cont.)

SHAPE 55, WIDE-MOUTH, 1933-1935

A number of these jugs were produced in Orcadia Ware a design of vivid streaked glazes which were allowed to run over the rims and down the inside and outside of the item. They have been found in two sizes.

Orcadia

Flowers

Leaves

Backstamp: **A.** Orange ink stamp "Wadeheath Orcadia Ware"
B. Black ink stamp "Wadeheath Orcadia Ware British Made"
C. Black ink stamp "Made in England" with impressed "55"
D. Black ink stamp "Wadeheath England" with lion

No.	Description	Colourways	Size	U.S.$	Can.$	U.K.£
1a	Orcadia	Brown/orange/brown streaks; brown base	180	100.00	125.00	55.00
1b	Orcadia	Orange/dark green streaks; grey base	180	100.00	195.00	55.00
1c	Orcadia	Orange/yellow/brown streaks; brown base	180	100.00	125.00	55.00
1d	Orcadia	Orange/yellow/green; grey-blue base; wide-mouth	180	100.00	125.00	55.00
2a	Flowers	Large orange/blue flowers; yellow lines; black panel, foot	195	95.00	125.00	60.00
2b	Leaves	Large orange leaves; black seeds, rim	195	95.00	155.00	60.00

SHAPE 76, DATES UNKNOWN

Backstamp: Black ink stamp "Wadeheath England" with a lion and impressed "76"

No.	Description	Colourways	Size	U.S.$	Can.$	U.K.£
1	Flowers	Cream; small orange/mauve flowers	208	60.00	80.00	30.00

WADE HEATH (cont.)

SHAPE 88, 1934-1937

Most of these jugs are hand-painted and have a spout that is moulded in a V shape.

Backstamp: **A.** Black ink stamp "WadeHeath England" with a lion and impressed shape number
B. Black ink stamp "Flaxman Ware Hand Made Pottery by Wadeheath, England" with impressed shape number
C. Black ink stamp "Wadeheath Ware England" with impressed shape number

Shape Nos.: 88M — Miniature
88MS — Medium
88 — Large

No.	Description	Colourways	Size	U.S.$	Can.$	U.K.£
1a	Flower	Yellow; large orange flower	Miniature/140	70.00	95.00	35.00
1b	Flowers	Cream; pink/blue flowers; green leaves	Miniature/140	70.00	95.00	35.00
1c	Flowers	Cream; pink/mauve flowers	Miniature/140	70.00	95.00	35.00
1d	Flowers	Cream; blue handle; pink flowers	Miniature/140	70.00	95.00	35.00
1e	Flowers	Cream; large orange/blue flowers	Miniature/140	70.00	95.00	35.00
1f	Flowers	Cream; yellow/orange flowers; grey cross stripes	Miniature/140	70.00	90.00	35.00
1g	Flowers	Cream; yellow/red flowers	Miniature/140	70.00	90.00	35.00
1h	Mottled	Mottled brown/light brown neck	Miniature/140	60.00	80.00	30.00
1i	Mottled	Mottled greens	Miniature/140	60.00	80.00	30.00
1j	Mottled	Mottled yellow/brown	Miniature/140	60.00	80.00	30.00
1k	Solid colour	Green	Miniature/140	60.00	80.00	30.00
1l	Streaks	Cream; dark brown/light brown streaks	Miniature/140	60.00	80.00	30.00
1m	Streaks	Cream; orange/yellow/brown streaks	Miniature/140	60.00	80.00	30.00
2a	Flowers	Cream; blue/yellow flowers	Medium/185	80.00	110.00	40.00
2b	Streaks	Streaked orange/yellow/brown; orange handle, bowl; brown base	Medium/185	80.00	110.00	40.00
2c	Windmill	Off white; red/yellow windmill; green trees	Medium/185	80.00	110.00	45.00
3a	Flowers	Cream; blue spout, handle; grey base; red/blue flowers; green leaves	Large/210	90.00	120.00	45.00
3b	Flying Heron	Green/yellow; blue/yellow flowers; brown flying Heron	Large/215	90.00	120.00	48.00

WADE HEATH (cont.)

SHAPE 89, 1934-1935

This jug has a long pointed spout and an impressed and embossed triangle design around the neck.

Photograph not available
at press time

Backstamp: **A.** Black ink stamp "WadeHeath England" with a lion and impressed "89"
B. Orange ink stamp "Wadeheath Orcadia Ware"

No.	Description	Colourways	Size	U.S.$	Can.$	U.K.£
1a	Flowers	Cream; blue/yellow/orange flowers; green leaves	160	130.00	175.00	65.00
1b	Orcadia	Orange/brown	155	120.00	160.00	60.00

SHAPE 90, 1934-1935

These jugs are similar to shape 89, but the spout extends down to the waist of the jug and the triangle design is around the waist.

Backstamp: **A.** Black ink stamp "WadeHeath England" with a lion and embossed "90" 1934-1935
B. Black ink stamp "Flaxman Ware Hand Made Pottery by Wadeheath England" 1935-1937

No.	Description	Colourways	Size	U.S.$	Can.$	U.K.£
1a	Bird	Cream; blue/yellow flowers; brown trees, bird	215	140.00	200.00	75.00
1b	Butterflies	Green; brown flowers, green leaves (top); blue/brown flowers; black outlined butterflies	215	140.00	200.00	75.00
1c	Flowers	Cream/green; blue/brown/yellow flowers	215	140.00	200.00	75.00
1d	Flowers	Cream/orange; orange/yellow flowers	215	140.00	200.00	75.00
1e	Flowers	Cream; yellow/blue flowers; green leaves	215	140.00	200.00	75.00
1f	Flowers	Green; blue flowers; brown/green leaves	215	140.00	200.00	75.00
1g	Humming birds	Green; brown flowers (top); blue flowers; brown tree outline, hummingbirds	215	150.00	210.00	85.00
1h	Streaks	Orange/brown/yellow streaks; orange band	215	90.00	120.00	45.00
2	Triangles	Green; blue spout, handle; blue/brown flowers; brown triangles	225	140.00	200.00	75.00

WADE HEATH (cont.)

SHAPE 92, 1935-c.1945

Backstamp: **A.** Black ink stamp "Wadeheath Ware England" with impressed "92"
B. Black ink stamp "Made in England" with impressed "92"

No.	Description	Colourways	Size	U.S.$	Can.$	U.K.£
1a	Flowers	Mottled brown foot, handle; yellow/orange bowl, flowers	204	80.00	110.00	45.00
1b	Streaks	Brown foot, handle; blue/yellow/orange streaks	204	80.00	110.00	45.00
1c	Streaks	Brown foot, handle; yellow/orange/grey streaks	204	80.00	110.00	45.00
1d	Streaks	Yellow foot, handle; orange/brown/yellow streaks	204	80.00	110.00	45.00

SHAPE 93, ELITE, 1934-1937, c1948-c1952, 1955
Various Decoration, 1934-1937

The shape name for these jugs is 'Elite,' they were issued over a twenty year period with many different decorations.

Bird   Flowers   Leaves

Backstamp: **A.** Black ink stamp "WadeHeath England" with a lion and embossed "Elite No 93," 1934-1935
B. Black ink stamp "Flaxman Ware Hand Made Pottery by Wadeheath England" with embossed "Elite 93"

No.	Description	Colourways	Size	U.S.$	Can.$	U.K.£
1a	Flowers	Cream; brown striped jug, handle; large orange flower; green/black/brown leaves	285	170.00	225.00	85.00
1b	Flowers	Cream; green/brown base, handle; maroon/mauve flowers	285	170.00	225.00	85.00
2a	Bird	Cream; green handle; blue/yellow flowers; brown/green tree; bird outlined in brown	295	170.00	225.00	85.00
2b	Flames	Cream; orange spout, handle; blue/orange/brown flames	295	170.00	225.00	85.00
2c	Leaves	Yellow; orange spout, base; brown handle; green leaves	295	170.00	225.00	85.00

WADE HEATH *(cont.)*

SHAPE 93 *(cont.)*
Peony Decoration, c.1948-c.1952

The flowers on these jugs were hand-painted, so no two jugs are identical.

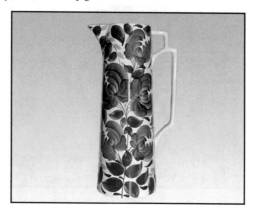

Backstamp: Black ink stamp "Harvest Ware Wade England" with the impressed "93"

No.	Description	Colourways	Size	U.S.$	Can.$	U.K.£
1	Peony	Cream; multicoloured flowers	280	90.00	120.00	45.00

Imperial Decoration, 1955

These jugs are decorated with large white seed cases highlighted in burnished gold.

Photograph not available
at press time

Backstamp: Circular print "Wade Made in England Hand Painted" and embossed "Elite 93"

No.	Description	Colourways	Size	U.S.$	Can.$	U.K.£
1	Imperial	Burgundy; white seed cases; gold highlights	285	130.00	175.00	65.00

WADE HEATH (cont.)

SHAPE 98/2, c.1928

The spout of this jug is short, and there are raised ribs running around the bowl.

Backstamp: Impressed "98/2 Made in England"

No.	Description	Colourways	Size	U.S.$	Can.$	U.K.£
1	Shape 98/2	Mottled turquoise/green/cream	205	110.00	145.00	55.00

SHAPE 100, ART DECO, 1934-c.1948

These jugs were either decorated with hand-painted designs or produced in all-over mottled colours.

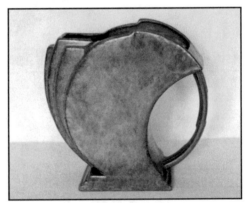

Cream, with large orange flower   Mottled blue and brown

Backstamp: **A.** Black ink stamp "Wadeheath England" with a lion and impressed "100"
               B. Impressed "Streamline 100 "

No.	Description	Colourways	Size	U.S.$	Can.$	U.K.£
1a	Flowers	Cream; orange handle, base; large orange flower	180	175.00	200.00	100.00
1b	Mottled	Mottled blue/brown	180	125.00	150.00	80.00

WADE HEATH (cont.)

SHAPE 106, 1934-c.1948

These jugs were either decorated with hand-painted designs or produced in an all-over mottled colours. There is a drainage hole inside the base under the handle.

Imari

Flowers, miniature size

Art Deco, large size

Parrot, large size

Backstamp: **A.** Black ink stamp "Wadeheath England" with a lion and impressed "106/30"
B. Black ink stamp "Flaxman Ware Hand Made Pottery by Wadeheath England" with impressed "106"
C. Black ink stamp "Flaxman Wade Heath England" with impressed "106"
D. Black ink stamp "Wadeheath Ware England" with impressed "106"
E. Black ink stamp "Made in England" with impressed "106"
Shape No.: 106 — Miniature, large; 106/30 — Medium

No.	Description	Colourways	Size	U.S.$	Can.$	U.K.£
1a	Flowers	Cream; green base, handle; large blue/yellow/orange flowers	Miniature/140	70.00	95.00	35.00
1b	Flowers	Cream; green base, handle; light brown leaves; small pink flower	Miniature/140	70.00	95.00	35.00
1c	Flowers	Cream; grey base; brown handle; large blue/yellow/orange flowers	Miniature/140	60.00	80.00	30.00
1d	Flowers	Cream; orange base; pink/mauve/blue flowers	Miniature/140	70.00	95.00	35.00
1e	Flowers	Cream; orange base; red/yellow/orange flowers	Miniature/140	70.00	95.00	35.00
1f	Flowers	Cream; pink base; brown/mauve flowers	Miniature/140	70.00	95.00	35.00
1g	Mottled	Mottled blue	Miniature/140	60.00	80.00	30.00
1h	Mottled	Mottled green	Miniature/140	60.00	80.00	30.00
1i	Mottled	Mottled orange/grey	Miniature/140	60.00	80.00	30.00
1j	Solid colour	Dark blue	Miniature/140	70.00	95.00	35.00
1k	Solid colour	Orange	Miniature/140	70.00	95.00	35.00
2a	Imari	White; dark blue handle; orange/dark blue flowers; gold lustre leaves	Medium/190	130.00	175.00	65.00
2b	Flowers	Cream; three multicoloured flowers	Medium/190	130.00	175.00	65.00
2c	Flowers	Cream; yellow flowers; green leaves	Medium/190	130.00	175.00	65.00
2d	Flowers	Cream; yellow/orange flowers; green leaves	Medium/190	130.00	175.00	65.00
2e	Mottled	Mottled dark green	Medium/190	80.00	110.00	40.00
2f	Mottled	Mottled cream/blue	Medium/190	80.00	110.00	40.00
2g	Streaks	Blue; brown streaks on base	Medium/190	80.00	110.00	40.00
2h	Tree's	Blue; brown trees	Medium/190	60.00	90.00	30.00
3a	Art Deco	Yellow/orange; orange handle; black/green/yellow squares; yellow flower	Large/222	160.00	240.00	75.00
3b	Flowers	Yellow; orange handle; orange/brown flowers; green leaves	Large/222	160.00	240.00	75.00
3c	Mottled	Mottled mustard/green/yellow; orange bands	Large/222	110.00	155.00	60.00
3d	Mottled	Mottled orange/yellow	Large/222	110.00	155.00	60.00
3e	Parrot	Cream; orange handle, parrot; green leaves	Large/222	160.00	240.00	75.00
3f	Parrot	Yellow; orange handle; orange/green parrot; green leaves	Large/222	160.00	240.00	75.00
3g	Trees	Blue; brown base, handle; brown/blue trees	Large/222	160.00	240.00	75.00

WADE HEATH *(cont.)*

SHAPE 110, 1934-1935

There are four ribbed bands around the waist of these jugs.

Backstamp: A. Black ink stamp "Wadeheath England" with a lion and embossed "110"
                   B. Orange ink stamp "Wadeheath Orcadia Ware"

No.	Description	Colourways	Size	U.S.$	Can.$	U.K.£
1a	Butterfly	Beige; rust spout; green flowers; outlined butterfly	230	145.00	180.00	65.00
1b	Cottage	Cream; grey rim, spout, handle, base; mauve flowers; brown gate, cottage	230	145.00	180.00	65.00
1c	Flowers	Cream; large orange/blue/green flowers	230	145.00	180.00	65.00
1d	Flowers	Cream; large orange/green flowers; brown/silver and green/silver leaves	230	145.00	180.00	65.00
1e	Flowers	Cream; purple/lilac/grey/yellow flowers; green grasses; orange-lustre spout, handle	230	145.00	180.00	65.00
1f	Mottled	Mottled yellow/green	230	70.00	95.00	45.00
1g	Orcadia	Orange/yellow/brown streaks; brown base	230	80.00	110.00	45.00
1h	Orcadia	Yellow; brown streaks	230	80.00	110.00	45.00
1i	Scrolls	Yellow; orange scrolls	230	80.00	110.00	45.00

WADE HEATH (cont.)

SHAPE 112, 1934-1935

These tall slender, hand-painted jugs, which taper at the top, have a handle consisting of a small and large triangle.

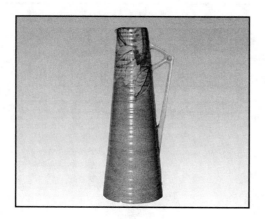

Backstamp: Black ink stamp "Wadeheath England" with a lion

No.	Description	Colourways	Size	U.S.$	Can.$	U.K.£
1a	Flowers	Cream; red house; red/orange flowers	285	90.00	120.00	45.00
1b	Flowers	Off white; blue/brown base, handle; pink/blue hollyhocks	285	170.00	225.00	85.00
1c	Leaves	Brown; green/grey/yellow leaves	285	90.00	120.00	45.00
1d	Leaves	Orange; green/grey/orange leaves	285	90.00	120.00	45.00
1e	Poppies	Off white; green handle; yellow corn; blue cornflowers; red poppies	285	170.00	225.00	85.00

WADE HEATH *(Cont.)*

SHAPE 113, 1934-c.1945

The body of these jugs is ribbed, which is hard to see on the mottled versions.

Backstamp: **A.** Black ink stamp "Wadeheath England" with a lion and impressed "113"
B. Black ink stamp "Flaxman Ware Hand Made—Pottery by Wadeheath England"
C. Black ink stamp "Made in England" with impressed "113"

No.	Description	Colourways	Size	U.S.$	Can.$	U.K.£
1a	Flowers	Cream; green base, handle; pink/ yellow flowers	Miniature/130	60.00	95.00	35.00
1b	Flowers	Cream; orange handle; small green and large orange flowers	Miniature/130	60.00	95.00	35.00
1c	Flowers	Cream; orange base; black/cream handle; black vine; orange/blue/green leaves	Miniature/130	60.00	95.00	35.00
1d	Flowers	Cream; pearlised orange base; cream/orange handle; orange/red/blue flowers; silver lustre	Miniature/130	60.00	95.00	35.00
1e	Flowers	Off white; orange flowers	Miniature/130	60.00	95.00	35.00
1f	Mottled	Green/mottled brown	Miniature/130	60.00	95.00	35.00
1g	Plain	Green	Miniature/130	50.00	70.00	25.00
1h	Plain	Orange/green	Miniature/130	50.00	70.00	25.00
1i	Plain	Yellow/mottled brown	Miniature/130	50.00	70.00	25.00
2a	Flower	Cream; black handle; orange base large orange flower; green leaves	Large/190	75.00	95.00	55.00
2b	Flowers	Cream; orange handle; small green and large orange flowers	Large/190	75.00	95.00	55.00
2c	Flowers	Cream; orange handle; orange/blue/yellow/ orange flowers; green leaves	Large/190	75.00	95.00	55.00
2d	Fruit	Green; yellow base, handle; yellow/ blue fruit	Large/190	75.00	95.00	55.00
2e	Mottled	Mottled Green	Large/190	101.00	145.00	55.00

WADE HEATH (cont.)

SHAPE 114, LONG-TAILED BIRD, 1934-1935

The tail of the moulded bird on the bowl of these jugs extends upward to form the handle.

Backstamp: Black ink stamp "Wadeheath England" with a lion

No.	Description	Colourways	Size	U.S.$	Can.$	U.K.£
1a	Long-tailed bird	Yellow; orange butterfly, flowers; green/yellow bird	180	180.00	240.00	90.00
1b	Long-tailed bird	Yellow; orange spout, base, butterfly; mauve/ orange flowers; light green/orange bird	180	180.00	240.00	90.00

SHAPE 119, 1935-1937

Backstamp: A. Black ink stamp "Flaxman Ware Hand Made Pottery by Wadeheath England" with embossed "119" and black ink stamp "Wadeheath England Registration No 812659"
B. Black ink stamp "Flaxman Ware Hand Made Pottery by Wadeheath England" with impressed "119"
C. Black ink stamp "Wadeheath England" with impressed "119"

No.	Description	Colourways	Size	U.S.$	Can.$	U.K.£
1a	Cottage	Yellow; green handle; brown/grey cottage; blue/yellow flowers	229	110.00	145.00	65.00
1b	Fruit	Green; blue/yellow/green fruit	229	110.00	145.00	55.00
1c	Mottled	Mottled cream/green	229	110.00	145.00	55.00
1d	Silver flower	Cream; green bands; silver lustre flower, lines	229	110.00	145.00	55.00
1e	Tree	White; blue/yellow tree, flowers	229	110.00	145.00	65.00

WADE HEATH *(cont.)*

SHAPE 120 , 1934-1937

A broad band runs diagonally down the jug from the spout to the base of the handle. It separates two panels of horizontal ribs.

Mottled

Flowers

Leaves

Backstamp: **A.** Black ink stamp "Wadeheath England" with a lion
B. Black ink stamp "Flaxman Ware Hand Made Pottery by Wadeheath England" with embossed "120"
C. Ink stamped "Wadeheath England" Sample "4044" with lion and impressed "120"

No.	Description	Colourways	Size	U.S.$	Can.$	U.K.£
1a	Flowers	Cream; orange handle; brown base; mauve/maroon/ yellow flowers	215	110.00	155.00	65.00
1b	Flowers	Cream; orange rim, base; orange/yellow flowers	215	110.00	155.00	65.00
1c	Flowers	Cream; yellow rim; brown handle, base; large maroon/ yellow flower	215	110.00	155.00	65.00
1d	Fruit	White; pale orange handle, base; blue/orange fruits	215	110.00	155.00	65.00
1e	Leaves	Mottled orange; brown rim, handle, foot; brown coffee, green leaves	215	110.00	155.00	65.00
1f	Mottled	Mottled green	215	90.00	130.00	55.00
1g	Mottled	Mottled green/cream	215	90.00	130.00	55.00
1h	Mottled	Mottled orange	215	90.00	130.00	55.00
1i	Mottled	Mottled yellow/golden brown	215	90.00	130.00	55.00

WADE HEATH (cont.)

SHAPE 121, 1934-1940

Cottage

Bands

Flowers

Backstamp: **A.** Grey ink stamp "Wadeheath England Registration No 812930" and embossed "121A"
B. Black ink stamp "Wadeheath England" with a lion and impressed "121A"
C. Black ink stamp "Flaxman Ware Hand Made Pottery by Wadeheath England" with embossed "121"
D. Black ink stamp "Wade Heath England" with embossed "121"

No.	Description	Colourways	Size	U.S.$	Can.$	U.K.£
1a	Bands	Cream; yellow/green/black bands; green/black handle; orange leaves	230	150.00	200.00	75.00
1b	Cottage	Cream; brown handle; grey/green trees; brown cottage; grey hill; orange/blue flowers	230	150.00	200.00	80.00
1c	Flowers	Cream; orange handle; blue/yellow tree; orange/blue flowers	230	150.00	200.00	80.00
1d	Flowers	Cream; yellow/green/orange bands; orange handle; blue/yellow/orange flowers	230	150.00	200.00	80.00
1e	Flowers	Cream; grey neck, handle; large orange/grey flowers	230	150.00	200.00	80.00
1f	Mottled	Mottled blue	230	150.00	200.00	75.00
1g	Mottled	Mottled cream top; turquoise bottom	230	150.00	200.00	75.00
1h	Mottled	Mottled green	230	150.00	200.00	75.00
1i	Mottled	Mottled orange	230	150.00	200.00	75.00
1j	Mottled	Mottled yellow/golden brown	230	150.00	200.00	75.00

WADE HEATH (cont.)

SHAPE 122, 1937-c.1945

Raised ribs run across the handle side of these jugs.

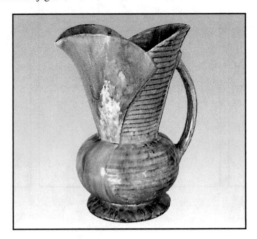

Backstamp: **A.** Black ink stamp "Wade Heath England" with embossed "122"
B. Black ink stamp "Flaxman Wade Heath England" with embossed "122"

No.	Description	Colourways	Size	U.S.$	Can.$	U.K.£
1a	Mottled	Mottled orange; blue/pink flowers	205	120.00	160.00	60.00
1b	Mottled	Mottled orange; mottled grey/brown base	205	120.00	160.00	60.00
1c	Mottled	Mottled turquoise/blue/beige	205	120.00	160.00	60.00

SHAPE 123, 1934-1937

These jugs have three embossed spirals extending down the body from the spout, with horizontal bands on the handle side.

Backstamp: **A.** Black ink stamp "Wadeheath England" with a lion and embossed "123"
B. Black ink stamp "Flaxman Ware Hand Made Pottery by Wadeheath England" with impressed "123"

No.	Description	Colourways	Size	U.S.$	Can.$	U.K.£
1a	Flowers	Cream; black/purple tree top; orange/yellow flowers; yellow/green cross bands	229	110.00	145.00	55.00
1b	Mottled	Mottled grey/turquoise	229	110.00	145.00	55.00
1c	Mottled	Mottled orange	229	110.00	145.00	55.00

WADE HEATH *(cont.)*

SHAPE 124, 1934-1937

These jugs have a broad band angled across the middle and a ribbed design around the body.

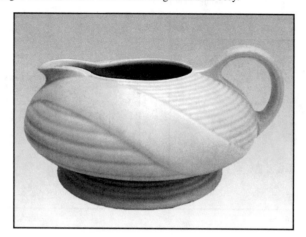

Backstamp: **A.** Black ink stamp "Wadeheath England" with a lion and embossed "124"
B. Black ink stamp "Flaxman Ware Hand Made Pottery by Wadeheath England" with impressed "124"

No.	Description	Colourways	Size	U.S.$	Can.$	U.K.£
1a	Flowers	Green/cream; silver diagonal stripe, flowers	75	60.00	80.00	30.00
1b	Mottled	Mottled green/mauve/cream	75	60.00	80.00	32.00
1c	Mottled	Mottled green/yellow	75	60.00	80.00	32.00
1d	Solid colour	Pale orange	75	60.00	80.00	32.00
1e	Solid colour	Pale yellow	75	60.00	80.00	32.00
1f	Solid colour	White	75	60.00	80.00	32.00

WADE HEATH (cont.)

SHAPE 125, RIBBED, 1934-1937

Similar to shape 120, this jug has horizontal ribs around the body.

Flowers	Mottled orange

Backstamp: **A.** Black ink stamp "Wadeheath England" with Lion and embossed "125"
B. Black ink stamp "Flaxman Ware Hand Made Pottery by Wadeheath England" with embossed "125"

No.	Description	Colourways	Size	U.S.$	Can.$	U.K.£
1a	Flowers	Cream; mauve/orange flowers; green leaves; orange lustre handle, foot	190	130.00	175.00	65.00
1b	Mottled	Mottled orange	190	130.00	175.00	65.00

SHAPE 127, 1934-1937

Backstamp: **A.** Black ink stamp "Wadeheath England" with a lion and embossed "127"
B. Black ink stamp "Flaxman Ware Hand Made Pottery by Wadeheath England" with impressed "127"
C. Orange ink stamp "Wadeheath Orcadia Ware"

No.	Description	Colourways	Size	U.S.$	Can.$	U.K.£
1a	Flowers	Cream; lilac/pink grasses; blue/yellow flowers; silver lustre	190	110.00	145.00	55.00
1b	Flowers	Cream; yellow/orange flowers; green/yellow grass	190	110.00	145.00	55.00
1c	Flowers	White; large yellow and small orange flowers; green leaves	190	110.00	145.00	55.00
1d	Mottled	Mottled blue	190	110.00	145.00	55.00
1e	Orcadia	Cream; maroon rim, handle; maroon/green/orange streaks	190	110.00	145.00	55.00

WADE HEATH (cont.)

SHAPE 128, 1935-1937

These tall jugs have a wavy handle consisting of three loops.

Mottled blue and green   Mottled brown, yellow and red

Backstamp: **A.** Black ink stamp "Flaxman Ware Hand Made Pottery by Wadeheath England" with impressed "128"
            B. Black ink stamp "Wadeheath England" with impressed "128"

No.	Description	Colourways	Size	U.S.$	Can.$	U.K.£
1a	Cottage	Cream; grey/orange tree; brown cottage; mauve flower	220	130.00	175.00	65.00
1b	Cottage	Cream; orange spout, handle; orange/ green trees; orange cottage, flowers	220	130.00	175.00	65.00
1c	Mottled	Mottled green/blue	220	130.00	175.00	65.00
1d	Mottled	Mottled brown/yellow/red				

WADE HEATH (cont.)

SHAPE 131, 1934-1940

These jugs have horizontal ribs running around the body and base.

Backstamp: A. Black ink stamp "WadeHeath England" with a lion and impressed "131"
B. Black ink stamp "Flaxman Ware Hand Made Pottery by Wadeheath, England" and impressed "131MIN" or "131MS"

No.	Description	Colourways	Size	U.S.$	Can.$	U.K.£
1a	Flowers	Cream; blue base; green band; blue flowers; brown leaves, branches	Miniature/135	90.00	175.00	55.00
1b	Mottled	Mottled blue	Miniature/135	70.00	110.00	40.00
1c	Mottled	Mottled green	Miniature/135	70.00	110.00	40.00
1d	Mottled	Mottled grey	Miniature/135	70.00	110.00	40.00
2a	Bands	Yellow; green crossed bands	Medium/184	70.00	110.00	40.00
2b	Cross bands	Grey; blue/brown crossed bands	Medium/184	70.00	110.00	40.00
2c	Mottled	Mottled blue	Medium/184	70.00	110.00	40.00
2d	Mottled	Mottled green/orange on yellow	Medium/184	70.00	110.00	40.00
3a	Bird	Light green; green/brown trees; brown bird	Large/215	150.00	200.00	75.00
3b	Cottage	Off white; bright orange base, handle, cottage; brown tree	Large/215	150.00	200.00	75.00
3c	Flowers	Cream; bright yellow base, handle; multicoloured flowers	Large/215	150.00	200.00	75.00
3d	Mottled	Mottled grey/mauve; mottled brown handle, base	Large/215	90.00	120.00	45.00
3e	Mottled	Mottled yellow/green/orange	Large/215	90.00	120.00	45.00
3f	Trees and sun	Green; orange sun; blue/green/orange trees	Large/215	90.00	120.00	45.00

WADE HEATH (cont.)

SHAPE 132, 1935-1937

These round jugs have an impressed design of wavy lines and swirls, except for style 2b, which is smooth.

Mottled colourways, wide base

Rabbits and Sunset, narrow base

Backstamp: Black ink stamp "Flaxman Ware Hand Made Pottery by Wadeheath, England" and an embossed "132"

Wide Base

No.	Description	Colourways	Size	U.S.$	Can.$	U.K.£
1a	Mottled	Mottled amber; brown leaves	Miniature/130	70.00	95.00	35.00
1b	Mottled	Mottled brown/green	Miniature/130	70.00	95.00	35.00
2a	Crossed lines	Pale blue; dull yellow crossed lines	Medium/192	120.00	160.00	60.00
2b	Sunflower	White; yellow sunflower, crossed lines	Medium/192	120.00	160.00	60.00

Narrow Base

No.	Description	Colourways	Size	U.S.$	Can.$	U.K.£
3a	Patches	Matt grey; dull yellow patches	Large/230	120.00	160.00	60.00
3b	Rabbits and sunset	Cream; light brown foot; yellow sun; brown rabbits; green grass	Large/230	120.00	160.00	65.00

184

WADE HEATH *(cont.)*

SHAPE 133, 1934-1937

These jugs have a raised band at the waist and an impressed crosshatch design at the neck and base.

Flowers Mottled	Wisteria

Backstamp: **A.** Black ink stamp "WadeHeath England" with a lion and embossed "133 MIN"
B. Black ink stamp "Flaxman Ware Hand Made Pottery by Wadeheath, England" and embossed "133 MIN"
C. Black ink stamp "Flaxman Ware Hand Made Pottery by Wadeheath, England" and embossed "133"

No.	Description	Colourways	Size	U.S.$	Can.$	U.K.£
1a	Flowers	Cream; grey neck band; green/orange flowers; green waist band	Miniature/135	70.00	95.00	35.00
1b	Flowers	Mottled pink; green stems, handle; lilac flowers	Miniature/135	70.00	95.00	35.00
1c	Flowers	Yellow; green handle; orange tulips	Miniature/135	70.00	95.00	35.00
1d	Mottled	Mottled green/beige	Miniature/135	60.00	80.00	30.00
1e	Mottled	Mottled green/orange	Miniature/135	60.00	80.00	30.00
1f	Mottled	Mottled orange	Miniature/135	60.00	80.00	30.00
2a	Mottled	Mottled blue/green	Large/230	90.00	120.00	45.00
2b	Mottled	Mottled orange/brown	Large/230	90.00	120.00	45.00
2c	Wisteria	Grey; brown vine; green leaves; orange/deep red flowers	Large/230	90.00	120.00	45.00

WADE HEATH (cont.)

SHAPE 134, 1935-1937

These six-sided jugs have four panels of raised lines and two framed panels on either side.

| Cottage | Mottled | Windmill |

Backstamp: **A.** Black ink stamp "Wadeheath England" with a lion and embossed "134"
B. "Flaxman Ware Hand Made Pottery by Wadeheath England" with embossed "134"

No.	Description	Colourways	Size	U.S.$	Can.$	U.K.£
1a	Cottage	Cream; brown cottage, tree	215	160.00	210.00	80.00
1b	Mottled	Mottled blue-green	215	80.00	110.00	60.00
1c	Mottled	Mottled brown/green	215	80.00	110.00	60.00
1d	Mottled	Mottled green	215	80.00	110.00	60.00
1e	Mottled	Mottled orange bands; mottled turquoise bands	215	80.00	110.00	60.00
1f	Mottled	Mottled orange/brown	215	80.00	110.00	60.00
1g	Windmill	Mottled green; blue/black windmill	215	80.00	110.00	70.00

WADE HEATH *(cont.)*

SHAPE 135, 1934-1937

These unusual jugs have four spouts around the rim.

| Cottage | Flower | Plain |

Backstamp: **A**. Black ink stamp "Wadeheath England" with a lion and embossed "135"
B. Black ink stamp "Flaxman Ware Hand Made Pottery by Wadeheath, England" with embossed "135"

No.	Description	Colourways	Size	U.S.$	Can.$	U.K.£
1a	Cottage	Pale green; brown handle, tree; brown/black cottage; multicoloured fruit	216	130.00	175.00	70.00
1b	Flowers	Pale yellow; large mauve flower, small red/yellow flowers	216	130.00	175.00	65.00
1c	Flowers	Pale yellow; large orange flowers; brown leaves	216	130.00	175.00	60.00
1d	Plain	Pale yellow top; light green bottom	216	130.00	175.00	60.00
1e	Rabbits	Pale blue; brown trees, rabbits	216	150.00	200.00	75.00

WADE HEATH (cont.)

SHAPE 143, BUDGIE HANDLE, 1935-1953

These jugs are shaped like a birdbath and are embossed with a brick design. A budgerigar sits on the rim, his tail and a rose stem form the handle. There are variations of the corner platform on which the budgie sits. It can be a small round platform, a small straight diagonal platform, or a large straight diagonal platform.

Round corner platform

Backstamp: **A.** Black ink "Flaxman Ware Hand Made Pottery by Wadeheath England"
B. Black ink stamp "Wadeheath Ware England"
C. Black ink stamp "Flaxman Wade Heath England" impressed "143"
D. Black ink stamp "Wade Heath England" with impressed "143"
E. Black ink stamp "Wade England"

Type One, Round Corner Platform, 1935

No.	Description	Colourways	Size	U.S.$	Can.$	U.K.£
1	Budgie	Pale green; green bird with blue/yellow feathers, black markings; pale blue/yellow flowers	Extra large/266	110.00	145.00	55.00

WADE HEATH (cont.)

SHAPE 143 (cont.)

Small diagonal platform

Type Two, Small Diagonal Corner Platform, 1935-1939

No.	Description	Colourways	Size	U.K.$	Can.$	U.K.£
1a	Budgie	Light blue; blue/green bird; blue flowers	Small/159	75.00	100.00	45.00
1b	Budgie	Yellow; green/yellow bird; blue flowers	Small/159	75.00	100.00	45.00
1c	Budgie	Yellow; yellow/blue bird; pink flowers	Small/159	75.00	100.00	45.00
2a	Budgie	Creamy-yellow; grey bird; blue flowers; brown handle	Medium.195	75.00	100.00	45.00
2b	Budgie	Grey; grey/blue bird; blue flowers	Medium./195	75.00	100.00	45.00
2c	Budgie	Green; green/blue bird; orange/blue flowers	Medium/195	75.00	100.00	45.00
3a	Budgie	Grey; grey/blue bird; blue flowers	Large/225	90.00	145.00	50.00
3b	Budgie	Pale blue; blue/green bird; blue flowers	Large/225	90.00	145.00	50.00
3c	Budgie	Yellow; grey bird; mauve flowers; brown handle	Large/225	90.00	145.00	50.00
3d	Budgie	Yellow; yellow/blue bird; mauve/purple flowers	Large/225	90.00	145.00	50.00
4a	Budgie	Yellow; yellow/blue bird; mauve flowers; green leaves	Extra large/266	90.00	145.00	50.00
4b	Budgie	Blue; blue/dark blue bird; dark yellow flowers	Extra large/266	110.00	145.00	50.00
4c	Budgie	Pale green; green/brown bird; blue/yellow flowers	Extra large/266	110.00	145.00	50.00
4d	Budgie	White: yellow/green bird; purple flowers	Extra large/266	110.00	145.00	50.00
4e	Budgie	Pale green; blue/dark blue bird; blue/yellow flowers	Extra large/266	110.00	145.00	50.00
4f	Budgie	Honey jug, bird; deep red flowers	Extra large/266	110.00	145.00	50.00

WADE HEATH (cont.)

SHAPE 143 (cont.)

Except for version 3d, these jugs were produced in one-colour glazes.

Large diagonal corner platform

Type Three, Large Diagonal Corner Platform, c.1948-1953

No.	Description	Colourways	Size	U.S.$	Can.$	U.K.£
1a	Budgie	Blue	Small/159	50.00	70.00	28.00
1b	Budgie	Cream	Small/159	50.00	70.00	28.00
1c	Budgie	Green	Small/159	50.00	70.00	28.00
1d	Budgie	Yellow	Small/159	50.00	70.00	28.00
2a	Budgie	Blue	Medium/195	60.00	80.00	35.00
2b	Budgie	Cream	Medium/195	60.00	80.00	35.00
2c	Budgie	Green	Medium/195	60.00	80.00	35.00
2d	Budgie	Orange	Medium/195	60.00	80.00	35.00
2e	Budgie	Pale orange	Medium/195	60.00	80.00	35.00
2f	Budgie	Yellow	Medium/195	60.00	80.00	35.00
3a	Budgie	Blue	Large/225	80.00	110.00	45.00
3b	Budgie	Green	Large/225	80.00	110.00	45.00
3c	Budgie	Turquoise	Large/225	80.00	110.00	45.00
3d	Budgie	Turquoise; dark blue handle	Large/225	80.00	110.00	45.00
3e	Budgie	Yellow	Large/225	80.00	110.00	45.00
4	Budgie	Green	Extra large/266	80.00	110.00	45.00

WADE HEATH *(cont.)*

SHAPE 144, c.1937-1948

This jug has an all-over design of embossed flowers, with a ribbed spout and rim. This jug was illustrated in an advertisement dated 1937.

Flowers

Solid colour

Backstamp: A. Black ink stamp "Wadeheath Ware England" c.1934-1937
B. Black ink stamp "Wade England" c.1940s-1953

No.	Description	Colourways	Size	U.S.$	Can.$	U.K.£
1a	Flowers	Pale green; blue/brown highlighted flowers	215	120.00	160.00	60.00
1b	Flowers	White; green/red flowers	215	140.00	185.00	70.00
1c	Flowers	White; yellow/mauve flowers	215	140.00	185.00	70.00
1d	Mottled	Mottled yellow/green	215	120.00	160.00	60.00
1e	Solid colour	Pale green	215	120.00	160.00	60.00
1f	Solid colour	Pale orange	215	120.00	160.00	60.00

WADE HEATH (cont.)

SHAPE 145, 1937-1939

There are ribs running around the body and base of these jugs, which have a swan neck handle.

Backstamp: **A.** Black print "Flaxman Wade Heath, England" with embossed "145"
B. Black ink stamp "Wade Heath England" with impressed "145"

No.	Description	Colourways	Size	U.S.$	Can.$	U.K.£
1a	Leaves and berries	Cream; pale green/brown leaves; yellow berries	242	120.00	160.00	60.00
1b	Mottled	Mottled lilac/turquoise	242	120.00	160.00	60.00
1c	Windmill	Cream; brown handle, windmill	242	120.00	160.00	70.00

SHAPE 146, SYCAMORE, 1935-c.1945

This jug has an embossed design of sycamore seed balls, leaves and small flowers.

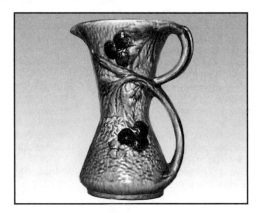

Backstamp: **A.** Black ink stamp "Flaxman Ware Hand Made Pottery by Wadeheath England" with embossed "146"
B. Black ink stamp "Flaxman Wade Heath, England" with embossed "146"
C. Green ink stamp "Wade Heath England" with embossed "146"

No.	Description	Colourways	Size	U.S.$	Can.$	U.K.£
1a	Sycamore	Brown; dark brown handle, leaves, seeds	230	90.00	120.00	45.00
1b	Sycamore	Mauve; light brown leaves; purple seeds	230	110.00	145.00	55.00
1c	Sycamore	Pale yellow; brown handle, leaves, seeds	230	110.00	145.00	55.00

WADE HEATH (cont.)

SHAPE 147, 1933-c.1940

These jugs have wavy, ribbed lines around the bowl.

Backstamp: **A**. Black ink stamp "Wadeheath England" with a lion and embossed "147"
B. Black ink stamp "Flaxman Wade Heath England"
C. Green ink stamp "Wade Heath England" with embossed "147"
D. Black ink stamp "Flaxman Ware Hand Made Pottery Wadeheath England" and impressed "147MIN"

No.	Description	Colourways	Size	U.S.$	Can.$	U.K.£
1a	Flowers	Green base; green/yellow/cream handles; yellow/green flowers; black leaves	Miniature/145	70.00	95.00	45.00
1b	Flowers	Grey base; orange/cream handles; orange/grey flowers; black leaves	Miniature/145	70.00	95.00	45.00
1c	Mottled	Mottled brown/green/cream	Miniature/145	70.00	95.00	38.00
1d	Mottled	Mottled green	Miniature/145	55.00	75.00	35.00
1e	Mottled	Mottled turquoise/brown	Miniature/145	55.00	75.00	35.00
1f	Plain	Green/purple	Miniature/145	55.00	75.00	35.00
2a	Butterfly	Cream; blue/pink flowers; orange butterfly	Medium/185	120.00	145.00	60.00
2b	Flowers	Blue base; blue/yellow/cream handles; blue/yellow flowers; black leaves	Medium/185	120.00	145.00	60.00
2c	Flowers	Cream; orange band; orange/black flowers; black leaves	Medium/185	120.00	145.00	60.00
2d	Budgie	Yellow	Medium/195	60.00	80.00	35.00
3a	Budgie	Blue	Large/225	80.00	110.00	45.00
3b	Budgie	Green	Large/225	80.00	110.00	45.00
3c	Budgie	Turquoise	Large/225	80.00	110.00	45.00
3d	Budgie	Turquoise; dark blue handle	Large/225	80.00	110.00	45.00
3e	Budgie	Yellow	Large/225	80.00	110.00	45.00
4	Budgie	Green	Extra large/266	80.00	110.00	45.00

WADE HEATH (cont.)

SHAPE 148, 1935-c.1945

There are four rows of indented ribs around the bowl of these jugs.

| Flowers | Mottled | Garland |

Backstamp: **A.** Black ink stamp "Flaxman Ware Hand Made Pottery by Wadeheath England"
B. Black ink stamp "Flaxman Wade Heath England"
C. Black ink stamp "Wade Heath England" with embossed "148"
D. Black ink stamp "Wade Heath England"

No.	Description	Colourways	Size	U.S.$	Can.$	U.K.£
1a	Flowers	Cream; black base; green/cream handle; green rim; orange/yellow flowers	Miniature/140	70.00	95.00	35.00
1b	Mottled	Mottled blue/brown	Miniature/140	60.00	80.00	30.00
1c	Mottled	Mottled blue/orange	Miniature/140	60.00	80.00	30.00
1d	Mottled	Mottled brown/green	Miniature/140	60.00	81.00	30.00
1e	Mottled	Mottled green/blue	Miniature/140	60.00	80.00	30.00
1f	Mottled	Mottled green/orange	Miniature/140	60.00	80.00	30.00
1g	Mottled	Mottled yellow/green	Miniature/140	60.00	80.00	30.00
2a	Flowers	Beige; red stripe; multicoloured flowers	Medium/195	70.00	95.00	35.00
2b	Mottled	Mottled blue/brown/cream	Medium/195	70.00	95.00	35.00
2c	Mottled	Mottled green	Medium/195	70.00	95.00	35.00
2d	Mottled	Mottled green/brown	Medium/195	70.00	95.00	35.00
2e	Mottled	Mottled yellow	Medium/195	70.00	95.00	35.00
3a	Flower	White; red handle, spots; yellow/black flower	Large/229	90.00	120.00	45.00
3b	Flower	Cream; orange/cream handle; large orange/ yellow/black flowers	Large/229	90.00	120.00	45.00
3c	Garland	Pale blue; blue/brown/yellow looped garland	Large/229	90.00	120.00	45.00

WADE HEATH *(cont.)*

SHAPE 149, 1935-.c1945

Two embossed bands with an impressed loop design run around the neck and the bottom of the body of these jugs. Variation 1h has a verse on one side, entitled "Memories Garden" within an oval surrounded by flowers.

Solid colour   Mottled

Verse

Backstamp: **A.** Black ink stamp "Flaxman Ware Hand Made Pottery by Wade Heath England" with impressed "149Min"
B. Black ink stamp "Flaxman Wade Heath England" with impressed "149Min"
C. Green ink stamp "Wade Heath England" with impressed "149"

No.	Description	Colourways	Size	U.S.$	Can.$	U.K.£
1a	Flowers	Cream; green base; green/cream handle; maroon/blue flowers	Miniature/145	50.00	70.00	25.00
1b	Mottled	Pale mottled turquoise/brown	Miniature/145	50.00	70.00	25.00
1c	Mottled	Mottled blue	Miniature/145	50.00	70.00	25.00
1d	Mottled	Mottled green	Miniature/145	50.00	70.00	25.00
1e	Patches	Orange; green patches	Miniature/145	50.00	70.00	25.00
1f	Solid colour	Light brown	Miniature/145	50.00	70.00	25.00
1g	Solid colour	Pale yellow	Miniature/145	50.00	70.00	25.00
1h	Verse	Cream; green trim, oval; yellow/blue flowers; black lettering	Miniature/145	50.00	70.00	25.00
2a	Mottled	Mottled brown/orange	Medium/190	60.00	80.00	30.00
2b	Mottled	Mottled green/cream	Medium/190	60.00	80.00	30.00
2c	Mottled	Mottled yellow	Medium/190	60.00	80.00	30.00
2d	Patches	Orange; green patches	Medium/190	60.00	80.00	30.00

WADE HEATH (cont.)

SHAPE 150, HORSE'S HEAD, 1934-1935

These jugs were moulded in the shape of a horse's head tilted forward onto its chest. They were produced in matt glazes, except for the large jug, which is in a high gloss glaze.

Horse heads

Backstamp: A. Black ink stamp "Flaxman Ware Hand Made Pottery by Wadeheath England" 1935-1937
B. Black ink stamp "Flaxman Wade Heath England" 1937 with impressed "150"

No.	Description	Colourways	Size	U.S.$	Can.$	U.K.£
1a	Horse's head	Blue	Small/100	75.00	100.00	45.00
1b	Horse's head	Green	Small/100	75.00	100.00	45.00
1c	Horse's head	Mottled green/orange	Small/100	75.00	100.00	45.00
1d	Horse's head	Orange	Small/100	75.00	100.00	45.00
1e	Horse's head	Pale blue	Small/100	75.00	100.00	45.00
1f	Horse's head	Pale yellow	Small/100	75.00	100.00	45.00
1g	Horse's head	White	Small/100	75.00	100.00	45.00
2a	Horse's head	Blue	Large/180	125.00	175.00	65.00
2b	Horse's head	Mottled blue/orange; gloss	Large/180	125.00	175.00	65.00

WADE HEATH (cont.)

SHAPE 152, SQUIRREL, SEATED, 1937-1939

Moulded in the shape of a seated squirrel, the spout is formed by its ears, and the tail curling forms the handle. Previously catalogued as shape 15, the correct number should be 152.

Backstamp: **A.** Black ink stamp "Flaxman Wade Heath England" with impressed "152"
B. Impressed "Made in England"

No.	Description	Colourways	Size	U.S.$	Can.$	U.K.£
1a	Flaxman	Mottled green/orange	Miniature/100	80.00	110.00	40.00
1b	Flaxman	Mottled mauve/green/yellow	Miniature/100	80.00	110.00	40.00
1c	Flaxman	Mottled turquoise/orange	Miniature/100	80.00	110.00	40.00
1d	Solid	Beige	Miniature/100	75.00	110.00	40.00
1e	Solid	Blue	Miniature/100	75.00	110.00	40.00
1f	Solid	Cream	Miniature/100	75.00	110.00	40.00
1g	Solid	Green	Miniature/100	75.00	110.00	40.00
1h	Solid	White	Miniature/100	70.00	95.00	35.00
1i	Solid	Yellow	Miniature/100	95.00	110.00	40.00
2	Flaxman	Mottled orange/green	Extra large/200	125.00	135.00	65.00

WADE HEATH (cont.)

SHAPE 154, SQUIRREL - BIRDS, 1936-c.1948

The **type one** jugs have a moulded squirrel sitting under a tree holding a nut. A pair of loverbirds are perched on top of the tree branch that forms the handle.

The **type two** jugs were issued in the late 1940s. They were produced in one-colour glazes and do not have the lovebirds on the handle.

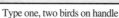

Type one, two birds on handle

Type two, no birds on handle

Backstamp: **A.** Black ink stamp "Flaxman Wade Heath England" with impressed "154"
B. Brown ink stamp "Flaxman Wade Heath England" with impressed "154"
C. Black ink stamp "Wade Heath England"
D. Black print "Wade England"

Type One: Squirrel and Birds

No.	Description	Colourways	Size	U.S.$	Can.$	U.K.£
1a	Squirrel/birds	Amber; honey-brown squirrel, birds; green leaves	220	140.00	195.00	75.00
1b	Squirrel/birds	Beige jug; brown squirrel, birds	220	140.00	195.00	75.00
1c	Squirrel/birds	Blue jug; blue/brown squirrel, birds	220	170.00	230.00	85.00
1d	Squirrel/birds	Green jug; green/brown squirrel	220	140.00	195.00	75.00
1e	Squirrel/birds	Honey-brown jug; honey/dark brown squirrel, birds	220	140.00	195.00	75.00
1f	Squirrel/birds	Orange jug; grey squirrel, birds	220	140.00	195.00	75.00
1g	Squirrel/birds	Turquoise jug; light brown squirrel, birds	220	140.00	195.00	75.00

Type Two: Squirrel

No.	Description	Colourways	Size	U.S.$	Can.$	U.K.£
2a	Squirrel	Blue	215	130.00	175.00	65.00
2b	Squirrel	Brown	215	130.00	175.00	65.00
2c	Squirrel	Green	215	130.00	175.00	65.00
2d	Squirrel	Orange	215	130.0	175.00	65.00
2e	Squirrel	Pale orange	215	130.00	175.00	65.00
2f	Squirrel	Yellow	215	130.00	175.00	65.00

WADE HEATH *(cont.)*

SHAPE 155, GOTHIC WARE, 1940, 1946-1953

These jugs are embossed with a design of swirling leaves and tulips. They were first decorated with matt colours; a 1940 advertisement has been found declaring a new series of 'Embossed-modelled Gothic Ornamental Ware,' and an advertisement for Gothic Wares in gloss colours with gold highlights has been found dated November 1946 with an advertised price of 12/6d.

Backstamp: A. Black ink stamp "Gothic Wade Heath England" with impressed "155"
B. Gold transfer print "Wade made in England - hand painted - Gothic" with impressed "155"

No.	Description	Colourways	Size	U.S.$	Can.$	U.K.£
1a	Gothic	Brown; dark brown leaves, flowers	230	100.00	145.00	55.00
1b	Gothic	Cream; lilac/pink flowers; green/yellow leaves; gold highlights	230	100.00	145.00	55.00
1c	Gothic	Pale green; cream leaves, flowers	230	100.00	145.00	55.00
1d	Gothic	Pale green; yellow/brown leaves; blue flowers	230	100.00	145.00	55.00
1e	Gothic	Pale yellow; green leaves, flowers	230	100.00	145.00	55.00

WADE HEATH *(cont.)*

SHAPE 157, GOTHIC WARE, 1940, 1946-1953

These jugs are embossed with a design of swirling leaves and tulips. They were first glazed in matt colours, then reissued in 1953 in gloss colours with gold highlighting.

Backstamp: **A.** Black ink stamp "Gothic Wade Heath England" with impressed "157"
B. Gold transfer print "Wade made in England - hand painted - Gothic" with impressed "157," 1947

No.	Description	Colourways	Size	U.S.$	Can.$	U.K.£
1a	Gothic	Cream; lilac/pink flowers; green/yellow leaves; gold highlights	290	125.00	15000	65.00
1b	Gothic	Pale orange	290	90.0	130.00	45.00
1c	Gothic	Pale yellow; pale green flowers/leaves	290	125.00	150.00	65.00

SHAPE 158, 1934-1935

Backstamp: Black ink stamp "Wadeheath England" with a lion and impressed "158"

No.	Description	Colourways	Size	U.S.$	Can.$	U.K.£
1a	Cottage	Yellow jug; orange handle; yellow/grey cottage; brown/green tree	195	120.00	160.00	60.00
1b	Leaves	Orange; yellow handle; orange/grey leaves	195	120.00	160.00	60.00

WADE HEATH (cont.)

SHAPE 164, ART DECO, 1936-1940

This art-deco jug has a small square handle that is crossed by a long loop handle and stands on a square foot.

Mottled blue and brown

Mottled brown and turquoise

Backstamp: Black ink stamp "Wade Heath England"

No.	Description	Colourways	Size	U.S$	Can.$	U.K.£
1a	Flowers	Cream; black/green rim, handle, base; green bands; orange/blue/yellow flowers	300	255.00	350.00	125.00
1b	Mottled	Blue/brown	300	175.00	200.00	85.00
1c	Mottled	Brown/turquoise	300	175.00	200.00	85.00

WADE HEATH *(cont.)*

SHAPE 168, DOVECOTE, 1936-.1940

These jugs were moulded in the shape of a wooden dovecote on a pole; the bird forms the top of the handle. Large lupins grow under the birdhouse; one flower forning the bottom of the handle. The jug 1a is decorated in an unusual high gloss glaze.

Backstamp: **A.** Black ink stamp "Flaxman Wade Heath England" with impressed "168"
        B. Black ink stamp "Wade Heath England" with impressed "168"

No.	Description	Colourways	Size	U.S.$	Can.$	U.K.£
1a	Dovecote, gloss	Cream jug, birds; brown pole; pink/lilac flowers	223	180.00	240.00	90.00
1b	Dovecote	Blue jug, birds; dark brown pole; yellow/ dark blue flowers; yellow handle	223	180.00	240.00	90.00
1c	Dovecote	Green jug; brown/pale blue birds; blue/yellow flowers; green handle	216	180.00	240.00	90.00
1d	Dovecote	Green jug, birds; dark brown pole; blue/yellow flowers; blue/green handle	223	180.00	240.00	90.00
1e	Dovecote	Green jug, birds; green/yellow bird; brown pole; yellow/blue flowers; yellow/green handle	223	180.00	240.00	90.00
1f	Dovecote	Yellow jug, birds; brown pole; blue/yellow flowers; blue handle	223	180.00	240.00	90.00
1g	Dovecote	Yellow jug, birds; golden brown pole; pink/blue flowers; pink/yellow handle	223	180.00	240.00	90.00

WADE HEATH (cont.)

SHAPE 169, 1936-c.1948

In **type one** the handle is shaped like a tree branch with a moulded bird feeding chicks in a nest. The **type two** jugs were issued in the late 1940s in one-colour glazes; they do not have the bird on the handle.

Bird on handle   No bird on handle

Backstamp: **A.** Green ink stamp "Wade Heath England" with impressed "169"
B. Black ink stamp "Wade England"

Type One: Handle With Bird

No.	Description	Colourways	Size	U.S.$	Can.$	U.K.£
1a	Rabbit/bird	Yellow; brown leaves, rabbit; blue/brown bird	190	180.00	225.00	85.00
1b	Rabbit/bird	Yellow jug, rabbit; green leaves; blue/yellow bird	190	180.00	225.00	85.00
1c	Rabbit/bird	Blue jug, bird; green leaves; grey rabbit	190	180.00	225.00	85.00
1d	Rabbit/bird	Orange; grey rabbit; blue bird	190	180.00	225.00	85.00

Type Two: Handle Without Bird

No.	Description	Colourways	Size	U.S.$	Can.$	U.K.£
2a	Rabbit	Blue	190	155.00	210.00	65.00
2b	Rabbit	Dark blue	190	155.00	210.00	65.00
2c	Rabbit	Green	190	155.00	210.00	65.00
2d	Rabbit	Orange	190	155.00	210.00	65.00
2e	Rabbit	Yellow	190	155.00	210.00	65.00
2f	Rabbit	Cream	190	155.00	210.00	65.00

WADE HEATH (cont.)

SHAPE 172, 1937-1939

This footed jug has a design of loops on one side above the handle.

Backstamp: Ink stamp "Flaxman Wade Heath England" with impressed "172"

No.	Description	Colourways	Size	U.S.$	Can.$	U.K.£
1	Mottled	Mottled blue/orange	190	110.00	145.00	55.00
2	Mottled	Mottled brown	235	110.00	145.00	55.00

SHAPE 173, 1937-c.1940

These jugs have an embossed basket-weave pattern on the body, an ornamental projection under the spout and above the handle, and three wavy lines running around the foot.

Backstamp: A. Black ink stamp "Flaxman Wade Heath England" with impressed "173"
               B. Black ink stamp "Wade Heath England" with impressed "173"

No.	Description	Colourways	Size	U.S.$	Can.$	U.K.£
1	Mottled	Mottled grey/blue/brown	117	110.00	145.00	55.00
2	Mottled	Mottled green	228	110.00	145.00	55.00

WADE HEATH (cont.)

SHAPE 301, 1937-1939

Mottled

Peony

Backstamp: Black ink stamp "Flaxman Wade Heath England" with impressed "301"

No.	Description	Colourways	Size	U.S.$	Can.$	U.K.£
1a	Mottled	Mottled blue	229	80.00	110.00	40.00
1b	Mottled	Mottled orange	229	80.00	110.00	40.00
1c	Peony	Multicoloured	229	100.00	145.00	65.00

SHAPE 302, 1937-1939

These jugs have a band of slanted ribs around the middle. They have been found in mottled and one-colour glazes.

Backstamp: Black ink stamp "Flaxman Wade Heath England" with impressed "S302"

No.	Description	Colourways	Size	U.S.$	Can.$	U.K.£
1a	Mottled	Mottled blue	230	80.000	110.00	42.00
1b	Mottled	Mottled green/orange	230	80.00	110.00	42.00
1c	Mottled	Mottled yellow	230	80.00	110.00	42.00
1d	Solid colour	Light green	230	80.00	110.00	42.00

WADE HEATH (cont.)

SHAPE 334, 1937-1939, 1955
Mottled and Peony decoration, 1937-1939

Mottled   Peony

Backstamp: A. Black ink stamp "Flaxman Wade Heath England"
B. Black ink stamp "Harvest Ware Wade England"

No.	Description	Coloueways	Size	U.S.$	CAN.$	U.K.£
1a	Mottled	Mottled cream/yellow	229	80.00	110.00	40.00
1b	Peony	Multicoloured	229	110.00	145.00	65.00
1c	Solid colour	White	229	80.00	110.00	40.00

Imperial Decoration, 1955

These jugs are decorated with large white seed cases highlighted in burnished gold.

Photograph not available
at press time

Backstamp: Circular print "Wade Made in England Hand Painted" and impressed "334"

No.	Description	Colourways	Size	U.S.$	Can.$	U.K.£
1	Imperial	Burgundy; white seed cases; gold highlights	229	80.00	110.00	40.00

WADE HEATH (cont.)

SHAPE 335, c.1952

These jugs are similar in shape to 302, but there are no ribs around the body. A black matt jug with a gold handle appears in a 1954 advertisment.

Backstamp: Circular print "Flaxman Wadeheath England" and impressed "335"

No.	Description	Colourways	Size	U.S.$	Can.$	U.K.£
1a	Matt	Matt black; gold handle	230	80.00	110.00	45.00
1b	Mottled	Mottled blue	230	80.00	110.00	40.00
1c	Mottled	Mottled green	230	80.00	110.00	40.00

SHAPE 371, c.1948-c.1952

These jugs are embossed with a flower design on the top and five wavy bands running diagonally across the bottom.

Backstamp: Black ink stamp "Wade England" with impressed "371"

No.	Description	Colourways	Size	U.S.$	Can.$	U.K.£
1a	Solid colour	Beige	225	85.00	120.00	55.00
1b	Solid colour	Dark blue	225	85.00	120.00	55.00
1c	Solid colour	Dark green	225	85.00	120.00	55.00
1d	Solid colour	Light green	225	85.00	120.00	55.00
1e	Solid colour	Orange	225	85.00	120.00	55.00
1f	Solid colour	Pale blue	225	85.00	120.00	55.00
1g	Solid colour	Pale orange	225	85.00	120.00	55.00

WADE HEATH (cont.)

SHAPE 401, EMPRESS, C.1948-1954, 1959-1961

Version 1a was issued in the late 1940s, 1b to 1d circa 1952 and version 1e in 1954.

Empress vase

Backstamp: **A.** Circular ink stamp "Royal Victoria Pottery Wade England"
B. Black ink stamp "Wade England"
C. Black ink stamp "Wade Empress England" with impressed "401"

No.	Description	Colourways	Size	U.S.$	Can.$	U.K.£
1a	Empress	Mottled green	170	80.00	110.00	40.00
1b	Empress	Blue; gold/cream stripes; gold handle	170	130.00	175.00	65.00
1c	Empress	Green; gold stripes, handle	170	130.00	175.00	65.00
1d	Empress	Maroon; gold stripes, handle	170	130.00	175.00	65.00
1e	Empress	White	170	80.00	110.00	40.00

REGENCY, 1959-1961

This miniature jug is a scaled down version of the Empress Jug.

Regency vase

Backstamp: **A.** Red print "Wade England"
B Black print "Wade England"

No.	Description	Colourways	Size	U.S.$	Can.$	U.K.£
1	Regency	White; gold handle, stripes on base	Miniature/110	30.00	40.00	15.00

WADE HEATH (cont.)

SHAPE 405, ACORN, c.1948-1953

Backstamp: Black ink stamp "Wade England" with impressed "405"

No.	Description	Colourways	Size	U.S.$	Can.$	U.K.£
1a	Acorn	Blue	138	60.00	90.00	35.00
1b	Acorn	Cream	138	60.00	90.00	35.00
1c	Acorn	Green	138	60.00	90.00	35.00
1d	Acorn	Orange	138	60.00	90.00	35.00
1e	Acorn	Orange; orange/black acorns; green handle, leaves	138	40.00	55.00	20.00
1f	Acorn	Pearlised jug; orange/brown acorns; green leaves	138	80.00	125.00	45.00

SHAPE 406, DAISY, c.1948-1953

Backstamp: Grey ink stamp "Wade England" with impressed "406"

No.	Description	Colourways	Size	U.S.$	Can.$	U.K.£
1a	Daisies	Blue	145	30.00	40.00	15.00
1b	Daisies	Cream; gold flowers	145	40.00	55.00	20.00
1c	Daisies	Cream; pink/yellow flowers	145	40.00	55.00	20.00
1d	Daisies	Green	145	30.00	40.00	15.00
1e	Daisies	Green; gold flowers	145	40.00	55.00	20.00
1f	Daisies	Orange; gold flowers	145	40.00	55.00	20.00
1g	Daisies	Pale orange	145	30.00	40.00	15.00
1h	Daisies	Pearlised mauve/yellow flowers; gold highlights	145	40.00	55.00	20.00

WADE HEATH *(cont.)*

SHAPE 407, PEBBLE, c.1948-c.1952

These jugs are embossed with a pebble design, curved diagonal bands and horizontal bands. Produced in matt glazes, only one example has been seen in a high gloss glaze.

Backstamp: Grey ink stamp "Wade England" and impressed "407"

Pebbled and Banded

No.	Description	Colourways	Size	U.S.$	Can.$	U.K.£
1a	Pebble/bands	Blue; matt	140	50.00	75.00	35.00
1b	Pebble/bands	Cream; gold bands; matt	140	50.00	75.00	35.00
1c	Pebble/bands	Cream; orange bands; matt	140	50.00	75.00	35.00
1d	Pebble/bands	Cream; orange/yellow/black bands; matt	140	50.00	75.00	35.00
1e	Pebble/bands	Green; matt	140	40.00	60.00	30.00
1f	Pebble/bands	Green/pink.blue/brown bands; gloss	140	60.00	85.00	45.00
1g	Pebble/bands	Orange; matt	140	40.00	60.00	30.00
1h	Pebble/bands	White; dark green bands; matt	140	40.00	60.00	30.00
1i	Pebble/bands	Yellow; matt	140	40.00	60.00	30.00

Banded Jugs

These jugs are the same shape as those above, but without the pebbled finish. There are curved bands on one side.

Photograph not available
at press time

Backstamp: Black ink stamp "Wade England" and impressed "407"

No.	Description	Colourways	Size	U.S.$	Can.$	U.K.£
1a	Bands	Beige	140	35.00	55.00	25.00
1b	Bands	Beige; gold bands	140	40.00	60.00	30.00
1c	Bands	Beige; orange bands	140	40.00	60.00	30.00
1d	Bands	Beige; orange/yellow bands	140	40.00	60.00	30.00
1e	Bands	Blue	140	40.00	60.00	30.00
1f	Bands	Green	140	40.00	60.00	30.00
1g	Bands	Orange	140	40.00	60.00	30.00
1h	Bands	Yellow	140	40.00	60.00	30.00

WADE HEATH (cont.)

SHAPE 411, GOTHIC WARE, 1940, 1946-1953

This jug is embossed with a design of swirling leaves and tulips and is glazed in gloss colours.

Gothic ware

Backstamp: **A.** Black ink stamp "Gothic Wade Heath England" with impressed "411"
B. Gold transfer print "Wade made in England - hand painted - Gothic" with impressed "411"

No.	Description	Colourways	Size	U.S.$	Can.$	U.K.£
1	Gothic	Cream; lilac/pink flowers; green/gold leaves	160	101.00	145.00	55.00

WADE HEATH (cont.)

HARMONY WARE, 1957-c.1962
Shape 433,

Shooting stars

Backstamp: **A**. Red print "Wade England" with impressed "England" and "433"
B. Red print "Wade England Fern" with impressed "England" and "433"
C. Black print "Wade England Parasol" with impressed "England" and "433"
D. Black print "Wade England" with impressed "England" and "433"
E. Black print "Wade England" and green shooting stars with impressed "England" and "433"
F. Impressed "Wade England" and "433"
G. Impressed "Wade England"

No.	Description	Colourways	Size	U.S.$	Can.$	U.K.£
1a	Carnival	White; yellow/red/green flowers	150	50.00	70.00	25.00
1b	Fern	White; black/red ferns	150	50.00	70.00	25.00
1c	Parasols	White; multicoloured parasols	150	50.00	70.00	25.00
1d	Shooting stars	White; multicoloured stars	150	50.00	70.00	25.00
1e	Solid colour	Black	150	40.00	55.00	20.00
1f	Solid colour	Green	150	40.00	55.00	20.00
1g	Solid colour	White	150	40.00	55.00	20.00
1h	Solid colour	Yellow	150	40.00	55.00	20.00
1i	Two tone	Green; peach inside	150	40.00	55.00	20.00
1j	Two tone	Grey; pink inside	150	40.00	55.00	20.00

WADE HEATH (cont.)

HARMONY WARE (cont.)
Shape 435, 1957-1962

Carnival

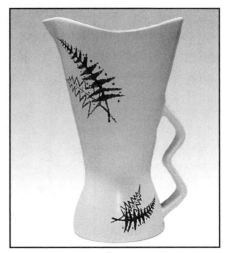

Fern

Backstamp: **A.** Red print "Wade England" with impressed "England" and "435"
B. Red print "Wade England Fern" with impressed "England" and "435"
C. Black print "Wade England Parasol" with impressed "England" and "435"
D. Black print "Wade England" with impressed "England" and "435"
E. Black print "Wade England" and green shooting stars with impressed "England" and "435"
F. Impressed "Wade England" and "435"
G. Impressed "Wade England"

No.	Description	Colourways	Size	U.S.$	Can.$	U.K.£
1a	Carnival	White; yellow/red/green flowers	225	80.00	110.00	40.00
1b	Fern	White; black/red ferns	225	80.00	110.00	40.00
1c	Parasols	White; multicoloured parasols	225	80.00	110.00	40.00
1d	Shooting stars	White; multicoloured stars	225	80.00	110.00	40.00
1e	Solid colour	Black	225	60.00	80.00	30.00
1f	Solid colour	Green	225	60.00	80.00	30.00
1g	Solid colour	White	225	60.00	80.00	30.00
1h	Solid colour	Yellow	225	60.00	80.00	30.00
1i	Two-tone	Green; peach inside	225	60.00	80.00	30.00
1j	Two-tone	Grey; pink inside	225	60.00	80.00	30.00

WADE HEATH (cont.)

**HARMONY WARE *(cont.)*
Shape 436, 1957-1962**

Solid colour

Backstamp: **A**. Red print "Wade England" with impressed "England" and "436"
B. Red print "Wade England Fern" with impressed "England" and "436"
C. Black print "Wade England Parasol" with impressed "England" and "436"
D. Black print "Wade England" with impressed "England" and "436"
E. Black print "Wade England" and green shooting stars with impressed "England" and "436"
F. Impressed "Wade England" and "436"
G. Impressed "Wade England"

No.	Description	Colourways	Size	U.S.$	Can.$	U.K.£
1a	Carnival	White; yellow/red/green flowers	177	60.00	80.00	30.00
1b	Fern	White; black/red ferns	177	60.00	80.00	30.00
1c	Parasols	White; multicoloured parasols	177	60.00	80.00	30.00
1d	Shooting stars	White; multicoloured stars	177	60.00	80.00	30.00
1e	Solid colour	Black	177	50.00	70.00	25.00
1f	Solid colour	Green	177	50.00	70.00	25.00
1g	Solid colour	White	177	50.00	70.00	25.00
1h	Solid colour	Yellow	177	50.00	70.00	25.00
1i	Two-tone	Green/peach	177	50.00	70.00	25.00
1j	Two-tone	Grey/pink	177	50.00	70.00	25.00

WADE HEATH *(cont.)*

HARMONY WARE *(cont.)*
Shape 453, 1957-1962

Harmony ware and souvenir jugs utilized shape 453.

Shooting stars

Two-tone

Backstamp: **A.** Red print "Wade England" with impressed "England" and "453"
B. Red print "Wade England Fern" with impressed "England" and "453"
C. Black print "Wade England Parasol" with impressed "England" and "453"
D. Black print "Wade England" with impressed "England" and "453"
E. Black print "Wade England" and green shooting stars with impressed "England" and "453"
F. Impressed "Wade England" and "453"
G. Impressed "Wade England"

No.	Description	Colourways	Size	U.S.$	Can.$	U.K.£
1a	Carnival	White; yellow/red/green flowers	130	25.00	35.00	12.00
1b	Fern	White; black/red ferns	130	25.00	35.00	12.00
1c	Parasols	White; multicoloured parasols	130	25.00	35.00	12.00
1d	Shooting stars	White; multicoloured stars	130	25.00	35.00	12.00
1e	Two-tone	Black; yellow inside	130	15.00	20.00	8.00
1f	Two-tone	Green; peach inside	130	15.00	20.00	8.00
1g	Two-tone	Grey; pink inside	130	15.00	20.00	8.00

WADE HEATH *(cont.)*

HARMONY WARE *(cont.)*
Shape 453 *(cont.)*
SOUVENIR , c.1958-c.1962

Backstamp: **A.** Black transfer print "A Dee Cee Souvenir by Wade"
B. Impressed "Wade 453 England" and a blue transfer print "A Desmond Cooper Souvenir by Wade"
C. Impressed "Wade 453 England" and a black transfer print "A Dee Cee Souvenir by Wade"
D. Red transfer print "Wade England"

No.	Description	Colourways	Size	U.S.$	Can.$	U.K.£
1a	Bognor Regis	White; red sail; blue water	130	25.00	35.00	12.00
1b	Bridlington	White; multicoloured parasols	130	25.00	35.00	12.00
1c	Cardiff	White; multicoloured parasols	130	25.00	35.00	12.00
1d	Douglas, Isle of Man	White; multicoloured parasols	130	25.00	35.00	12.00
1e	Dunnose cottage, I W	White; multicoloured parasols	130	25.00	35.00	12.00
1f	Eastbourne	White; multicoloured parasols	130	25.00	35.00	12.00
1g	Great Yarmouth	White; multicoloured parasols	130	25.00	35.00	12.00
1h	Great Yarmouth	White; red spots	130	25.00	35.00	12.00
1i	Jersey	White; multicoloured parasols	130	25.00	35.00	12.00
1j	New Brunswick map	White; gold rim, handle; multicoloured map; violet flowers	130	25.00	35.00	15.00
1k	Nova Scotia map	White; gold rim, handle; multicoloured map; violet flowers	130	25.00	35.00	15.00
1l	Romsey	White; red sail boat; blue water	130	25.00	35.00	12.00
1m	Truro	White; red sail boat; blue water	130	25.00	35.00	12.00
1n	York	White; red sail boat; blue water	130	25.00	35.00	12.00

WADE HEATH *(cont.)*

SHAPE 465, 1957-c.1962

The Black Frost Series jug was issued from 1957 to c.1962, a variety of British wild flowers can be found on these jugs. The Zamba Series jug was issued in 1957 only. A date for the all-over copper lustre jug has not been found.

| Black Frost | Copper | Zamba |

Backstamp: **A.** White "Wade England"
 B. Red transfer print "Wade England"

No.	Description	Colourways	Size	U.S.$	Can.$	U.K.£
1a	Black Frost	Black; white flowers; gold rim	145	35.00	50.00	25.00
1b	Copper	Copper lustre	145	20.00	30.00	15.00
1c	Zamba	White; black print	145	70.00	95.00	40.00

SHAPE 470, 1957

Zamba

Backstamp: **A.** Red transfer print "Wade England" with impressed "England 470"
 B. Black transfer print "Wade England" with impressed "England 470"

No.	Description	Colourways	Size	U.S.$	Can.$	U.K.£
1	Zamba	White; black print	Miniature/124	40.00	55.00	25.00

WADE HEATH (cont.)

BIG BAD WOLF AND THE THREE LITTLE PIGS JUGS, 1937-1939

The Big Bad Wolf forms the handle of these cartoon jugs, which can be found with or without a musical box fitted in the base. The jug is hand painted, so no two are identical (for example, the top of the door on the pig's house is square on one jug, rounded on another). The musical jug plays "Whose Afraid of the Big Bad Wolf" or "The Teddy Bear's Picnic."

Musical jug - round door

Muscial jug - square door

Backstamp: Black hand painted "Wadeheath England"

No.	Description	Colourways	Size	U.S.$	Can.$	U.K.£
1a	Jug	Cream/multicoloured; brown wolf; orange trousers; green braces	245	1,200.00	1,600.00	600.00
2a	Musical jug, round door	Cream/multicoloured; brown wolf; orange trousers; green braces; round door	260	1,400.00	1,850.00	700.00
2b	Musical jug, square door	Cream/multicoloured; brown wolf; orange trousers; green braces; square door	260	1,400.00	1,850.00	700.00

WADE HEATH (cont.)

EDWARDIAN WATER JUG AND BOWL

This set was created in the style of an Edwardian water jug and wash basin. The floral fayre design consists of small pink flowers; the fuchsia design is of fuchsias and leaves, the Queensway design is of large white flowers. For matching items in these designs please see Edwardian Photograph Frame, Planters and Vases.

Backstamp: Red print "Wade England" with two red lines

No.	Name	Colourways	Size	U.S.$	Can.$	U.K.£
1a	Floral fayre	White; pink/green print	153	25.00	35.00	12.00
1b	Fuchsia	White; pink/yellow/grey print	153	25.00	35.00	12.00
1c	Queensway	White; white/green print	153	25.00	35.00	12.00
2a	Floral fayre	White; pink/green print	180	25.00	35.00	12.00
2b	Fuchsia	White; pink/yellow/grey print	180	25.00	35.00	12.00
2c	Queensway	White; white/green	180	25.00	35.00	12.00

WADE HEATH (cont.)

EROS JUGS, 1933-c.1940

The Wade shape name for these jugs is Eros, the rim is scalloped, and they have a round curved-edge base.

Eros, six-panel neck

Eros, smooth neck

Eros, Six-panel Neck

Backstamp: **A:** Red ink stamp "Wades England" with a lion (1927-1933)
B: Red ink stamp "Wadeheath England" with a lion (1933-1940)

No.	Description	Colourways	Size	U.S.$	Can.$	U.K.£
1	Flowers	Yellow; large orange /blue flowers; green leaves; black base	Small/145	35.00	50.00	25.00
2	Flowers	Yellow; blue rim, base; large purple/blue flowers	Medium/165	38.00	55.00	30.00
3	Pansies	Yellow; grey/blue/orange pansies; brown tree; black base	Large/177	38.00	55.00	30.00
4a	Flowers	Grey-green; green handle, base; large orange flowers	Ex large/190	45.00	70.00	35.00
4b	Leaves	Cream; black rim, base; large orange leaves	Ex large/190	45.00	70.00	35.00
4c	Wavy lines	Cream; royal blue handle, leaves; gold/orange wavy lines	Ex large/190	45.00	70.00	35.00

Eros, Smooth Neck

Backstamp: Red ink stamp "Wadeheath England" with a lion

No.	Description	Colourways	Size	U.S.$	Can.$	U.K.£
1a	Flowers; smooth neck	Cream; black base; large orange leaves; grey/black flowers	Ex large/190	45.00	70.00	35.00
1b	Flowers; smooth neck	Cream; large orange/yellow/blue flowers; green leaves	Ex large/190	45.00	70.00	35.00

WADE HEATH *(cont.)*

GALLERY COLLECTION, 1995-1996, 1999-2000

There were five jug designs in this series: "nouvelle" is an art-deco design with a lily-type flower; the "Japanese garden" features a tall tree with flowers around the base; the "orange grove" consists of large oranges; "sunburst" has large orange marigold-type flowers and the "paradise" design includes a large blue bird with oranges.

Jacobean

Japanese garden

Backstamp: Black and orange print "The Gallery Collection inspired by original 1930s Wade Heath Designs - Wade made in England" with the pattern name and two red lines, all within a frame composed of elements of the pattern

No.	Description	Colourways	Size	U.S.$	Can.$	U.K.£
1a	Jacobean	White; red/black design	180	22.00	30.00	15.00
1b	Japanese garden	White; blue/green/orange design	180	22.00	30.00	15.00
1c	Nouvelle	White; orange/green/yellow/black design	180	22.00	30.00	15.00
1d	Orange grove	White; orange/green/black design	180	22.00	30.00	15.00
1e	Paradise	White; blue/orange/green/black design	180	22.00	30.00	15.00
1f	Sunburst	White; orange/black design	180	22.00	30.00	15.00

WADE HEATH (cont.)

GOTHIC WARE, c.1947-c.1953

This jug in Gothic gloss colours is a derivative of the shape-360 vase, with a handle added to the side. To date no shape number has been found for this jug.

Backstamp: Gold printed "Wade Made in England Hand Painted Gothic"

No.	Description	Colourways	Size	U.S.$	Can.$	U.K.£
1	Gothic jug	Cream; pink/yellow flowers; green/yellow leaves	223	130.00	175.00	65.00

IMPERIAL, 1955

These jugs are decorated with large white seed cases highlighted in burnished gold. The handle of number 4 is shaped like the number 3. The Dandy shaped jug was originally produced between 1938 - 1962 as a tableware item.

Deco Imperial Jug

Backstamp: Circular print "Wade Made in England Hand Painted"

No.	Description	Colourways	Size	U.S.$	Can.$	U.K.£
1	Dandy	Black; white seed pods; gold highlights	130	45.00	60.00	30.00
2	Deco	Burgundy; white seed pods; gold highlights	140	45.00	60.00	30.00
3	Round foot	Burgundy; white seed pods; gold highlights	140	60.00	80.00	40.00
4	3-shaped handle	Burgundy; white seed pods; gold highlights	140	70.00	95.00	35.00

WADE HEATH (cont.)

LEANING, 1935

The body of these jugs curves inward at the handle, while the mouth juts upward in three steps.

Photograph not available
at press time

Backstamp: Black ink stamp "Flaxman Ware Hand Made Pottery by Wadeheath"

No.	Description	Colourways	Size	U.S.$	Can.$	U.K.£
1a	Leaning	Yellow; orange fruit	160	170.00	225.00	85.00
1b	Leaning	Off white; orange flowers; brown bird; green leaves; blue branch	160	170.00	225.00	85.00

MEDALLIONS, c.1948-c.1952

These jugs have flattened sides and are embossed with two circular rows of dots around the edges of each side. They were either hand painted or glazed in matt colours.

Backstamp: Black ink stamp "Wade England"

No.	Description	Colourways	Size	U.S.$	Can.$	U.K.£
1a	Copper, barley	Copper lustre; yellow barley ears	Small/125	90.00	120.00	45.00
1b	Fawn	Cream; brown outline of fawn; orange flowers	Small/125	60.00	80.00	35.00
1c	Flowers	Cream; orange flowers	Small/125	60.00	80.00	35.00
1d	Solid colour	Blue	Small/125	50.00	70.00	25.00
1e	Solid colour	Cream	Small/125	50.00	70.00	25.00
1f	Solid colour	Green	Small/125	50.00	70.00	25.00
2a	Copper, barley	Copper lustre; yellow barley ears	Medium/153	90.00	120.00	45.00
2b	Gold ring	Cream; gold ring	Medium/153	90.00	120.00	45.00
2c	Solid colour	Blue	Medium/153	60.00	80.00	30.00
2d	Solid colour	Cream	Medium/153	60.00	80.00	30.00
2e	Solid colour	Green	Medium/153	60.00	80.00	30.00
3a	Copper, barley	Copper lustre; yellow barley ears	Large/175	100.00	145.00	55.00
3b	Gold ring	Cream; gold ring	Large/175	70.00	95.00	35.00
3c	Solid colour	Blue	Large/175	70.00	95.00	35.00
3d	Solid colour	Cream	Large/175	70.00	95.00	35.00
3e	Solid colour	Green	Large/175	70.00	95.00	35.00

WADE HEATH (cont.)

MINIATURE JUG - TYPE 1

Type 1 jug has a ball-shaped body. The shape number for this jug has not been found

Backstamp: Black ink "Flaxman Wade Heath England"

No.	Description	Colourways	Size	U.S.$	Can.$	U.K.£
1	Type 1	Cream/turquoise/ orange/pale green	137	32.00	45.00	22.00

MINIATURE JUG - TYPE 2

Type 2 jug has a flattened, circular body. The shape number for this jug has not been found

Backstamp: Black ink "Flaxman Wade Heath England"

No.	Description	Colourways	Size	U.S.$	Can.$	U.K.£
1	Type 2	White	132	32.00	45.00	22.00

WADE HEATH (cont.)

OIL JUGS, 1956-c.1962

The following series, African Animals, Souvenirs of Canada and England, and Veteran Cars all utilize the same shape jug.

South Africa, 1956-c.1962

These miniature oil jugs have transfer prints of African animals on the front.

Backstamp: Red transfer print "Wade England"

No.	Description	Colourways	Size	U.S.$	Can.$	U.K.£
1a	Eland	Amber; silver lustre; brown/white print	95	25.00	35.00	12.00
1b	Giraffe	Amber; silver lustre; multicoloured print	95	25.00	35.00	12.00
1c	Lion	Amber; silver lustre; multicoloured print	95	25.00	35.00	12.00
1d	Zebra	Amber; multicoloured print	95	25.00	35.00	12.00

Souvenir of Canada, 1956-c.1962

This oil jug was decorated with the provincial crest of Nova Scotia, Canada.

Photograph not available
at press time

Backstamp: **A.** Red transfer print "Wade England"
B. Red transfer print "Wade Ireland"

No.	Description	Colourways	Size	U.S.$	Can.$	U.K.£
1	Nova Scotia crest	Amber; silver lustre; black print	95	30.00	40.00	15.00

WADE HEATH (cont.)

OIL JUGS (cont.)
Souvenirs of England, c.1962

These oil jugs were decorated with black transfer prints of London and other UK landmarks.

Backstamp: A. Red transfer print "Wade England"
B. Red transfer print "Wade Ireland"

No.	Description	Colourways	Size	U.S.$	Can.$	U.K.£
1a	Big Ben	Amber; silver lustre; black print	95	30.00	40.00	15.00
1b	Eros, Piccadilly Circus	Amber; silver lustre; black print	95	30.00	40.00	15.00
1c	Hastings	Amber; silver lustre; black print/lettering	95	30.00	40.00	15.00
1d	London Coat of Arms	Amber; silver lustre; red/black print	95	30.00	40.00	15.00
1e	Southend	Amber; silver lustre; black print/lettering	95	30.00	40.00	15.00
1f	Tower Bridge	Amber; silver lustre; black print	95	30.00	40.00	15.00
1g	Trafalgar Square	Amber; silver lustre; black print	95	30.00	40.00	15.00
1h	Wadebridge	Amber; silver lustre; black print/lettering	95	30.00	40.00	15.00

WADE HEATH *(cont.)*

OIL JUGS *(cont.)*
Veteran Cars, c.1958-c.1975

These oil jugs were produced in the same amber glaze used for the Veteran Car Series tankards and have silver lustre rims, handles and bases. They are decorated on the front with transfer prints of veteran and vintage racing cars and were produced in the Wade England and Wade Ireland potteries. Printed on the base is "Authenticated by the Veteran Car Club of Great Britain."

Ford; Series 1   Sunbeam; Series 2

Backstamp: **A.** Black print "A Moko product by Wade of England"
B. Black print "An RK Product by Wade of Ireland"

Series 1

No.	Description	Colourways	Size	U.S.$	Can.$	U.K.£
1a	Benz	Amber; silver lustre; black print	90	20.00	30.00	10.00
1b	Darracq	Amber; silver lustre; black print	90	20.00	30.00	10.00
1c	Ford	Amber; silver lustre; black print	90	20.00	30.00	10.00

Series 2

No.	Description	Colourways	Size	U.S.$	Can.$	U.K.£
2a	Baby Peugeot	Amber; silver lustre; black print	90	20.00	30.00	10.00
2b	Rolls-Royce	Amber; silver lustre; black print	90	20.00	30.00	10.00
2c	Sunbeam	Amber; silver lustre; black print	90	20.00	30.00	10.00

Series 3

No.	Description	Colourways	Size	U.S.$	Can.$	U.K.£
3a	De Dion Bouton	Amber; silver lustre; black print	90	20.00	30.00	10.00
3b	Lanchester	Amber; silver lustre; black print	90	20.00	30.00	10.00
3c	Spyker	Amber; silver lustre; black print	90	20.00	30.00	10.00

WADE HEATH *(cont.)*

OIL JUGS *(cont.)*
Veteran Cars (cont.)
Series 4

No.	Description	Colourways	Size	U.S.$	Can.$	U.K.£
4a	Cadillac	Amber; silver lustre; black print	90	20.00	30.00	10.00
4b	Oldsmobile	Amber; silver lustre; black print	90	20.00	30.00	10.00
4c	White Steam Car	Amber; silver lustre; black print	90	20.00	30.00	10.00

Series 5

No.	Description	Colourways	Size	U.S.$	Can.$	U.K.£
5a	Bugatti	Amber; silver lustre; multicoloured print	90	20.00	30.00	10.00
5b	Itala	Amber; silver lustre; multicoloured print	90	20.00	30.00	10.00
5c	Sunbeam, 1914	Amber; silver lustre; multicoloured print	90	20.00	30.00	10.00

Series 6

No.	Description	Colourways	Size	U.S.$	Can.$	U.K.£
6a	Alfa Romeo	Amber; silver lustre; multicoloured print	90	20.00	30.00	10.00
6b	Bentley	Amber; silver lustre; multicoloured print	90	20.00	30.00	10.00
6c	Bugatti, 1927	Amber; silver lustre; multicoloured print	90	20.00	30.00	10.00

228

WADE HEATH *(cont.)*

PINCHED-MOUTH, 1935-1937
Type 1

The mouth of these jugs is pinched in at the centre. They were produced in four sizes.

Bands

Bird on branch

Streaks

Backstamp:A. Black ink stamp "Wadeheath Ware Regd Shape No. 787794 Made in England"
B. Orange ink stamp "Wadeheath Orcadia Ware"
C. Black ink stamp "Flaxman Ware Hand Made Pottery by Wadeheath England "

No.	Description	Colourways	Size	U.S.$	Can.$	U.K.£
1a	Bands	Brown/blue/yellow/orange bands	Small/140	90.00	135.00	50.00
1b	Bands	Cream; brown base; orange handle; brown/ orange/blue/greens bands	Small/140	90.00	135.00	50.00
1c	Flowers	Cream; orange base, handle; brown/orange flowers	Small/140	90.00	135.00	60.00
1d	Flowers	Mottled brown; large orange/yellow flowers	Small/140	90.00	135.00	60.00
2a	Bird on branch	Cream; amber bird; blue flowers	Medium/165	120.00	160.00	60.00
2b	Orcadia	Green/orange streaks; blue base	Medium/165	90.00	135.00	60.00
2c	Striped bands	Cream; orange/green/blue striped bands	Medium/165	90.00	135.00	50.00
3a	Flowers	Cream; black base; blue/yellow/orange flowers	Large/185	90.00	135.00	60.00
3b	Fruit	Cream; brown neck; cream/brown handle; blue/yellow/orange fruit	Large/185	90.00	135.00	60.00
3c	Orcadia	Green; orange streaks	Large/185	90.00	135.00	60.00
4a	Balls	Cream; black/orange handle, bands; blue/green/yellow squares; orange/blue balls	Ex large/205	90.00	135.00	65.00
4b	Flowers	Brown; orange/yellow flowers	Ex large/205	90.00	135.00	65.00
4c	Orcadia	Blue/brown/yellow; orange streaks	Ex large/205	90.00	135.00	65.00
4d	Orcadia	Maroon/green/yellow/orange streaks	Ex large/205	90.00	135.00	65.00
4e	Orcadia	Orange/yellow/brown streaks	Ex large/205	90.00	135.00	65.00
4f	Streaks	Orange/yellow/blue streaks	Ex large/205	90.00	135.00	65.00
4g	Streaks	Green/orange/green/blue streaks	Ex large/205	90.00	135.00	65.00

WADE HEATH (cont.)

PINCHED-MOUTH (cont.)
Type 2

The mouth of this jug is pinched in at the centre and it has a long straight body.

Backstamp: Black ink stamp "Wades England" with Lion

No.	Description	Colourways	Size	U.S.$	Can.$	U.K.£
1	Pinched-mouth, straight body	Cream; black base; black striped handle; large orange/yellow flowers	Small/140	120.00	160.00	60.00

PLYMOUTH, 1953-c.1962

This jug resembles a wooden keg.

Backstamp: Red transfer print "Wade England"

No.	Description	Colourways	Size	U.S.$	Can.$	U.K.£
1	Plymouth	Amber; silver-lustre bands	95	15.00	20.00	12.00

WADE HEATH (cont.)

SNOW WHITE AND THE SEVEN DWARFS, 1938

This musical jug has Snow White and the Seven Dwarfs moulded around the front with the dwarfs' cottage on the back. A squirrel and a pair of bluebirds sit on the handle. Two tunes have been reported, "Whistle While You Work" and "Someday My Prince Will Come."

Snow White, face

Snow White, back

Backstamp: Black ink stamp "Wade Heath England"

No.	Description	Colourways	Size	U.S.$	Can.$	U.K.£
1	Snow White	Cream; multicoloured figures	225	1,200.00	1,600.00	630.00

WADE HEATH (cont.)

WIDE-MOUTH, 1933-1934

On type 1 the jugs resemble the woodpecker jug, shape 13, they have a wide mouth and the top of the handle is looped, on type 2 the jug is narrower and the top of the handle is straight.

| Fruit and leaves, type 1 | Fruit and squares, type 1 | Flowers, type 2 |

Type 1 - Round Top Handle

Backstamp: Red ink stamp "Wadeheath England" with a lion

No.	Description	Colourways	Size	U.S.$	Can.$	U.K.£
1a	Fruit and leaves	Cream; brown rim; cream/brown base; large orange/ yellow/purple fruit; green leaves	180	90.00	120.00	45.00
1b	Fruit and squares	Cream; cream/brown base; large orange/yellow/ blue fruit; small orange/brown/blue squares	180	90.00	120.00	45.00

Type 2 - Straight Top Handle

No.	Description	Colourways	Size	U.S.$	Can.$	U.K.£
2	Flowers	Cream; grey/yellow patches; large orange flowers	202	90.00	120.00	45.00

WADE HEATH (cont.)

ZEBRA-STRIPED JUGS, 1955

Deco

3-shaped handle

Backstamp: Circular transfer print "Royal Victoria Pottery Wade England"

No.	Description	Colourways	Size	U.S.$	Can.$	U.K.£
1	Deco	Bright yellow/black stripes	140	70.00	95.00	40.00
2a	3-shaped handle	Blue/black stripes	140	70.00	95.00	40.00
2b	3-shaped handle	Bright yellow/black stripes	140	70.00	95.00	40.00

LAMPS
1959-1995

Since this book was first published a large assortment of c.1940s-1960s lamps have been found, the shape numbers or names of which are mostly unknown. Lamps that are derivatives of vases with shape numbers are listed first. A number of Wade lamps were produced from 1991 to 1999 for sale in British department stores and were also supplied to a lighting company called Astbury Lighting. Lamps with no shape numbers are listed in alphabetical order by shape or design name when known.

Wade Heath
Wade Ireland

BACKSTAMPS

Transfer Prints

Prior to 1953 ink stamp backstamps were used on lamps.

After 1953 transfer prints were used, with the majority of lamps being produced from 1991-1995 and are marked with the gold "Wade" transfer print.

WADE HEATH

SHAPE 69, HARVEST WARE

This Harvest Ware lamp is a derivative of shape number 69 vase.

Backstamp: Ink stamp "Wade England"

No.	Description	Colourways	Size	U.S.$	Can.$	U.K.£
1	Peony	Cream; multicoloured flowers	205	130.00	175.00	65.00

SHAPE 244, GOTHIC WARE, c. 1953

The triangular-shaped lamp is a variation of the flower holder vase shape number. 244. It is decorated with the embossed design of swirling leaves and tulips characteristic of Gothic Ware.

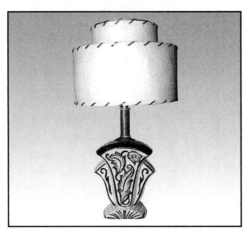

Backstamp: Gold transfer print "Wade made in England Hand Painted Gothic"

No.	Description	Colourways	Size	U.S.$	Can.$	U.K.£
1	Gothic ware	Cream; lilac/pink flowers; green/gold leaves	150	95.00	125.00	55.00

WADE HEATH *(cont.)*

SHAPE 333, GEORGIAN OAK

This lamp is a derivative of the shape number 333 vase.

Backstamp: Gold printed semi circular "Wade made in England Hand Painted" c.early 1953-1960s

No.	Description	Colourways	Size	U.S.$	Can.$	U.K.£
1	Georgian Oak	Copper lustre; white oak leaves/acorns	220	45.00	65.00	35.00

SHAPE 359, GOTHIC WARE, c. early 1950s

This Gothic Ware lamp is a derivative of shape number 359 vase.

Backstamp: A. Green ink stamp "Wade England Gothic" with impressed "359"
               B. Gold printed "Wade Made in England Hand Painted Gothic"

No.	Description	Colourways	Size	U.S.$	Can.$	U.K.£
1a	Gloss	Cream; pink/yellow flowers; blue/green leaves; gloss	170	130.00	175.00	65.00
1b	Matt	Cream; pink/yellow flowers; blue/green leaves; matt	170	130.00	175.00	65.00

WADE HEATH *(cont.)*

SHAPE 360, GOTHIC WARE c.early 1950s

This Gothic Ware lamp is a derivative of shape number 360 vase.

Backstamp: Gold printed "Wade Made in England Hand Painted Gothic"

No.	Description	Colourways	Size	U.S.$	Can.$	U.K.£
1	Gothic ware	Cream; pink/yellow flowers; blue/green leaves; gloss	220	130.00	175.00	65.00

SHAPE 362

This lamp is a derivative of shape number 362 vase.

Flowers   Leaves

Backstamp: Green ink stamp "Wade England"

No.	Description	Colourways	Size	U.S.$	Can.$	U.K.£
1a	Flowers	White; pink rim, base; multicoloured flower spray	230	130.00	175.00	65.00
1b	Leaves	Cream; brown leaves; blue berries	230	130.00	175.00	65.00

WADE HEATH (cont.)

SHAPE 407

This lamp is a derivative of shape number 407 jug.

Backstamp: Black ink stamp "Wade England"

No.	Description	Colourways	Size	U.S.$	Can.$	U.K.£
1	Banded	Cream; gold bands	165	60.00	75.00	35.00

BARREL LAMP, c.1962

Backstamp: Red transfer print "Wade England"

No.	Description	Colourways	Size	U.S.$	Can.$	U.K.£
1	Barrel	Amber; silver bands	Unknown	50.00	70.00	25.00

WADE HEATH *(cont.)*

BRAMBLE WARE LAMPS, c.1948-c.1953

The Bramble Ware lamp was produced in two sizes. The design was first seen on Wade tableware between 1948 and 1962. The small lamp is in the Bramble Ware colours; the large is in the popular Gold Blush Bramble Ware colourway.

Small Bramble ware lamp

Large Bramble ware lamp

Backstamp: A. Black ink stamp "Wade England"
B. Black ink stamp "Made in England"

No.	Description	Colourways	Size	U.S.$	Can.$	U.K.£
1	Bramble Ware	Creamy beige; purple berries; green leaves	85	75.00	100.00	45.00
2	Bramble Gold Blush	Creamy beige; rose red berries /leaves; gold highlights	155	85.00	110.00	55.00

BULBOUS LAMPS, c.1948 and c.1962

The first of these bulbous lamps has a transfer decorated design called Cambridge which was used on Wade tablewares c.1955-1962, the second lamp has a hand painted design seen on Wade Heath vases and plates c.late 1940s.

Cambridge print

Daisy and peony

Backstamp: A. Green or grey ink stamped "Wade England"
B. Black printed "Wade England"

No.	Description	Colourways	Size	U.S.$	Can.$	U.K.£
1a	Cambridge	White; gold flowers	130	38.00	60.00	28.00
1b	Daisy and peony	White; pink daisy; yellow peony flowers; green leaves	145	80.00	110.00	40.00

WADE HEATH (cont.)

CANDY TWIST LAMPS, 1991-2000

The shape name for these lamps is Candy Twist, they were produced in two sizes, small and large for British department stores Debenhams and British Home Stores and were also available from the Wade factory shop.

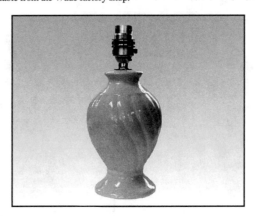

Backstamp: Transfer print "Wade England "

No.	Description	Colourways	Size	U.S.$	Can.$	U.K.£
1a	Solid colour	Pale green	Small/unknown	25.00	30.00	15.00
1b	Solid colour	Pale pink	Small/unknown	25.00	30.00	15.00
1c	Solid colour	White	Small/unknown	25.00	30.00	15.00
2a	Solid colour	Pale green	Large/340	35.00	50.00	25.00
2b	Solid colour	Pale pink	Large/340	35.00	50.00	25.00
2c	Solid colour	White	Large/340	35.00	50.00	25.00

WADE HEATH (cont.)

ELY LAMPS, 1991-2000

The shape name for these lamps is Ely, they were produced for British department stores Debenhams and British Home Stores and were also available from the Wade factory shop during 2000 at £25.00 for the small size, £35.00 for the medium size and £40.00 for the large size.

Backstamp: Transfer print "Wade England"

No.	Description	Colourways	Size	U.S.$	Can.$	U.K.£
1a	Blue peacock	White; blue peacocks; brown tree	Small/unknown	35.00	50.00	25.00
1b	Gold peacock	White; gold peacocks; brown tree	Small/unknown	35.00	50.00	25.00
2a	Blue peacock	White; blue peacocks; brown tree	Medium/unknown	50.00	70.00	35.00
2b	Gold peacock	White; gold peacocks; brown tree	Medium/unknown	50.00	70.00	35.00
3a	Blue peacock	White; blue peacocks; brown tree	Large/405	55.00	80.00	40.00
3b	Gold peacock	White; gold peacocks; brown tree	Large/405	55.00	80.00	40.00

EMPRESS LAMP, c.1953-c.1955

Decorated in the colours of the Empress vases, the shape number for this lamp is not known.

Backstamp: Transfer print "Wade 'Empress' England" inside a scalloped frame

No.	Description	Colourways	Size	U.S.$	Can.$	U.K.£
1	Empress	Maroon; gold/ white stripes	220	130.00	175.00	65.00

WADE HEATH (cont.)

GILBEY'S BARREL LAMPS, 1959-1961

These lamps were made from Gilbey's Gin wine barrels (see *The Charlton Standard Catalogue of Wade, Volume Four, Liquor Containers*), which had the name of a different spirit printed on the front. A lamp kit and five Gilbey lamp shades were first sold at the Ideal Home Exhibition in London in March 1959 and went on sale to the general public the next month.

Backstamp: Transfer print "Royal Victoria Pottery, Wade England"

No.	Description	Colourways	Size	U.S.$	Can.$	U.K.£
1a	Gin	White; gold/blue bands; grey border; black lettering	Half bottle/115	40.00	55.00	20.00
1b	Port	White; gold/maroon bands; grey border; black lettering	Half bottle/115	40.00	55.00	20.00
1c	Scotch	White; gold/red bands; brown border; black lettering	Half bottle/115	40.00	55.00	20.00
1d	Sherry	White; gold/green bands; brown border; black lettering	Half bottle/115	40.00	55.00	20.00
2	Cognac	Black; gold bands, frame, lettering	Quart/133	50.00	70.00	25.00

WADE HEATH *(cont.)*

GINGER JAR LAMPS, 1991-1995

The shape name for these lamps is Ginger Jar. They were produced in three sizes and were decorated in designs called Kawa and Wisteria. They are part of a giftware line that was decorated in this style.

Kawa

Wisteria

Backstamp: Unknown

No.	Description	Colourways	Size	U.S.$	Can.$	U.K.£
1a	Kawa	White; pale pink flowers; pale green bamboo	Small/230	35.00	55.00	25.00
1b	Wisteria	Cream; blue wisteria; pale pink flowers	Small/230	35.00	55.00	25.00
2a	Kawa	White; pale pink flowers; pale green bamboo	Medium/290	50.00	75.00	40.00
2b	Wisteria	Cream; blue wisteria; pale pink flowers	Medium/290	50.00	75.00	40.00
3a	Kawa	White; pale pink flowers; pale green bamboo	Large/340	75.00	95.00	50.00
3b	Wisteria	Mushroom; blue wisteria; pale pink flowers	Large/340	75.00	95.00	50.00

GRAPE LAMPS, 1948-c 1962

Wade Heath produced a range of tableware called Grape which was produced in various colourways, the lamps are in the Regal White and Rubytone Grape design and were produced in two different shapes.

Type one, Regal white

Type two, Rubytone

Backstamp: **A.** Hand painted "Made in England"
B. Hand painted "Made in England"

No.	Description	Colourways	Size	U.S.$	Can.$	U.K.£
1	Type one	White; gold bands, grapes, leaves	155	90.00	120.00	45.00
2	Type two	Ruby red; gold bands, grapes, leaves	155	90.00	120.00	45.00

WADE HEATH (cont.)

GREEK VASE LAMPS, 1991-1999

The shape name of these lamps is Greek Vase. They were produced in a mushroom craquelle glaze in designs of English Bouquet, Hana, and Zakuro. The Zakuro design is of flowers and seedpods, with a floral band around the neck, as well as two bands of 24-karat gold. They are fitted with a brass lamp holder and riser and a gold cable and sit on a hardwood plinth. The price direct from the Wade factory shop in the year 2000 was small £20, medium £35, and large £48.

English bouquet

Hana

Zakuro

Backstamp: Gold transfer print "Wade"

No.	Description	Colourways	Size	U.S.$	Can.$	U.K.£
1a	English bouquet	White; gold bands; pale pink/blue/beige flowers	Small/355	30.00	40.00	20.00
1b	Hana	White; mauve band; gold bands; multicoloured flowers	Small/355	30.00	40.00	20.00
1c	Zakuro	Mushroom; pale yellow/pink flowers; blue/green leaves; gold/blue band	Small/355	30.00	40.00	20.00
2a	English bouquet	White; gold bands; pale pink/blue/beige flowers	Medium/405	45.00	70.00	35.00
2b	Hana	White; mauve band; gold bands; multicoloured flowers	Medium/405	45.00	70.00	35.00
2c	Zakuro	Mushroom; pale yellow flowers; blue/green leaves; gold/blue band	Medium/405	45.00	70.00	35.00
3a	English bouquet	White; gold bands; pale pink/blue/beige flowers	Large/455	80.00	90.00	48.00
3b	Hana	White; mauve band; gold bands; multicoloured flowers	Large/455	70.00	90.00	48.00
3c	Zakuro	Mushroom; pale yellow flowers; blue/green leaves; gold/blue band	Large/455	70.00	90.00	48.00

WADE HEATH (cont.)

HANDLED LAMP

This handled lamp has a slightly ribbed rim and foot similar to the Wade Regency wares.

Backstamp: Green ink stamp "Wade Made in England"

No.	Description	Colourways	Size	U.S.$	Can.$	U.K.£
1	Handled lamp	Maroon	215	50.00	75.00	38.00

JACOBEAN LAMPS, 1991-1995

Backstamp: Gold transfer print "Wade"

No.	Description	Colourways	Size	U.S.$	Can.$	U.K.£
1	Jacobean	White; gold bands; rust/black flowers	Small/355	50.00	75.00	35.00
2	Jacobean	White; gold bands; rust/black flowers	Medium/405	60.00	90.00	45.00
3	Jacobean	White; gold bands; rust/black flowers	Large/455	70.00	105.00	50.00

WADE HEATH (cont.)

PANELLED LAMPS, 1991

These hexangular lamps were produced with a wooden plinth and were available in a large variety of colours and designs.

Oriental butterfly

Blue peacock

Backstamp: Unknown

No.	Description	Colourways	Size	U.S.$	Can.$	U.K.£
1a	Oriental butterfly and flowers	White; yellow/green butterfly; multicoloured flowers	Small/215	30.00	40.00	20.00
1b	Oriental butterfly and swallow	White; blue butterfly, bird, flowers	Small/215	30.00	40.00	20.00
2a	Solid colour	Dark green	Medium/265	50.00	70.00	35.00
2b	Solid colour	Pale green	Medium/265	50.00	70.00	35.00
2c	Solid colour	Pastel Pink	Medium/265	50.00	70.00	35.00
2d	Solid colour	White	Medium/265	50.00	70.00	35.00
3a	Blue peacock	White; blue peacock; pink flowers	Large/300	70.00	100.00	48.00
3b	Green peacock	White; green peacock; pink flowers	Large/300	70.00	100.00	48.00
3c	Red peacock	White; Red peacock; pink flowers	Large/300	70.00	100.00	48.00

WADE HEATH (cont.)

RECTANGULAR LAMPS, 1991

These rectangular lamps have a decorative band around the top and base and were produced with a wooden plinth.

Butterfly and flowers

Butterfly, swallow and flowers

Backstamp: Unknown

No.	Description	Colourways	Size	U.S.$	Can.$	U.K.£
1a	Oriental butterfly and flowers	White; yellow/white/green butterfly; multicoloured	Large/405	50.00	70.00	35.00
1b	Oriental butterfly, swallow and flowers	White; blue butterfly, bird, flowers	Large/405	50.00	70.00	35.00

REGENCY LAMP

This lamp is a derivative of the Regency shaped coffee-pot.

Backstamp: Gold printed "Wade England"

No.	Description	Colourways	Size	U.S.$	Can.$	U.K.£
1	Regency lamp	Maroon; gold edging	185	50.00	75.00	38.00

WADE HEATH (cont.)

TEMPLE JAR LAMPS, 1991-2000

The shape name for these lamps is Round Temple, they were produced for British department stores Debenhams and British Home Stores and are also available from the Wade factory shop. They were produced in a craquelle glaze of pale blue or mushroom and are found decorated in various designs with a floral band around the neck and base, as well as two bands of 24-karat gold. They are fitted with a brass lamp holder and riser and a gold cable, they were also produced with and without a hardwood plinth. They are found in three sizes, and are listed alphabetically by the Pattern name / colour. Prices direct from Wade were as follows.

Ko-eda print

Mariko print

Backstamp: Gold transfer print "Wade England" between two gold lines

No.	Description	Colourways	Size	U.S.$	Can.$	U.K.£
1a	Black	Black	Small/240	30.00	45.00	25.00
1b	Blue	Pale blue	Small/240	30.00	45.00	25.00
1c	Burgundy	Burgundy	Small/240	30.00	45.00	25.00
1d	Jade	Green	Small/240	30.00	45.00	25.00
1e	Kawa	White; pale pink flowers; pale green bamboo blue/yellow band	Small/240	110.00	145.00	55.00
1f	Ko-eda	Pale blue; pastel pink/blue flowers blue/yellow band	Small/240	110.00	145.00	55.00
1g	Mariko	Mushroom; pale pink/yellow peonies; blue/yellow band	Small/240	110.00	145.00	55.00
1h	Navy blue	Navy blue	Small/240	30.00	45.00	25.00
1i	Peacocks	Gold peacocks; multicoloured flowering tree; blue/yellow band	Small/240	110.00	145.00	55.00
1j	Pink	Pink	Small/240	30.00	45.00	25.00
2a	Black	Black	Medium/285	30.00	45.00	25.00
2b	Blue	Pale blue	Medium/285	30.00	45.00	25.00
2c	Burgundy	Burgundy	Medium/285	30.00	45.00	25.00
2d	Jade	Green	Medium/285	30.00	45.00	25.00
2e	Kawa	White; pale pink flowers; pale green bamboo; blue/yellow band	Medium/285	110.00	145.00	55.00
2f	Ko-eda	Pale blue; pastel pink/blue flowers; blue/yellow band	Medium/285	110.00	145.00	55.00
2g	Mariko	Mushroom; pale pink/yellow peonies; blue/yellow band	Medium/285	110.00	145.00	55.00
2h	Navy blue	Navy blue	Medium/285	30.00	45.00	25.00

WADE HEATH (cont.)

TEMPLE JAR LAMPS (cont.)

Kawa print

Jade print

No.	Description	Colourways	Size	U.S.$	Can.$	U.K.£
2i	Peacocks	Gold peacocks; multicoloured flowering tree; blue/yellow band	Medium/285	110.00	145.00	55.00
2j	Pink	Pink	Medium/285	30.00	45.00	25.00
3a	Black	Black	Large/385	30.00	45.00	25.00
3b	Blue	Pale blue	Large/385	30.00	45.00	25.00
3c	Burgundy	Burgundy	Large/385	30.00	45.00	25.00
3d	Jade	Green	Large/385	30.00	45.00	25.00
3e	Kawa	White; pale pink flowers; pale green bamboo; blue/yellow band	Large/385	110.00	145.00	55.00
3f	Ko-eda	Pale blue; pastel pink / blue flowers; blue/yellow band	Large/385	110.00	145.00	55.00
3g	Mariko	Mushroom; pale pink/yellow peonies; blue/yellow band	Large/385	110.00	145.00	55.00
3h	Navy blue	Navy blue	Large/385	30.00	45.00	25.00
3i	Peacocks	Gold peacocks; multicoloured flowering tree; blue/yellow band	Large/385	110.00	145.00	55.00
3j	Pink	Pink	Large/385	30.00	45.00	25.00

WADE HEATH *(cont.)*

VINTAGE CARS LAMP

The base of this tubular-shaped lamp is decorated with transfer prints of vintage cars.

Vintage cars lamp

Backstamp: Red transfer print "Wade England"

No.	Description	Colourways	Size	U.S.$	Can.$	U.K.£
1a	Ford/Morris/Rolls Royce	White/black; multicoloured prints	165	70.00	95.00	40.00
1b	Austin/Daimler/Wolseley	White/black; multicoloured prints	165	70.00	95.00	40.00

WADE IRELAND

IRISH WADE LAMP c.1960s

This Irish Wade lamp base has an embossed design of knurls, shamrocks and linked chains.

Backstamp: Impressed "Irish Porcelain made in Ireland by wade Co Armagh"

No.	Description	Colourways	Size	U.S.$	Can.$	U.K.£
1	Knurled lamp	Grey green	150 dia.	65.00	85.00	45.00

WADE (IRELAND) LTD
ONE OF THE WADE GROUP

Registered Office:

WATSON STREET
PORTADOWN
CO. ARMAGH BT 63 5AH
NORTHERN IRELAND

TELEPHONE:
(0762) 332288
TELEX: 747128

SHAMROCK RANGE
1. SR01 Half Pint Tankard
2. SR02 One Pint Tankard

3. SR17 Large Ashtray with Gold Rim
4. SR18 Small Ashtray without Gold Rim

SHEET S6

5. SR12 Candlestick

MISCELLANEOUS DECORATIVE WARES

c.1955-1993

The items in this section vary from bells to clocks to picture frames and tiles. The potteries in England and Ireland are represented here. The items are listed in alphabetical order within their respective country of origin.

Wade Heath
Wade Ireland

BACKSTAMPS

Impressed Backstamps

Wade Ireland used impressed backstamps on its inkstand, produced in the mid 1950s , and in 1962 on its rhinoceros decanter.

Transfer Prints

Wade used transfer-printed backstamps on a variety of miscellaneous items from the late 1950s to 1992.

Embossed Backstamps

Embossed backstamps appear on the 1962 Wade Ireland rhinoceros decanter and on the Romance Series photo frames and pomanders, produced from 1983 to 1985.

WADE HEATH

BELLS

CHRISTMAS BELLS, 1997

Sold at the Wade Christmas Extravaganza in November 1998, these bells have multicoloured transfer prints of Christmas scenes.

Backstamp: Printed "Wade Made in England"

No.	Description	Colourways	Size	U.S.$	Can.$	U.K.£
1a	Holly and bows	White; gold band; multicoloured print	130	4.00	6.00	3.00
1b	Merry Christmas in mistletoe wreath	White; gold band; green wreath	130	4.00	6.00	3.00

MILLENNIUM BELLS, 1999-2000

Issued as part of the Millennium Series these bells were produced in two colours.

Backstamp: Printed "Wade England" between two lines

No.	Description	Colourways	Size	U.S.$	Can.$	U.K.£
1a	Black/gold	Black; gold decorative print	130/diam	25.00	40.00	20.00
1b	Blue/silver	Dark blue; silver decorative print	130/diam	25.00	40.00	20.00

WADE HEATH *(cont.)*

BROOCHES
Cameo Brooch

A cameo portrait plaque of a woman with loose hair and a 'v-necked' dress edged with white lace has been found that has a brooch pin glued to the back.

Photograph not available
at press time

Backstamp: Unmarked

No.	Description	Colourways	Shape No./Size	U.S.$	Can.$	U.K.£
1	Cameo brooch	Grey; green dress; white lace	70 x 50	20.00	30.00	10.00

Guitar Brooches, 1960

First issued in August 1960, this set of brooches depict the British teenage heart throbs of the time. For matching cameo plaques, see Plaques; for matching heart-shaped caskets, see Boxes. The original price of the brooches was 4/11d.

Backstamp: Black print "Wade Porcelain Made in England"

No.	Description	Colourways	Size	U.S.$	Can.$	U.K.£
1a	Cliff Richard	White; multicoloured portrait; gold trim	60		Rare	
1b	Tommy Steele	White; multicoloured portrait; gold trim	60		Rare	
1c	Frankie Vaughan	White; multicoloured portrait; gold trim	60		Rare	
1d	Marty Wilde	White; multicoloured portrait; gold trim	60		Rare	

WADE HEATH *(cont.)*

BROOCHES *(cont.)*
Identification Brooches, 1996-1997

Porcelain identification brooches were produced for the first jointly held Wade and Jim Beam Bottle Collectors Society Show which was held in Seattle, Washington, July 1996. The following brooches were produced: Wade staff - Ralph, Adele, Jenny and Kim; authors - Pat Murray, Mike Posgay and Ian Warner; Seattle co-ordinator for Wade - Molly Newman.

Further identification brooches were produced for Wade personnel attending the Dunstable Show, 1996, and Trentham Gardens, 1997.

A brooch was also produced for Alan Cooper, for the 1997 Oconomowoc, Wisconsin, Wade - Jim Beam Show.

Backstamp: Embossed in rectangle "S52/5S"

Seattle, Washington, U.S.A. July 1996

No.	Description	Colourways	Size	U.S.$	Can.$	U.K.£
1a	Adele	White; red/black lines and lettering	35 dia.			
1b	Ian	White; red/black lines and lettering	35 dia.			
1c	Jenny	White; red/black lines and lettering	35 dia.		One	
1d	Kim	White; red/black lines and lettering	35 dia.		of a	
1e	Mike	White; red/black lines and lettering	35 dia.		kind	
1f	Molly	White; red/black lines and lettering	35 dia.			
1g	Pat	White; red/black lines and lettering	35 dia.			
1h	Ralph	White; red/black lines and lettering	35 dia.			

Dunstable, Bedfordshire, U.K. September 1996

No.	Description	Colourways	Size	U.S.$	Can.$	U.K.£
1i	Caryl	White; red/black lines and lettering	35 dia.			
1j	Helen	White; red/black lines and lettering	35 dia.		One	
1k	Joy	White; red/black lines and lettering	35 dia.		of a	
1l	Nina	White; red/black lines and lettering	35 dia.		kind	
1m	Paul	White; red/black lines and lettering	35 dia.			

Trentham Gardens, Staffordshire, U.K. April 1997

No.	Description	Colourways	Size	U.S.$	Can.$	U.K.£
1n	Cheryl	White; red/black lines and lettering	35 dia.			
1o	Dave	White; red/black lines and lettering	35 dia.		One	
1p	Mandy	White; red/black lines and lettering	35 dia.		of a	
1q	Stephen	White; red/black lines and lettering	35 dia.		kind	
1r	Sue	White; red/black lines and lettering	35 dia.			
1s	Tony	White; red/black lines and lettering	35 dia.			

The last brooch added was that of Alan Cooper former managing director and one of the three new owners of Wade Ceramics in 1999.

No.	Description	Colourways	Size	U.S.$	Can.$	U.K.£
1t	Alan	White; red/black lines and lettering	35 dia.		Unique	

WADE HEATH *(cont.)*

BROOCHES *(cont.)*
Zamba Brooch, c.Late 1950s

An unusual find is this oval Zamba brooch. There is a plain gold-coloured pin glued on the back. No other information has been found.

Backstamp: None

No.	Description	Colourways	Size	U.S.$	Can.$	U.K.£
1	Zamba brooch	White; black dancer print; gold trim	55		Rare	

WADE HEATH (cont.)

BUSINESS CARD HOLDER, 1999

This rectangular business card holder has a triangular Art Nouveau design along the base.

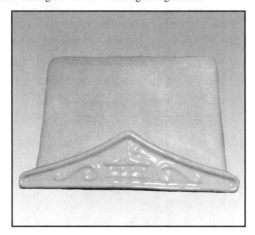

Backstamp: Black printed "Wade England" between two lines

No.	Description	Colourways	Size	U.S.$	Can.$	U.K.£
1	Business card holder	Cream	80 x 135	10.00	15.00	7.00

CLOCKS, 1990-1992, 1999-2000

The Jacobean design is of enamelled exotic flowers and Kawa is a Japanese design of peonies and bamboo stems. The Kawa design clock was still available from the Wade factory shop during 1999-2000 for £20.00.

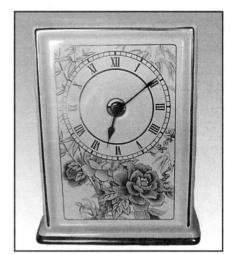

Jacobean transfer print   Kawa transfer print

Backstamp: **A.** Red transfer print "Wade England" with two red lines and "Jacobean"
B. Gold transfer print "Wade England" with two gold lines and "Kawa"

No.	Description	Colourways	Size	U.S.$	Can.$	U.K.£
1a	Jacobean print	White; red/black print, clock face	160	50.00	70.00	25.00
1b	Kawa print	White; pastel pink/green print; gold highlights, clock face	160	30.00	40.00	20.00

WADE HEATH *(cont.)*

EXECUTIVE DESK SET, 1993

These items were part of an eight-piece executive desk set produced by Wade for companies to present to their clients. They have a stylised lily emblem in the centre of each item. The inkwell is similar in shape to the Pusser's miniature rum jug.

Backstamp: Unknown

No.	Description	Colourways	Size	U.S.$	Can.$	U.K.£
1.	Ashtray	Black; godl edge, emblem	Unk.	5.00	8.00	3.00
2.	Bosun's decanter	Black; gold edge, emblem	Unk.	40.00	55.00	20.00
3	Desk tidy	Black; gold edge, emblem	Unk.	30.00	40.00	15.00
4.	Half-pint tankard	Black; gold edge, emblem	Unk.	10.00	15.00	5.00
5	Inkwell	Black; gold edge, emblem	63	14.00	20.00	10.00
6	Letter rack	Black; gold edge, emblem	100	40.00	55.00	20.00
7	Pencil holder pot	Black; gold edge, emblem	100	10.00	15.00	5.00
8	Trinket box	Black; gold edge, emblem	63	30.00	40.00	15.00

WADE HEATH (cont.)

HOUSE DECORATIONS
Bed Knobs, 1999-2000

These hollow porcelain bed knobs were produced in two sizes and intended as decoration for the top of bedposts.

Backstamp: Unmarked

No.	Description	Colourways	Size	U.S.$	Can.$	U.K.£
1a	Gold bands	White; gold bands	70	3.00	4.00	2.00
1b	Mallow flowers	White; gold leaves; blue and pink flowers	60	3.00	4.00	2.00

WADE HEATH *(cont.)*

HOUSE DECORATIONS *(cont.)*
Doorknobs, 1997-2000

Doorknobs in three sizes, are sold in the Wade factory shop from £1.99 to £3.99 a pair, depending on size. Measurement is by height.

Flowers

Flowers, gold frame

Backstamp: **A.** Embossed "S43/2"
B. Embossed "S111/2"
C. Embossed "K2"
D. None

No.	Description	Colourways	Size	U.S.$	Can.$	U.K.£
1a	Rose	White; pink rose; green leaves	Small/25	3.00	4.00	1.99
1b	Rose and forget-me-nots	Cream; pink rose; blue forget-me-nots	Small/25	3.00	4.00	1.99
2a	Dog rose	Cream; pink rose; green leaves	Medium/35	4.00	6.00	2.99
2b	Roman lady	Cream; brown; sepia print	Medium/35	4.00	6.00	2.99
2c	Rose	White; pink rose; green leaves	Medium/35	4.00	6.00	2.99
3a	Flowers	White; multicoloured flowers	Large/45	6.00	8.00	3.99
3b	Flowers, gold frame	White; gold frame; pink/red flowers	Large/45	6.00	8.00	3.99
3c	Rose	White; pink rose; green leaves	Large/45	6.00	8.00	3.99
3d	Rosebud	White; pink rose; small blue/white flowers	Large/45	6.00	8.00	3.99
3e	Wild flowers	Cream; pink/blue flowers; green leaves	Large/45	6.00	8.00	3.99
3f	Wild flowers	White; pink/blue/white flowers; green leaves	Large/45	6.00	8.00	3.99

WADE HEATH (cont.)

HOUSE DECORATIONS (cont.)
Door Number Plates, 1999-2000

These items were produced in two shapes Arched and Oval. They were sold in the Wade factory shop and were also a line produced for retail stores.

Arched door number plate, flower design

Oval door number plate "Myosotis scorpioides"

Backstamp: **A.** Embossed "England 5107/1a" on rim
B. Red printed "Wade England"

No.	Description	Colourways	Size	U.S.$	Can.$	U.K.£
1	Flower bouquet	White; multicolour flowers	Arched/120 x 165	12.00	18.00	3.99
2a	Blackberries	White; black/purple berries	Oval/165	12.00	18.00	3.99
2b	Carnations	White; red flowers	Oval/165	12.00	18.00	3.99
2c	Chestnuts/hazel nuts	White; brown print	Oval/165	12.00	18.00	3.99
2d	"Myosotis scorpioides" (Forget-Me-Nots)	White; blue flowers; black lettering	Oval/165	12.00	18.00	3.99
2e	Solid colour	Black	Oval/165	8.00	12.00	3.99
2f	Wild flowers	White; blue/pink flowers	Oval/165	12.00	18.00	3.99

WADE HEATH *(cont.)*

HOUSE DECORATIONS *(cont.)*
Door Plates, 1997-2000

The door plates could be purchased at the Wade factory shop for £3.95 a pair, and were an off-the-shelf line produced by Wade for retail stores. The Dog rose door plate has a Rothley China, Staffordshire backstamp.

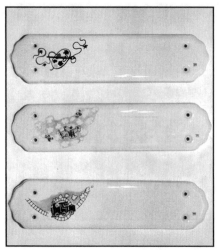

Needle/thread/button, Aeroplane and Train patterns

Willow and marbled patterns

Backstamp: **A.** Embossed "England 5107/1a"
B. Embossed "Wade Ceramics England 5103/ia"
C. Red "Wade Made in England"
D. Embossed "Rothley China Staffordshire England S71/1"

No.	Description	Colourways	Size	U.S.$	Can.$	U.K.£
1a	Aeroplane	White; multicoloured print	330	5.00	8.00	3.95
1b	Artist paint palette	White; multicoloured print	330	5.00	8.00	3.95
1c	Dog Rose	White; multicoloured print	330	5.00	8.00	3.95
1d	Marbled	White; brown marbled print	330	5.00	8.00	3.95
1e	Needle, thread and button	White; multicoloured print	330	5.00	8.00	3.95
1f	Rose	White; pink rose; green leaves	330	5.00	8.00	3.95
1g	Train	White; multicoloured print	330	5.00	8.00	3.95
1h	Willow pattern	White; blue design	330	5.00	8.00	3.95
2	Handle plate	Black; gold edging	275	3.00	4.00	2.00

WADE HEATH (cont.)

HOUSE DECORATIONS (cont.)
Keyhole Covers, 1997-2000

Door keyhole covers could be purchased from the Wade factory shop at £1.25 a pair.

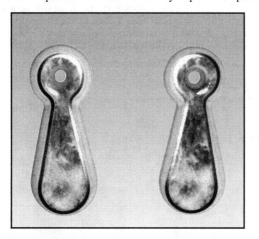 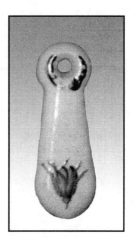

Backstamp: **A.** Embossed "S10373"
B. Embossed "S27/4"
C. None

No.	Description	Colourways	Size	U.S.$	Can.$	U.K.£
1a	Flowers	White; gold line; multicoloured flowers	60 x 25	6.00	9.00	5.00
1b	Solid colour	White; gold line	60 x 25	5.00	8.00	3.00
1c	Rose	White; red rose	60 x 25	6.00	9.00	5.00
1d	Rosebud	White; green/pink rosebud	60 x 25	6.00	9.00	5.00

Light Switch Plates, 1999-2000

Light switch plates were available from the Wade factory shop at a cost of £1.95 during 1999-2000.

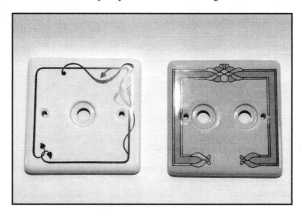

Backstamp: **A.** Embossed "Pat applied for 50093" on one hole plate
B. Embossed "Pat applied for 50094" on two hole plate

No.	Description	Colourways	Size	U.S.$	Can.$	U.K.£
1	Banded (2 hole)	White; gold/grey band	90	3.00	4.00	1.95
2	Solid colour (1 hole)	White; silver grey line	90	3.00	4.00	1.95

WADE HEATH *(cont.)*

HOUSE DECORATIONS *(cont.)*
Wall Tiles, c.1930s

In late 1927 Albert J. Wade, brother to George Wade, formed his own company known as the Flaxman Tile Works to produce decorative wall tiles and ceramic tiled fireplaces. With the popularity of gas fires increasing in the late 1950s, tile fireplaces and wall tile production began a steady decline eventually forcing the Flaxman Tile Works to close down in 1970. Although hundreds-of-thousands of tiles must have been produced between 1927 and 1970, only a few examples have been seen. The face of the Clock tile shows Roman numerals, and has a hole at the centre for clock hands. The Flying Pheasants tile is a transfer print often used by Wade Ireland on ashtrays and tankards.

Assorted sizes and styles

Backstamp: **A.** Embossed "Flaxman"
B. Embossed "Flaxman England"
C. Embossed "Flaxman RD 165617"
D. Embossed "BCM Wades England"
E. Embossed "Wade England"

No.	Description	Colourways	Size	U.S.$	Can.$	U.K.£
1a	Art Nouveau vase	Brown/blue/cream/green/mauve	153 x 153	95.00	110.00	50.00
1b	Art Nouveau leaves	Grey	153 x 153	95.00	110.00	50.00
1c	Clock face	Off white; multicoloured print	153 x 153	70.00	90.00	50.00
1d	Flying pheasants	Mottled grey; multicoloured print	115 x 115	20.00	30.00	15.00
1e	Geometric leaf	Brown	153 x 153	145.00	150.00	135.00
1f	Landscape	White; multicoloured print	150 x 305	145.00	150.00	135.00
1g	Windmill	Cream; brown windmill	153 x 76	145.00	150.00	135.00
1h	Windmill	Green; blue windmill	153 x 76	145.00	150.00	135.00

WADE HEATH (cont.)

MINIATURES, c.1962

Backstamp: Black or Red transfer print "Wade England"

No.	Description	Colourways	Size	U.S.$	Can.$	U.K.£
1	Coal box	Gold	45	25.00	35.00	12.00
2a	Coal scuttle	Gold	90	25.00	35.00	12.00
2b	Coal scuttle	Silver	90	25.00	35.00	12.00
3	Flagon	Gold	90	25.00	35.00	12.00
4	Oil jug	Gold	90	25.00	35.00	12.00

WADE HEATH *(cont.)*

PICTURE FRAMES
Edwardian Photograph Frames, 1986-1990

Floral fayre   Nasturtium

Backstamp: A. Red "Wade England" with two red lines
B. Printed "Floral Fayre Wade England"

No.	Description	Colourways	Size	U.S.$	Can.$	U.K.£
1a	Floral fayre	White; pink flowers; green leaves	145	25.00	35.00	12.00
1b	Fuchsia	White; pink/yellow flowers	145	25.00	35.00	12.00
1c	Nasturtium	White; grey/pink/yellow flowers	145	25.00	35.00	12.00
1d	Queensway	White; white flowers; green leaves	145	25.00	35.00	12.00

Romance Picture Frames, 1983-1985

Square frames   Heart frame

Backstamp: Raised "Wade Made in England"

No.	Description	Colourways	Size	U.S.$	Can.$	U.K.£
1a	Frame	Cream; blue/grey/fawn flowers	Rectangular/142	40.00	60.00	30.00
1b	Frame	Fawn; grey/yellow/white flowers	Rectangular/142	40.00	60.00	30.00
2a	Frame	Cream; blue/grey/fawn flowers	Rectangular/170	40.00	60.00	30.00
2b	Frame	Fawn; grey/yellow/white flowers	Rectangular/170	40.00	60.00	30.00
3a	Frame	Cream; blue/grey/fawn flowers	Heart/150	40.00	60.00	30.00
3b	Frame	Fawn; grey/yellow/white flowers	Heart/150	40.00	60.00	30.00

WADE HEATH (cont.)

ROMANCE POMANDER, 1983-1985

This round pomander has a mottled glaze on the top, with fluted ribs around the body and lid. It was sold with a sachet of herbs or lavender. The top of the lid, which is embossed with a pebbled design, has vents to allow the scent to escape. The original price was £2.50.

Pomander

Backstamp: Raised "Wade Made in England"

No.	Description	Colourways	Size	U.S.$	Can.$	U.K.£
1a	Pomander	Mottled blue/grey/fawn top; cream bottom	Round/52	30.00	38.00	18.00
1b	Pomander	Mottled grey/yellow/white top; fawn bottom	Round/52	30.00	38.00	18.00

SOAP DISH, 1999

This scallop shell soap dish was available from the Wade factory shop during 1999, the design name is 'Spring Bouquet'

Backstamp: Printed "Wade Spring Bouquet Made in England Dishwasher and Microwave Safe"

No.	Description	Colourways	Size	U.S.$	Can.$	U.K.£
1	Spring bouquet	Off white; pink/white crocuses; green leaves	145	4.00	5.00	2.00

WADE IRELAND

IRISH PORCELAIN

BELLS OF IRELAND, SHAPE SR03, 1983-1986

These seven porcelain bells are decorated on the front with transfer prints, mostly of Irish scenes. The Bunratty Castle bell has a short history of the Castle on the back of the bell.

Backstamp: Unknown

No.	Description	Colourways	Shape No./Size	U.S.$	Can.$	U.K.£
1a	Blarney Castle	White; gold bands; multicoloured print; black lettering	SR03/1/146	60.00	80.00	30.00
1b	Bunratty Castle	White; gold bands; multicoloured print; black lettering	SR03/3/146	60.00	80.00	30.00
1c	Christmas tree	White; gold bands; multicoloured print;	SR03/7/146	50.00	70.00	25.00
1d	Ross Castle	White; gold bands; multicoloured print; black lettering	SR03/2/146	60.00	80.00	30.00
1e	Shamrocks	White; gold bands; green shamrocks	SR03/5/146	50.00	70.00	25.00
1f	Thatched cottage	White; gold bands; multicoloured print;	SR03/8/146	60.00	80.00	30.00
1g	Woman with spinning wheel	White; gold bands; multicoloured print; black lettering "Souvenir of Ireland"	SR03/4/146	60.00	80.00	30.00

IRISH PORCELAIN (cont.)

INK STAND, c.1955

This small rectangular inkstand from Wade Ireland has an embossed design of shamrocks on it. It includes a round lid and two grooves for pens.

Backstamp: Impressed "Irish Porcelain" curved over a shamrock leaf with "Made in Ireland" in a straight line underneath

No.	Description	Colourways	Size	U.S.$	Can.$	U.K.£
1	Ink stand	Blue-grey	55	54.00	70.00	30.00

RHINOCEROS DECANTERS, 1962

Although the Rhinoceros decanter has been found with whisky inside, a 1960s advertisment shows it as an ashtray. These are novelty models of a comic rhinoceros with a wide-open mouth. A design fault (especially prominant in the large version, with its front toes curled upward) causes them to be top heavy, and they topple over unless filled with liquid or sand to keep them upright. They have a black stopper in the hole in the base, which has "Chekaleke Regd No 698795" and "14" impressed in it.

Backstamp: A. Embossed "Irish Porcelain Made in Ireland" in an Irish knot oval frame and impressed "Chekaleke Regd No 698795" and "14" on stopper
  B. Impressed "Irish Porcelain Made in Ireland" with a shamrock leaf and impressed "Chekaleke Regd No 698795" and "14" on stopper

No.	Description	Colourways	Size	U.S.$	Can.$	U.K.£
1	Rhinoceros	Blue/grey/green	Small/140	300.00	400.00	200.00
2	Rhinoceros	Blue/grey/green	Medium/180	300.00	400.00	200.00
3	Rhinoceros	Blue/grey/green	Large/220	350.00	500.00	250.00

IRISH PORCELAIN (cont.)

VETERAN CAR MINIATURE OIL FUNNEL, c.1958

A small quantity of miniature oil funnels were produced in the Veteran Car Series during the late 1950s. They are in the same amber glaze as the oil jugs. They are decorated with transfer prints of veteran cars.

Backstamp: A. Black print "A Moko product by Wade of England"
B. Black print "An RK Product by Wade of Ireland"

Series 1

No.	Description	Colourways	Size	U.S.$	Can.$	U.K.£
1a	Benz	Amber; silver lustre; black print	92	30.00	40.00	15.00
1b	Darracq	Amber; silver lustre; black print	92	30.00	40.00	15.00
1c	Ford	Amber; silver lustre; black print	92	30.00	40.00	15.00

Series 2

No.	Description	Colourways	Size	U.S.$	Can.$	U.K.£
1d	Baby Peugeot	Amber; silver lustre; black print	92	30.00	40.00	15.00
1e	Rolls-Royce, 1907	Amber; silver lustre; black print	92	30.00	40.00	15.00
1f	Sunbeam	Amber; silver lustre; black print	92	30.00	40.00	15.00

Series 3

No.	Description	Colourways	Size	U.S.$	Can.$	U.K.£
1g	De Dion Bouton	Amber; silver lustre; black print	92	30.00	40.00	15.00
1h	Lanchester	Amber; silver lustre; black print	92	30.00	40.00	15.00
1i	Spyker	Amber; silver lustre; black print	92	30.00	40.00	15.00

PLANTERS AND FLOWERPOTS

1935-1992

Most of these planters and flowerpots were made in England, although a couple were produced at Wade Ireland beginning in the 1950s. Several items are part of a series that include matching bowls, dishes and vases. The planters and flowerpots are listed in alphabetical order for the Wade Heath items and in shape number order for the Wade Ireland issues.

Wade Heath
Wade Ireland

BACKSTAMPS

Ink Stamps

From 1935 to 1937, Wade Heath used an ink stamp on its Flaxman Ware tulip planter. From the mid 1950s to the 1980s, Wade Ireland used an ink stamp on some of its jardinieres.

Impressed Backstamps

Wade Ireland used impressed backstamps on its flower potholder and on some of its jardinieres, from the early 1950s to the 1980s.

Embossed Backstamp

As well as using ink stamps and impressed backstamps, Wade Ireland also put an embossed backstamp on some of its jardinieres.

Transfer Prints

Most of the items in this section were marked with a transfer-printed backstamp. They were used from 1957 to 1992.

WADE HEATH

BLACK FROST FLOWERPOT AND WATER TRAY, 1957-c.1962

Backstamp: Red or white transfer print "Wade England"

No.	Description	Colourways	Size	U.S.$	Can.$	U.K.£
1	Black Frost	Black; white flowers; gold rim	65	20.00	28.00	12.00
2	Black Frost	Black; white flowers; gold rim	115	30.00	45.00	20.00

EDWARDIAN PLANTERS

The floral fayre design consists of small pink flowers, the fuchsia design is of fuchsias and leaves, and the Queensway design is of large white flowers. These planters have two moulded handles. For matching items in these patterns please see Edwardian photograph frames (page 270), and vases (page 361).

Backstamp: Red transfer print "Wade England" with two red lines

No.	Description	Colourways	Size	U.S.$	Can.$	U.K.£
1a	Floral fayre	White; pink/green print	Small/88	20.00	30.00	10.00
1b	Fuchsia	White; pink/yellow/grey print	Small/88	20.00	30.00	10.00
2a	Floral fayre	White; pink/green print	Medium/108	40.00	55.00	20.00
2b	Fuchsia	White; pink/yellow/grey print	Medium/108	40.00	55.00	20.00
3a	Floral fayre	White; pink/green print	Large/127	40.00	55.00	20.00
3b	Fuchsia	White; pink/yellow/grey print	Large/127	40.00	55.00	20.00

WADE HEATH (cont.)

FLOWERPOTS, c.1958-c.1962

These flowerpots were produced by the Wade Heath Pottery and could be purchased with a matching water tray. Styles 1, 3 and 5 are footed pots. Each design can be found in a variety of sizes and style.

Backstamp: Red transfer print "Wade England"

No.	Description	Colourways	Shape/Size	U.S.$	Can.$	U.K.£
1a	Cherry blossom	White; pink flowers; pink inside	Small, footed/67	12.00	18.00	8.00
1b	Ivy	White; light/dark green; black inside	Small, footed/67	12.00	18.00	8.00
2a	Banded	Unknown	Small/67	12.00	18.00	8.00
2b	Bella Donna	White; green/yellow leaves; red berries; red inside	Small/67	12.00	18.00	8.00
2c	Bella Donna	White; green/yellow leaves; red berries; yellow inside	Small/67	12.00	18.00	8.00
2d	Bella Donna	White; green/yellow leaves; red berries; black inside	Small/67	12.00	18.00	8.00
2e	Etched	Black; red inside	Small/67	12.00	18.00	8.00
2f	Leaves	White; green/red/blue leaves; red inside	Small/67	12.00	18.00	8.00
2g	Leaves	White; green/red/blue leaves; black inside	Small/67	12.00	18.00	8.00
2h	Strawberries	White; red strawberries; red inside	Small/67	12.00	18.00	8.00
2i	White rose	Black; white rose; pink inside	Small/67	12.00	18.00	8.00
3	Cherry blossom	White; pink flowers; pink inside	Medium, footed/108	22.00	35.00	15.00
4a	Banded	Unknown	Medium/108	22.00	35.00	15.00
4b	Bella Donna	White; green/yellow leaves; red berries; black inside	Medium/108	22.00	35.00	15.00
4c	Bella Donna	White; green/yellow leaves; red berries; green inside	Medium/108	22.00	35.00	15.00
4d	Etched	Unknown	Medium/108	22.00	35.00	15.00
4e	Virginia creeper	White; green/white vine; green inside	Medium/108	22.00	35.00	15.00
4f	White rose	Black; white rose; pink inside	Medium/108	22.00	35.00	15.00
5a	Cherry blossom	White; pink flowers; pink inside	Large, footed/133	28.00	42.00	18.00
5b	Ivy	White; light/dark green; black inside	Large, footed/133	28.00	42.00	18.00
6a	Etched	Unknown	Large/133	25.00	35.00	12.00
6b	Virginia creeper	White; green/white vine; green inside	Large/133	28.00	42.00	18.00
6c	White rose	Black; white rose; pink inside	Large/133	28.00	42.00	18.00

WADE HEATH *(cont.)*

FOOTED PLANTER, c.1998

The shape and series name of this planter is unknown. It is square-shaped, has four feet and has been found in two sizes.

Fern

Unknown flowers

Wild flowers

Backstamp: Gold transfer print "Royal Victoria Pottery, Wade England"

No.	Description	Colourways	Size	U.S.$	Can.$	U.K.£
1a	Fern	White; yellow/green ferns	Small/135	18.00	25.00	12.00
1b	Unknown flowers	White; white/grey flowers; grey/green leaves	Small/135	18.00	25.00	14.00
2	Wild flowers	White; mauve/red flowers; green leaves	Large/165	18.00	25.00	14.00

JACOBEAN AND KAWA PLANTERS, 1990-1992

The Jacobean design consists of enamelled exotic flowers, and Kawa is a Japanese design of peonies and bamboo stems.

Photograph not available
at press time

Backstamp: **A.** Red "Wade England" with two red lines and "Jacobean"
B. Gold "Wade England" with two gold lines and "Kawa"

No.	Description	Colourways	Size	U.S.$	Can.$	U.K.£
1a	Jacobean	White; enamelled red/black print	Small/88	30.00	40.00	15.00
1b.	Kawa	White; pastel pink/green print; gold highlights	Small/88	30.00	40.00	15.00
2a	Jacobean	White; enamelled red/black print	Medium/108	40.00	55.00	20.00
2b	Kawa	White; pastel pink/green print; gold highlights	Medium/108	40.00	55.00	20.00
3a	Jacobean	White; enamelled red/black print	Large/127	50.00	70.00	25.00
3b	Kawa	White; pastel pink/green print; gold highlights	Large/127	50.00	70.00	25.00

WADE HEATH (cont.)

ORCHID PLANTER 1999

The shape and series name of this round planter is unknown. It was sold through the Wade factory shop during 1999.

Backstamp: None

No.	Description	Colourways	Size	U.S.$	Can.$	U.K.£
1	Orchid planter	White; pink orchids	138	18.00	25.00	12.00

REGENCY PLANTER

This large heavy planter has the same ribbed design seen on the Regency wares.

Backstamp: Black ink stamp "Wade England Flaxman" with two red lines

No.	Description	Colourways	Size	U.S.$	Can.$	U.K.£
1	Regency planter	Green	180 x 210	90.00	145.00	55.00

WADE HEATH *(cont.)*
ROSE TRELLIS PLANTER

Backstamp: Red transfer print "Wade England" with two red lines

No.	Description	Colourways	Size	U.S.$	Can.$	U.K.£
1	Rose trellis	White; dark pink/green print	Small/88	20.00	30.00	10.00
2	Rose trellis	White; dark pink/green print	Medium/108	20.00	30.00	10.00
3	Rose trellis	White; dark pink/green print	Large/127	30.00	40.00	15.00

SUMMER FESTIVAL PLANTERS, 1986-1988

This bowl-shaped planter was available in three sizes and three colourways: Clementine–flowers and leaves; Dauphine–orchids, and plain white

Photograph not available
at press time

Backstamp: Red transfer print "Wade England" with two red lines

No.	Description	Colourways	Size	U.S.$	Can.$	U.K.£
1a	Clementine	White; pale pink/grey print	Small/88	13.00	18.00	5.00
1b	Dauphine	White; cream/yellow print	Small/88	13.00	18.00	5.00
1c	White	White	Small/88	13.00	18.00	5.00
2a	Clementine	White; pale pink/grey print	Medium/108	20.00	28.00	8.00
2b	Dauphine	White; cream/yellow print	Medium/108	20.00	28.00	8.00
2c	White	White	Medium/108	20.00	28.00	8.00
3a	Clementine	White; pale pink/grey print	Large/127	25.00	35.00	10.00
3b	Dauphine	White; cream/yellow print	Large/127	25.00	35.00	10.00
3c	White	White	Large/127	25.00	35.00	10.00

WADE HEATH (cont.)

TULIP PLANTER, 1935-1937

This rectangular planter is embossed with tulips and leaves, which form the top rim.

Photograph not available
at press time

Backstamp: Black ink stamp "Flaxman Ware Hand Made Pottery by Wadeheath England," 1935-1937

No.	Description	Colourways	Size	U.S.$	Can.$	U.K.£
1	Tulip planter	Mottled green/orange	115 x 255	150.00	200.00	75.00

VENETIAN FLOWERPOTS, c.1958-c.1962

These pots have a fluted rib design running down the outside of the pot.

Backstamp: Red transfer print "Wade England"

No.	Description	Colourways	Size	U.S.$	Can.$	U.K.£
1a	Venetian	Black; red inside	Small/63	20.00	30.00	10.00
1b	Venetian	Blue; olive green inside	Small/63	20.00	30.00	10.00
2	Venetian	Black; red inside	Medium/108	20.00	30.00	10.00
3	Venetian	Black; grey inside	Large/133	30.00	40.00	15.00

WADE IRELAND

IRISH PORCELAIN

SHAPE I.P.37, FLOWERPOT HOLDER, c.1952-1979

This flowerpot holder has five rows of knurls and shamrock leaves on it. It was reissued in the 1970s and discontinued in 1979.

Backstamp: Impressed "Irish Porcelain" curved over a shamrock with "Made in Ireland" impressed in a straight line underneath

No.	Description	Colourways	Size	U.S.$	Can.$	U.K.£
1	Planter	Brown/blue	101	40.00	55.00	20.00

SHAPE C.302, JARDINIERES, c.1955-c.1985

These two-handled jardinieres have an embossed design of raindrops around the bottom of the oval bowl. They originally came packaged in a brown cardboard box with a green label that reads "Irish Porcelain Created by Wade of Ireland." They were first issued in the mid 1950s, then again in the 1970s and 1980s.

Backstamp: **A.** Impressed "Irish Porcelain" over a shamrock and "Wade Co Armagh" impressed underneath
B. Embossed "Irish Porcelain" over a small shamrock with embossed "Made in Ireland," all inside a wreath of Irish knots
C. Black ink stamp "Irish Porcelain" over a shamrock with black ink stamp "Made in Ireland" underneath

No.	Description	Colourways	Size	U.S.$	Can.$	U.K.£
1	Jardiniere	Grey/blue/green	Small/65	25.00	35.00	12.00
2	Jardiniere	Grey/blue/green	Large/100	38.00	50.00	20.00

Wade Ireland, Violet Posy Bowl

POSY BOWLS AND LOGS

1934-1988

Posy bowls and logs are usually low containers meant to hold short-stemmed flowers. The items in this section range from 28-millimetres to 120-millimetres high. They come in several novelty shapes, including a caterpillar posy bowl, a donkey and cart, and a duck posy bowl.

The first measurement given in the listings is the height of the piece, the second is its width or length. The items are listed in alphabetical order.

Wade Heath
Wade Ireland

BACKSTAMPS

Ink Stamps

Embossed Backstamps

Most of the ink stamps found on posy bowls are from Wade Heath and range from 1934 to 1937. Wade Ireland used a black ink stamp on some of its duck posy bowls from 1954 to the 1960s.

Impressed Backstamps

The majority of backstamps used on posy bowls are embossed, and most of them read "Wade England." They were primarily used in the 1950s, but also appear on the log bowl produced in 1988. Wade Ireland used an embossed backstamp for its 1957 to 1958 Valencia posy bowls.

All the impressed backstamps used on posy bowls were produced by Wade Ireland. They range in dates from the early 1950s to the mid 1980s.

WADE HEATH

POSY BOWLS

ASCOT POSY BOWLS, 1957-1958

These fluted bowls have a 25-millimetre-high model of a horse standing on a plinth in the centre. They were created by Paul Zalman, who also designed the cherub posy bowls. They were first issued in August 1957 and withdrawn in January 1958.

Backstamp: Embossed "Wade Porcelain Made in England"

No.	Description	Colourways	Size	U.S.$	Can.$	U.K.£
1a	Ascot	Blue; white horse	50 x 105	80.00	110.00	40.00
1b	Ascot	Brown; white horse	50 x 105	80.00	110.00	40.00
1c	Ascot	Grey; white horse	50 x 105	80.00	110.00	40.00
1d	Ascot	Turquoise; white horse	50 x 105	80.00	110.00	40.00

BARGE POSY BOWLS, SHAPE S25 AND 32, 1954, 1972

The canal barges were issued in two different styles.

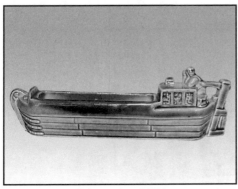

Style one - issued 1954

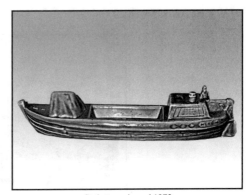

Style two - issued 1972

Backstamp: **A.** Embossed "Wade England Regd in Gt. Britain No 871886"
B. Embossed "Wade England"

No.	Description	Colourways	Size	U.S.$	Can.$	U.K.£
1a	Style one	Beige	60 x 195	30.00	40.00	15.00
1b	Style one	Green	60 x 195	30.00	40.00	15.00
2	Style two	Beige	40 x 198	50.00	70.00	25.00

WADE HEATH *(cont.)*

BRIDGE POSY BOWLS, SHAPE S25/31, 1954-1958

Two styles of bridge posy bowls were produced due to the replacement of a broken die. The top of the bridge on style one is curved and has a swallow on it. The bridge on style two has a straight top and the bird has been omitted. They were withdrawn in January 1958.

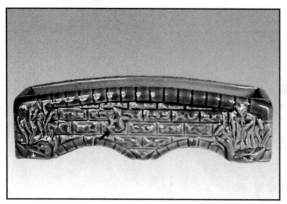

Style one, curved bridge

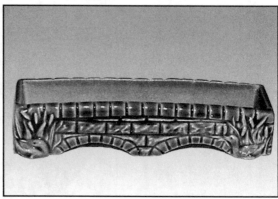

Style two, straight bridge

Backstamp: Embossed "Wade England Regd in Gt. Britain No 871653"

No.	Description	Colourways	Size	U.S.$	Can.$	U.K.£
1a	Curved bridge/swallow	Beige	43 x 150	30.00	40.00	15.00
1b	Curved bridge/swallow	Green	43 x 150	30.00	40.00	15.00
1c	Curved bridge/swallow	Honey brown/brown	43 x 150	40.00	55.00	20.00
1d	Curved Bridge/swallow	White	43 x 150	40.00	55.00	20.00
2a	Straight bridge	Beige	43 x 150	30.00	40.00	15.00
2b	Straight bridge	Green	43 x 150	30.00	40.00	15.00

CATERPILLAR POSY BOWLS, 1935-1937

Backstamp: Black ink stamp "Flaxman Ware Hand Made Pottery by Wadeheath"

No.	Description	Colourways	Size	U.S.$	Can.$	U.K.£
1a	Caterpillar	Beige	73 x 290	90.00	120.00	48.00
1b	Caterpillar	Pale orange	73 x 290	90.00	120.00	48.00

WADE HEATH (cont.)

CHERUB POSY BOWLS, 1957-1959

These bowls were modelled by Paul Zalman. They were first issued in August 1957 for a price of 4/6d, then withdrawn in January 1959. For similar bowls without the cherub and swan, see primrose posy bowls.

Backstamp: Embossed "Wade Porcelain Made in England"

No.	Description	Colourways	Size	U.S.$	Can.$	U.K.£
1a	Cherub	Green outside; yellow inside; flesh-coloured cherub; white swan	100 x 100	90.00	120.00	45.00
1b	Cherub	Grey outside; yellow inside; flesh-coloured cherub; white swan	100 x 100	90.00	120.00	45.00

CHEVALINE POSY BOWLS, 1955-1959

These crescent-shaped bowls have an embossed design of horses and leafy branches on both sides and handles that resemble curled knots. They were first issued in September 1955.

Backstamp: Embossed "Wade England"

No.	Description	Colourways	Size	U.S.$	Can.$	U.K.£
1a	Chevaline	Beige	65 x 155	38.00	55.00	22.00
1b	Chevaline	Green	65 x 155	38.00	55.00	22.00

WADE HEATH (cont.)

CHIMPANZEE POSY BOWL, 1959-1960

This posy bowl was first issued in September 1959 for an original price of 3/6d.

Backstamp: Embossed "Wade Porcelain Made in England"

No.	Description	Colourways	Size	U.S.$	Can.$	U.K.£
1	Chimpanzee	Green trunk; grey-brown chimpanzee	80 x 90	75.00	100.00	40.00

FLAT-BACKED POSY BOWL, 1955-1959

This posy bowl, with a flat back, although not marked Wade is decorated in the typical 1950s green glaze and style of Wade posy bowls. Embossed on the base is Dee Cee Ware England, Dee Cee being the trade name of Desmond Cooper whose backstamp is found on a large number of Wade souvenir and decorative wares. It also has a similarity with the Wade Traditional Posy bowl (see page 297).

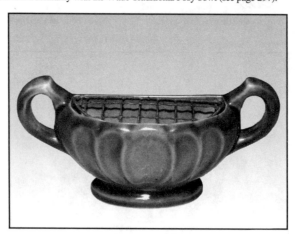

Backstamp: Embossed "DEE CEE Ware England" in the hollow of the base

No.	Description	Colourways	Size	U.S.$	Can.$	U.K.£
1	Flat-backed posy bowl	Green	110 x 210	22.00	30.00	15.00

WADE HEATH (cont.)

GLOBE POSY BOWL, SHAPE 216, 1934-1937

These bowls have six flower pockets around the outside. The 1934 bowls were hand painted but from 1935 they were issued in mottled Flaxman glazes.

Butterfly design

Flower design

Backstamp: **A.** Black ink stamp "WadeHeath England" with a lion and impressed "216"
B. Black ink stamp "Flaxman Ware Hand Made Pottery by Wadeheath England" with impressed "216"

No.	Description	Colourways	Size	U.S.$	Can.$	U.K.£
1a	Butterfly	Cream; blue/pink/yellow flowers; yellow/brown butterfly	120 x 150	130.00	175.00	65.00
1b	Cottage	White; orange/yellow cottage, flowers	120 x 150	130.00	175.00	65.00
1c	Flowers	Cream/orange; blue/pink/orange flowers	120 x 150	130.00	175.00	65.00
1d	Flowers	Cream; orange pockets; orange/blue flowers; blue base	120 x 150	130.00	175.00	65.00
1e	Mottled	Mottled blue/dark blue flecks	120 x 150	90.00	120.00	45.00
1f	Mottled	Mottled brown/yellow/green	120 x 150	90.00	120.00	45.00
1g	Mottled	Mottled dark brown/light brown	120 x 150	90.00	120.00	45.00
1h	Mottled	Mottled green/brown	120 x 150	90.00	120.00	45.00
1i	Mottled	Mottled green/dark green flecks	120 x 150	90.00	120.00	45.00
1j	Mottled	Mottled orange/dark green	120 x 150	90.00	120.00	45.00

WADE HEATH (cont.)

GRECIAN URN POSY BOWLS, 1955-1959

These posy bowls have an embossed decoration of oval stones and dots around the top rim and the stem. They also have a six-sided foot. The bowl shown has a fitted double-wire frame, which holds small flowers in place. Some of these bowls have been found with small holes in the top rim. These are for a single-wire flower frame.

Backstamp: Embossed "Wade" in the hollow of the base

No.	Description	Colourways	Size	U.S.$	Can.$	U.K.£
1a	Grecian urn	Marbled blue	80 x 110	32.00	45.00	20.00
1b	Grecian urn	Green	80 x 110	32.00	45.00	20.00
1c	Grecian urn	Beige	80 x 110	32.00	45.00	20.00

KOALA BEAR POSY BOWL, 1957-1959

This bowl was first issued in March 1957, when it sold for 2/11d, and was withdrawn in January 1959.

Backstamp: Embossed "Wade Porcelain Made in England"

No.	Description	Colourways	Size	U.S.$	Can.$	U.K.£
1	Koala bear	Green; brown koala	55 x 80	55.00	80.00	35.00

WADE HEATH (cont.)

LOG POSY BOWLS, 1988

Two log-shaped posy bowls were produced by Wade in early February 1988, they were advertised as "Woodlands Log Posy Bowls".

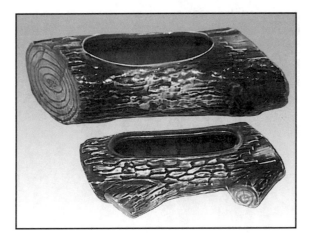

Backstamp: Embossed "Wade England"

No.	Description	Colourways	Size	U.S.$	Can.$	U.K.£
1	Log	Light brown/dark brown/grey	Small /57 x 177	20.00	30.00	10.00
2	Log	Light brown/dark brown/grey	Large/101 x 255	30.00	40.00	15.00

MERMAID POSY BOWLS, 1955-1959

These bowls have an embossed design of starfish, seahorses and seaweed on them. Mermaids form the handles of the bowl, each one looking to her right. These bowls were first issued in September 1955.

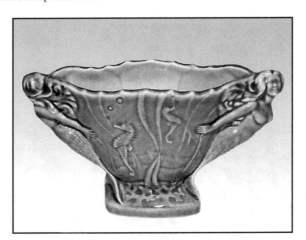

Backstamp: Embossed "Wade England"

No.	Description	Colourways	Size	U.S.$	Can.$	U.K.£
1a	Mermaid	Beige	Small/60 x 100	38.00	55.00	18.00
1b	Mermaid	Green	Small/60 x 100	38.00	55.00	18.00
2a	Mermaid	Beige	Large/90 x 150	45.00	65.00	22.00
2b	Mermaid	Green	Large/90 x 150	45.00	65.00	22.00

WADE HEATH *(cont.)*

PALERMO POSY BOWLS, 1957-1959

These posy bowls were first issued in August 1957 and withdrawn in January 1959.

Backstamp: Embossed "Wade Porcelain Made in England"

No.	Description	Colourways	Size	U.S.$	Can.$	U.K.£
1a	Palermo	Beige	85 x 155	30.00	40.00	15.00
1b	Palermo	Green	85 x 155	30.00	40.00	15.00
1c	Palermo	White	85 x 155	30.00	40.00	15.00

PEGASUS POSY BOWL, 1958-1959

The open wings of this mythical flying horse form the posy bowl. It was first issued in January 1958 and sold for 10/6d. It was withdrawn in January 1959.

Backstamp: Embossed "Wade Porcelain Made in England"

No.	Description	Colourways	Size	U.S.$	Can.$	U.K.£
1	Pegasus	Yellow; blue mane, hooves, tail	110 x 145	130.00	175.00	65.00

WADE HEATH (cont.)

POPPY POSY BOWLS, 1957-1959

These small bowls, first advertised in January 1954, are shaped in the form of an open four-petalled poppy with embossed petals and stamens.

Backstamp: Unmarked

No.	Description	Colourways	Size	U.S.$	Can.$	U.K.£
1a	Poppy	Bright yellow/white; green stamens	45	44.00	60.00	25.00
1b	Poppy	Dull yellow/white; black stamens	45	44.00	60.00	25.00
1c	Poppy	Red/white; green stamens	45	44.00	60.00	25.00

PRIMROSE POSY BOWLS, 1957-1959

These are the same shape as the cherub posy bowls, but without the centre pillar and cherub. The first style still has the square indentation in the middle where the pillar would fit; there is no indentation in the second style. They were first issued in August 1957 and withdrawn in January 1959.

Primrose bowl with indentation   Primrose bowl without indentation

Backstamp: Embossed "Wade Porcelain Made in England"

No.	Description	Colourways	Size	U.S.$	Can.$	U.K.£
1	Indentation	Pale blue outside; yellow inside	50 x 100	30.00	40.00	15.00
2a	No indentation	Cream outside; light green inside	50 x 100	30.00	40.00	15.00
2b	No indentation	Cream outside; pale blue inside	50 x 100	30.00	40.00	15.00
2c	No indentation	Dark green outside; pink inside	50 x 100	30.00	40.00	15.00
2d	No indentation	Grey outside; yellow inside	50 x 100	30.00	40.00	15.00

WADE HEATH *(cont.)*

SWALLOW POSY BOWLS, 1957-1961

These bowls were modelled by William Harper and first issued in August 1957. The original cost was 4/6d.

Backstamp: Unknown

No.	Description	Colourways	Size	U.S.$	Can.$	U.K.£
1a	Swallow	Brown; blue/white bird	105 x 105	60.00	80.00	30.00
1b	Swallow	Green; blue/white bird	105 x 105	60.00	80.00	30.00
1c	Swallow	White; blue/white/green bird	105 x 105	60.00	80.00	30.00

WADE HEATH *(cont.)*

TRADITIONAL POSY BOWL, SHAPE S.25/26, 1954-1959

The small bowl originally cost 2/3d, and the large bowl cost 3/11d. They were withdrawn in January 1959.

Backstamp: Embossed "Wade England"

No.	Description	Colourways	Size	U.S.$	Can.$	U.K.£
1a	Traditional	Beige	Small/45 x 100	15.00	22.00	10.00
1b	Traditional	Green	Small/45 x 100	15.00	22.00	10.00
1c	Traditional	White	Small/45 x 100	15.00	22.00	10.00
2a	Traditional	Beige	Large/70 x 155	24.00	35.00	15.00
2b	Traditional	Dark Green	Large/70 x 155	24.00	35.00	15.00
2c	Traditional	Mint green	Large/70 x 155	28.00	40.00	18.00
2d	Traditional	Mottled grey-blue	Large/70 x 155	24.00	35.00	15.00
2e	Traditional	Pink	Large/70 x 155	24.00	35.00	15.00
2f	Traditional	Royal blue	Large/70 x 155	24.00	35.00	15.00
2g	Traditional	White	Large/70 x 155	24.00	35.00	15.00

VALENCIA POSY BOWLS, 1957-1958

Valencia posy bowls were produced by Wade and Wade Ireland during the same period. The slight size variation is due to the replacement of worn dies. They were first issued in August 1957 for a price of 3/6d, and withdrawn in January 1958.

Valencia posy bowl

Backstamp: Embossed "Wade Porcelain made in England"

No.	Description	Colourways	Size	U.S.$	Can.$	U.K.£
1a	Valencia	Beige	65 x 148	10.00	15.00	5.00
1b	Valencia	Green	65 x 148	10.00	15.00	5.00
1c	Valencia	White	65 x 148	10.00	15.00	5.00

WADE HEATH (cont.)

POSY LOGS

C-SHAPED POSY LOGS, SHAPE S.25/24, 1954-1959

These posy logs are finished with a bark and wood-knots design. They originally sold for 2/3d. The log posy bowls were first advertised in January 1954 and were withdrawn in January 1959.

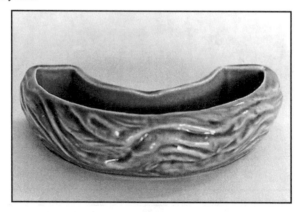

Backstamp: Embossed "Wade England"

No.	Description	Colourways	Size	U.S.$	Can.$	U.K.£
1a	C-shape	Beige	30 x 140	14.00	18.00	7.00
1b	C-shape	Green	30 x 140	14.00	18.00	7.00
1c	C-shape	Pale blue	30 x 140	14.00	18.00	7.00

C-SHAPED POSY LOGS WITH RABBIT OR SQUIRREL, 1954-1959

These posy logs are similar to the C-shaped posy logs with the addition of a rabbit or squirrel sitting on one end of the log. The rabbit model was first produced in January 1954, and the squirrel was added in 1955. The original price was 2/11d.

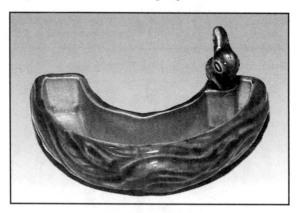

Backstamp: Embossed "Wade England"

No.	Description	Colourways	Size	U.S.$	Can.$	U.K.£
1a	Rabbit	Beige	60 x 140	22.00	32.00	12.00
1b	Rabbit	Green	60 x 140	22.00	32.00	12.00
2a	Squirrel	Beige	60 x 140	22.00	32.00	12.00
2b	Squirrel	Green	60 x 140	22.00	32.00	12.00

WADE HEATH *(cont.)*

S-SHAPED POSY LOGS, SHAPE S.25/25, 1954-1959

These posy logs are embossed with a bark and wood-knots design. When they were first issued, they sold for 2/3d. The log posy bowls were first advertised in January 1954 and were withdrawn in January 1959.

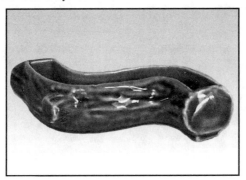

Backstamp: Embossed "Wade England"

No.	Description	Colourways	Size	U.S.$	Can.$	U.K.£
1a	S-shape	Brown	30 x 140	10.00	15.00	5.00
1b	S-shape	Dark green	30 x 140	10.00	15.00	5.00
1c	S-shape	Ming green	30 x 140	10.00	15.00	5.00
1d	S-shape	Pale blue	30 x 140	10.00	15.00	5.00
1e	S-shape	Royal blue	30 x 140	10.00	15.00	5.00
1f	S-shape	Salmon pink	30 x 140	10.00	15.00	5.00
1g	S-shape	White	30 x 140	10.00	15.00	5.00

S-SHAPED POSY LOGS WITH RABBIT OR SQUIRREL, 1954-1959

These logs combine the S-shaped posy logs with a model of a seated rabbit or squirrel. The rabbit model was used first; in 1955 the squirrel was added to the range. They originally sold for 2/11d. These models were withdrawn in January 1959.

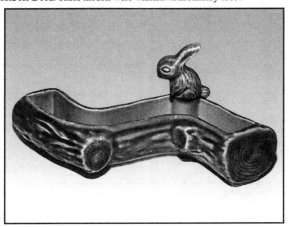

Backstamp: Embossed "Wade England"

No.	Description	Colourways	Size	U.S.$	Can.$	U.K.£
1a	Rabbit	Beige	60 x 140	22.00	32.00	12.00
1b	Rabbit	Green	60 x 140	22.00	32.00	12.00
2a	Squirrel	Beige	60 x 140	22.00	32.00	12.00
2b	Squirrel	Green	60 x 140	22.00	32.00	12.00

WADE HEATH *(cont.)*

STRAIGHT POSY LOGS, SHAPE S.25/10, 1954-1959

Backstamp: Embossed "Wade England"

No.	Description	Colourways	Size	U.S.$	Can.$	U.K.£
1a	Straight log	Beige	28 x 120	10.00	15.00	5.00
1b	Straight log	Green	28 x 120	10.00	15.00	5.00
1c	Straight log	Ming green	28 x 120	10.00	15.00	5.00
1d	Straight log	Pale blue	28 x 120	10.00	15.00	5.00
1e	Straight log	Royal blue	28 x 120	10.00	15.00	5.00
1f	Straight log	Salmon pink	28 x 120	10.00	15.00	5.00
1g	Straight log	Turquoise	28 x 120	10.00	15.00	5.00
1h	Straight log	White	28 x 120	10.00	15.00	5.00

STRAIGHT POSY LOGS WITH RABBIT OR SQUIRREL, 1954-1959

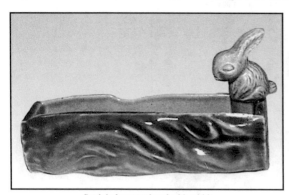
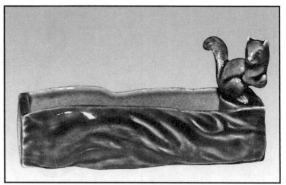

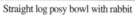
Straight log posy bowl with rabbit   Straight log posy bow with squirrel

Backstamp: Embossed "Wade England"

No.	Description	Colourways	Size	U.S.$	Can.$	U.K.£
1a	Rabbit	Beige	60 x 120	25.00	35.00	10.00
1b	Rabbit	Green	60 x 120	25.00	35.00	10.00
2a	Squirrel	Beige	60 x 120	25.00	35.00	10.00
2b	Squirrel	Green	60 x 120	25.00	35.00	10.00
2c	Squirrel	White	60 x 120	25.00	35.00	10.00

WADE HEATH (cont.)

POSY RINGS

POSY RING, SHAPE No. UNKNOWN, 1937

This posy ring has a trough for short-stemmed flowers and is decorated with a rolling scroll design around the outside.

Photograph not available
at press time

Backstamp: Black ink stamp "Flaxman Ware Hand Made Pottery by Wadeheath England"

No.	Description	Colourways	Size	U.S.$	Can.$	U.K.£
1	Posy ring	Mottled green/grey	70 x 229	50.00	70.00	25.00

WADE IRELAND

A small range of Wade Ireland posy bowls were introduced and reissued throughout the 30-plus years of production. Only approximate dates can be given as very often the original moulds, which included impressed and embossed marks, were reissued with the same marks. With the exception of the shamrock range, and a small series of Mourne vases, the posy bowls were produced in the easily recognizable Irish Wade blues and brownish green glazes. The posy bowls are listed by shape number first, followed by the series or shape name if known. Almost all the Wade Ireland vases have a shape number (*I.P.* stands for Irish porcelain; *S.R.* for Shamrock Range). Items found without shape numbers are listed in order of shape.

IRISH PORCELAIN, POSY BOWLS

SHAPE I.P.34
Violet Posy Bowl, c.1952, c.1975-c.1985

This miniature model has three rows of impressed and embossed knurls, dots and shamrocks on it. Although it is actually a thistle-shaped vase, Wade Ireland catalogued it as a bowl.

Backstamp: Impressed "Irish Porcelain" over a shamrock, impressed "Made in Ireland" underneath, with "H" inside the shamrock

No.	Description	Colourways	Size	U.S.$	Can.$	U.K.£
1	Violet bowl	Grey/blue	65 x 40	10.00	15.00	5.00

IRISH PORCELAIN (cont.)

SHAPES I.P.40, I.P.41, I.P.42 and I.P.43
Killarney Urn Posy Bowls, C.1953-c.1985

These posy bowls are decorated with an embossed design of knurls, dots and shamrocks.

Backstamp: A. Impressed "Irish Porcelain" over a shamrock and "Made in Ireland" underneath in a curved shape
B. Impressed "Irish Porcelain" curved above a shamrock and "Made in Ireland" in a straight line underneath
C. Impressed "Made in Ireland Irish Porcelain Wade eire tir a dheanta" in a circle with a shamrock and crown design

No.	Description	Colourways	Size	U.S.$	Can.$	U.K.£
1	Killarney urn, I.P.43	Grey/blue	Miniature/78	10.00	15.00	5.00
2	Killarney urn, I.P.42	Grey/blue	Small/114	20.00	30.00	10.00
3	Killarney urn, I.P.41	Grey/blue	Medium/153	20.00	30.00	10.00
4	Killarney urn, I.P.40	Grey/blue	Large/202	30.00	40.00	15.00

SHAPE I.P.602
Three-legged Posy Bowl, c.1955, c.1975-c.1985

The three-legged posy bowl has an impressed design of shamrocks around the middle.

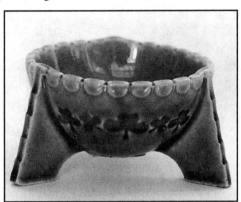

Backstamp: Impressed "Irish Porcelain" curved over a shamrock with "Made in Ireland" impressed in a straight line underneath

No.	Description	Colourways	Size	U.S.$	Can.$	U.K.£
1a	Three legs	Blue/green	45 x 65	10.00	15.00	5.00
1b	Three legs	Light brown	45 x 65	10.00	15.00	5.00

IRISH PORCELAIN *(cont.)*

SHAPE I.P.603
Irish Cooking Pot Posy Bowl c.1955, c.1975-1986

There are two types of the Irish cooking pot. When it was first issued in the 1950s it had a flat base, then, when a new mould was made, three feet were added. The Cooking pots were also sold as sugar bowls with matching cream jugs (see *The Charlton Standard Catalogue of Wade, Volume Three, Tableware*). It was re-issued in the 1970s until the 1980s. (For cooking pot with green Shamrock design see Shamrock Range page 305).

Cooking pot with feet

Backstamp: Impressed "Irish Porcelain" curved over a shamrock with "Made in Ireland, Wade Co. Armagh" underneath

No.	Description	Colourways	Size	U.S.$	Can.$	U.K.£
1	Cooking pot, flat	Greenish brown/blue	60 x 70	10.00	15.00	5.00
2	Cooking pot, feet	Greenish brown/blue	60 x 70	10.00	15.00	5.00

DUCK POSY BOWLS, 1954-c.1965

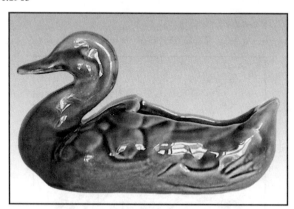

Irish porcelain duck

Backstamp: **A.** Impressed "Irish Porcelain Made in Ireland" with a shamrock leaf
B. Black ink stamp "Irish Porcelain Made in Ireland" with a shamrock leaf
C. Unmarked

No.	Description	Colourways	Size	U.S.$	Can.$	U.K.£
1	Duck	Grey/blue	105 x 173	60.00	80.00	30.00
2	Duck	Grey/blue/green	100 x 180	60.00	80.00	30.00

SHAMROCK RANGE

POSY BOWLS

SHAPE S.R.19
Shamrock Urn Posy Bowl, 1983-1986

The Shamrock Range was issued from 1983-1986. The Shamrock Urn is similar to the Irish Porcelain Killarney Urn, but does not have an embossed design.

Photograph not available
at press time

Backstamp: Printed "Made in Ireland eire tir A dheanta Porcelain Wade" over a shamrock and crown design

No.	Description	Colourways	Size	U.S.$	Can.$	U.K.£
1	Shamrock urn	White; green shamrocks	S.R.19/202	30.00	40.00	15.00

SHAPE S.R.20
Shamrock Cooking Pot Posy Bowl, 1983-1986

The three-legged cooking pot is similar to the Irish Porcelain cooking pot, but does not have an embossed design (see page 304).

Backstamp: Green printed "Made in Ireland eire tir A dheanta Porcelain Wade" over a shamrock and crown design

No.	Description	Colourways	Size	U.S.$	Can.$	U.K.£
1	Shamrock cooking pot	White; green shamrocks	S.R.20/60 x 70	30.00	40.00	15.00

SHAMROCK RANGE (cont.)

SHAPE C.338
Donkey And Cart Posy Bowls, 1956-1961

These items are part of the Shamrock Pottery Series, which included the pink elephant, the Irish comical pig, the shamrock cottage and the pixie dish (see *The Charlton Standard Catalogue of Wade Whimsical Collectables*). The first style of this posy bowl has an open back on the cart with the shafts not touching the neck, and the second style has a solid back with the shafts touching the neck.

Style one, open back

Style two, closed back

Backstamp: Embossed "Shamrock Pottery Made in Ireland"

No.	Description	Colourways	Size	U.S.$	Can.$	U.K.£
1	Open back	Grey/blue/green	100 x 158	70.00	100.00	45.00
2	Closed back	Grey/blue/green	91 x 168	65.00	95.00	35.00

VASES AND URNS

1933-1992

All of the vases produced up to World War II were made by Wade Heath. When production of decorative ware resumed following the war, production was spread out amongst all Wade's potteries, including Wade Ireland beginning in the 1950s.

Those items with shape numbers are listed first, in number order. The rest of the vases and urns follow in alphabetical order, with the Wade Ireland vases at the end of the listing.

Wade Heath
Wade Ireland

BACKSTAMPS

Ink Stamps

Transfer Prints

From 1957 to 1992 Wade used a variety of black, black and red, and red and gold transfer prints. Some of these backstamps incorporated impressed marks, often the shape number, as well.

Impressed Backstamps

Impressed backstamps can be found on some Harmony Ware vases produced from 1957 to the early 1960s. Wade Ireland used impressed marks on its vases from 1950 to the mid 1980s.

Embossed Backstamps

Wade England began using embossed backstamps in 1962, and by 1959 they could also be found on Wade Ireland vases until 1982.

Many of the vases in this section were produced in the 1930s and are marked with a Wade Heath backstamp, which often includes a lion and an impressed shape number. These stamps are predominantly black, but may also be found in orange, red and green.

From the 1940s to the early 1950s, black Harvest Ware and green Gothic Ware ink stamps were used. The standard Wade England ink stamps, in green or black, appeared from the late 1940s to the mid 1960s. Wade Ireland used an ink stamp intermittently until the mid 1980s.

WADE HEATH

SHAPE 17, ORCADIA WARE, 1933-1934

This vase, shape 17, was issued in two colourways. The flowered vase is green with yellow hand-painted flowers, while Orcadia Ware was produced in vivid streaked glazes that were allowed to run over the rims and down the inside and outside of the vases. With this method of decoration no two items are identical.

Orcadia ware

Backstamp: **A.** Black ink stamp "WadeHeath England" with a lion and impressed "17"
B. Orange ink stamp "Wadeheath Orcadia Ware"
C. Black ink stamp "British Roskyl Pottery"

No.	Description	Colourways	Size	U.S.$	Can.$	U.K.£
1	Orcadia	Orange/green/yellow streaks	190	150.00	200.00	75.00
2	Orcadia	Green/orange/yellow streaks	215	150.00	200.00	75.00
3a	Flowers	Green; yellow flowers	230	150.00	200.00	75.00
3b	Orcadia	Green/orange/yellow streaks	230	150.00	200.00	75.00

WADE HEATH (cont.)

SHAPE 18, ORCADIA WARE, 1933-1937

Numbers 1d - 1f of these two handled vases have an unusual sponged-shell like design. The colours are listed in order from top to bottom. The Orcadia ware decorated vase was produced between 1933 and 1935. The brightly coloured splash design looks almost like crocus flowers.

Bands

Marigolds

Sponged shell

Backstamp: **A.** Orange ink stamp "Wades Orcadia Ware" with a lion, 1933-1934
B. Black ink stamp "WadeHeath England" with a lion and impressed "18, 1933-1935"
D. Black ink stamp "Wadeheath, England" with impressed "18"

No.	Description	Colourways	Size	U.S.$	Can.$	U.K.£
1a	Bands	Orange handles; orange/yellow/brown horizontal bands; orange/yellow/brown streaks	171	65.00	100.00	50.00
1b	Orcadia	Orange handles; brown/yellow/orange streaks	171	65.00	100.00	50.00
1c	Splash	Orange handles; turquoise with yellow/orange splashes	171	65.00	100.00	50.00
1d	Sponged shells	Mottled blue handles; blue/green/yellow/orange shell design	171	65.00	100.00	50.00
1e	Sponged shells	Mottled purple handles; purple/green/yellow/ orange shell design	171	65.00	100.00	50.00
1f	Sponged shells, marigolds	Brown handles; orange and yellow marigolds; brown shell design	171	65.00	100.00	50.00

WADE HEATH (cont.)

SHAPE 19, FLAXMAN AND ORCADIA WARE, 1933-1937

Orcadia ware vases were produced between 1933 and 1935. No 1n has an unusual sponged shell like design.

Art Nouveau

Orcadia ware

Sponged shells

Backstamp: **A.** Orange ink stamp "Wades Orcadia Ware" with a lion, 1933
B. Orange ink stamp "Wadeheath Orcadia Ware", 1933-1934
C. Black ink stamp "WadeHeath England" with a lion and impressed "19", 1933-1935
D. Black ink stamp "Flaxman Ware Hand Made Pottery by Wadeheath, England" with impressed "19", 1935-1937

No.	Description	Colourways	Size	U.S.$	Can.$	U.K.£
1a	Art Nouveau	Orange; brown leaf design	120	110.00	145.00	58.00
1b	Bird	Cream; brown rim, handles, tree stump; orange bird	120	130.00	165.00	65.00
1c	Bird	Green/cream; orange/mauve flowers; brown bird	120	130.00	165.00	65.00
1d	Bird	Yellow; blue flower; brown bird (tube lined)	120	130.00	165.00	65.00
1e	Flowers	Brown; orange/yellow flowers	120	130.00	165.00	65.00
1f	Flowers	Green handles; brown flecks; pink flowers; green leaves	120	130.00	165.00	65.00
1g	Flowers	Orange; blue flowers; green leaves	120	130.00	165.00	65.00
1h	Leaves	Mustard; brown leaves	120	130.00	165.00	65.00
1i	Mottled	Mottled orange	120	70.00	95.00	35.00
1j	Mottled	Turquoise; brown/turquoise/green design	120	110.00	145.00	55.00
1k	Orcadia	Green/orange	120	90.00	120.00	50.00
1l	Orcadia	Orange/yellow	120	90.00	120.00	50.00
1m	Orcadia	Orange/yellow/brown streaks	120	70.00	95.00	50.00
1n	Sponged shells	Blue handles; blue/yellow/green/orange shells	120	130.00	165.00	65.00
1o	Stripes	Orange top, handles; bright blue/orange/green/ yellow/purple stripes	120	110.00	145.00	55.00

WADE HEATH *(cont.)*

SHAPE 21/12, FLAXMAN AND ORCADIA WARE, 1935-1937

These grooved vases have an unusual double shape number. The hand painted Rabbits at Sunset design has also been found on a ribbed wall plaque. The brightly coloured splash design looks almost like crocus flowers.

Orcadia ware

Rabbits at sunset

Splashes

Backstamp: **A.** Black ink stamp "Wadeheath, England" with Lion and impressed "21/12" c.1934-1937
B. Black ink stamp "Flaxman Ware Hand Made Pottery Wadeheath, England" with impressed "21/12" c.1935-1937
C. Orange ink stamp "Wadeheath Orcadia Ware"

No.	Description	Colourways	Size	U.S.$	Can.$	U.K.£
1	Orcadia	Mustard/brown/orange streaks	Small/170	120.00	160.00	60.00
2a	Orcadia	Mustard/brown/orange streaks	Large/295	200.00	290.00	80.00
2b	Orcadia	Blue/brown/yellow/orange streaks	Large/295	200.00	290.00	80.00
2c	Rabbits at sunset	Pale blue; brown rabbits; orange sun	Large/295	200.00	290.00	80.00
2d	Splashes	Brown/yellow/orange splashes	Large/295	200.00	290.00	80.00

WADE HEATH (cont.)

SHAPE 23, FLAXMAN AND ORCADIA WARE, 1935-1937

These vases with moulded feet were previously catalogued as shape 11. A new example has been found with a clearly impressed "23."

Art Nouveau

Heron

Backstamp: **A.** Black ink stamp "Flaxman Ware Hand Made Pottery by Wadeheath, England" with impressed "23"
B. Orange ink stamp "Wadeheath Orcadia Ware"

No.	Description	Colourways	Size	U.S.$	Can.$	U.K.£
1a	Art Nouveau	Amber; brown/green foliage; orange/brown flowers	150	120.00	160.00	65.00
1b	Heron	Cream; green foliage; orange/blue flowers; brown outline of heron	150	120.00	160.00	65.00
1c	Orcadia	Green streaked top, base; orange streaked middle	150	120.00	160.00	60.00

SHAPE 36, BRITISH ROSKYL, 1935-c.1952

This vase with an orb-shaped body, and a round foot, has the unusual British Roskyl Pottery backstamp.

Tree and flowers

Backstamp: Black ink stamp "British Roskyl Pottery" with impressed "36"

No.	Description	Colourways	Size	U.S.$	Can.$	U.K.£
1	Tree and flowers	Cream; green tree; orange/yellow blue flowers	190	80.00	110.00	45.00

WADE HEATH *(cont.)*

SHAPE 60, ORCADIA WARE, 1933-c.1935

This pot-shaped vase is decorated in the popular Orcadia Ware design, which was produced between 1933 and 1935.

Orcadia ware

Backstamp: Orange ink stamp "Wadeheath Orcadia Ware" with impressed "60"

No.	Description	Colourways	Size	U.S.$	Can.$	U.K.£
1	Orcadia ware	Brown/green streaks	185	80.00	110.00	40.00

SHAPE INDEX

Shape 460

Shape 462

Shape 464

Shape 465

Shape 467

Shape 468

Shape 469

Shape 470

Shape 474

Shape 478

Shape 483

Shape 484

Shape 513

Shape 528

Shape 531

Shape 532

ASHTRAYS

Knurled Rim Pipe Ashtray

"Happy" Ashtray

Crinkled Edge Ashtray

Rose Rim Ashtray

Shamrocks and Irish-Knots Rim Ashtray

Souvenir Ashtray, Niagara Falls, Canada

BOXES

Gothic Ware Trinket Box

Wade Ireland Candy Box, Paddy McGredy, Floribunda Roses

CANDLESTICKS

Ribbed Candlestick

Decorative Candlestick

Crosses and Raised Knurls Candlestick

DISHES

Shell Dish, Rose print

Nova Scotia Souvenir Dish

Charactors of London Dish "Beefeater"

Oak Leaf Dish

Trinket Tray, Doberman

FLOWERS

Binnie Pot: Pansies, Rose, Wild Rose

Flower Centre: Anemones, Long Stemmed

Spherical Bowl: Wild Roses

Menu Holders: Water Lily (left), Rose (right)   Posy Ring

Triangular Vase, Stepped base

Flower Centre: Anemones, Pansies and Poppies, Short Stemmed

JARS

Jacobean Ginger Jar

Lidded Jar "Splash"

Topline Jar, Duryea Phaeton, 1904

LAMPS

Shape 407. "Banded" design

Shape 69. Harvest Ware Lamp "Peony"

Panelled Lamp "Oriental Butterfly"

Temple Jar Lamp "Kawa"

Bramble Ware Lamp, "Gold Blush" design

Regency Lamp

JUG COLOURWAYS

Pinched-mouth: Type 2, Flowers

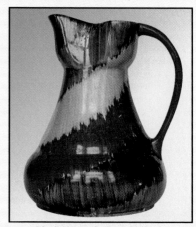

Pinched-mouth: Type 1, Bands

Pinched-mouth: Type 1, Bands

Pinched-mouth: Type 1, Bird on Branch

Pinched-mouth: Type 1, Streaks

Pinched-mouth: Type 1, Streaks

VASES

Shape 18, Orcadian Ware

Shape 69, "Splash" design

Shape 332, Harvest Ware, "Leaves" design

Shape 21, "Rabbits at Sunset"

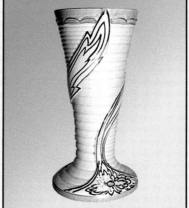

Shape 310, "Silver Flower and Leaf" design

Shape 156, Gothic Ware

Tapered Vase, "Nouvelle" design

"Egyptian Theme" design

Ovoid Shape Vase

WALL PLAQUES

Pearlstone, Butterfly

Shoveller, Female

Bottles and Jars

WALL PLATES (CHARGERS)

"Cottage"

"Blue Bird"

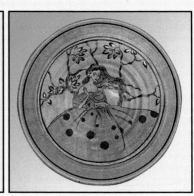

"Autumn Lady"

WALL POCKETS

Shape 229, Tulip

Shape 159, Gothic Ware

Shape 228, Blocks

WADE HEATH *(cont.)*

SHAPE 61, BRITISH ROSKYL, FLAXMAN AND ORCADIA WARE, 1933-1937

The small size Orcadia (1d) vase has a British Roskyl Pottery backstamp.

Orcadia ware

Backstamp: **A.** Black ink stamp "Wadeheath England" with a lion
B. Black ink stamped "Flaxman Ware Hand Made Pottery by Wadeheath England" with impressed No "61" (1935-1937)
C. Orange ink stamp "Wadeheath Orcadia Ware"
D. Orange ink stamp "British Roskyl Pottery"

No.	Description	Colourways	Size	U.S.$	Can.$	U.K.£
1a	Flowers	Pale yellow; black square; large mauve/orange/ blue flowers; green leaves	Small/165	180.00	245.00	75.00
1b	Heron	Cream; orange/green grass; brown flying heron	Small/165	180.00	245.00	75.00
1c	Heron flowers	Cream; green trees; orange, blue flowers; brown flying heron	Small/165	180.00	245.00;	75.00
1d	Orcadia	Grey-blue/orange/green/blue	Small/160	110.00	145.00	55.00
2a	Flowers	Pale yellow; large orange flower; green leaves	Large/170	180.00	245.00	75.00
2b	Orcadia	Green/orange	Large/170	110.00	145.00	55.00
2c	Orcadia	Grey-blue/orange/yellow	Large/170	110.00	145.00	55.00
2d	Splash	Orange; blue/green/mauve splashes	Large/170	110.00	145.00	55.00
2e	Orcadia	Yellow/orange	Large/170	110.00	145.00	55.00

WADE HEATH (cont.)

SHAPE 69, FLAXMAN, HARVEST AND ORCADIA WARE, 1935-c.1952

Orcadia ware vases were produced between 1933 and 1935. The Flaxman ware vases were produced from 1935 to 1939. The peony design vases were produced between the late 1940s and the early 1950s. The brightly coloured splash design looks almost like crocus flowers. Vase 2e has an unusual sponged shell like design.

  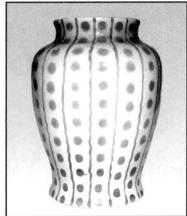

| Blue tulip | Splash | Spots |

Backstamp: **A.** Black ink stamp "Harvest Ware Wade England" with impressed "69," late 1940s-early 1950s
B. Black ink stamp "Flaxman Ware Hand Made Pottery by Wadeheath England" with impressed "69," 1935-1937
C. Black ink stamp "Flaxman Wade Heath England" with impressed "69," 1937-1939
D. Green ink stamp "Wade England" with impressed "69," late 1940s-early 1950
E. Orange ink stamp "Wadeheath Orcadia Ware"

No.	Description	Colourways	Size	U.S.$	Can.$	U.K.£
1	Orcadia	Green/brown/yellow streaks; dark brown base	Small/125	80.00	110.00	40.00
2a	Blue tulip	Cream; blue tulips	Large/200	70.00	95.00	55.00
2b	Peony	Cream; multicoloured flowers	Large/200	90.00	120.00	65.00
2c	Splash	Orange; mauve/blue/green splashes; brown base	Large/200	70.00	95.00	45.00
2d	Speckled	Blue/yellow brown speckles	Large/200	90.00	120.00	45.00
2e	Sponged shell	Cream; green/mauve shells; orange base	Large/200	65.00	80.00	40.00
2f	Spots	White; blue spots; grey lines	Large/200	70.00	95.00	45.00

WADE HEATH (cont.)

SHAPE 94, RICHMOND WITH HANDLES, 1934-1935, 1937-1939

These vases have horizontal ribs on the neck. One vase has been found that is slightly larger than the others.

| Art Nouveau | Feather and flowers | Heron |

Backstamp: **A.** Black ink stamp "WadeHeath England" with a lion and embossed "94 Richmond," 1934-1935
B. Black ink stamped "Flaxman Ware Hand Made Pottery by Wadeheath England" (1935-1937)
C. Black ink stamp "Flaxman Wade Heath England" 1937-1939
D. Black ink stamped "Flaxman Wade Heath England" embossed "94" impressed "M" (1937-1939)

No.	Description	Colourways	Size	U.S.$	Can.$	U.K.£
1a	Art Nouveau	Brown neck/base; yellow handle; brown/ yellow/green leaves and heart shape design	160	100.00	150.00	50.00
1b	Bands	Yellow; orange bands; blue/orange streaks; blue dots, cross lines	160	100.00	150.00	50.00
1c	Circles	Yellow; orange rim, handle, base, circles; blue/green leaves	160	100.00	150.00	50.00
1d	Feather/flowers	Orange, black bands; orange/blue spotted; feather; orange/mauve flowers	160	100.00	150.00	50.00
1e	Flowers	Blue/green with chevron, flowers	160	100.00	150.00	50.00
1f	Flowers	Blue/green; blue handle, flower; golden brown triangles	160	100.00	150.00	50.00
1g	Flowers	Off white; pink/blue/yellow flowers	160	100.00	150.00	50.00
1h	Orcadia	Green/yellow; brown streaks at base	160	100.00	150.00	50.00
1i	Squares	Green/blue; brown fan; blue/brown squares	160	100.00	150.00	50.00
2	Heron	Cream; green trees; orange, mauve flowers; brown flying heron	172	100.00	150.00	50.00

WADE HEATH (cont.)

SHAPE 95, RICHMOND VASE WITHOUT HANDLES, 1934-1935

Photograph not available
at press time

Backstamp: Black ink stamp "WadeHeath England" with a lion and embossed "95 Richmond"

No.	Description	Colourways	Size	U.S.$	Can.$	U.K.£
1	Stripes	Green; green/yellow top stripe; brown bottom stripe	Unknown		Unknown	

SHAPE 99, PINE, 1935-1937

The pot-shaped vase 1b has a streaked design similar to Orcadia ware.

Art Deco

Streaks

Backstamp: Black ink stamp "Flaxman Ware Hand Made Pottery by Wadeheath England" with impressed "99 Pine"

No.	Description	Colourways	Size	U.S.$	Can.$	U.K.£
1a	Art Deco	Green; blue flowers; brown deco triangles	140	80.00	130.00	50.00
1b	Streaks	Brown/green/yellow streaks	140	80.00	120.00	40.00

WADE HEATH (cont.)

SHAPE 107, 1934-1935

This vase has two handles that end on the round footed base.

Birds and flowers   Flowers

Backstamp: A. Black ink stamp "Wadeheath England" with a lion and embossed "107"
B. Black ink stamp "Flaxman Ware Hand Made Pottery by Wadeheath England" with embossed "107"

No.	Description	Colourways	Size	U.S.$	Can.$	U.K.£
1a	Bird and Flowers	White; orange bird; blue flowers; brown handles/foot/tree	225	80.00	110.00	55.00
1b	Flowers and triangles	White; pink/blue/yellow triangles and flowers	225	80.00	110.00	55.00
1c	Flower	Cream; pink flower; green leaves; grey trees/base	225	95.00	130.00	50.00
1d	Mottled	Yellow/brown/orange	225	70.00	95.00	35.00

SHAPE 129, 1934-1935

This art deco-shaped vase has two half handles, one on the upper section, the other on the opposite lower section.

Leaves   Trees and rectangles

Backstamp: Black ink stamp "Wadeheath England" with a lion and embossed "129"

No.	Description	Colourways	Size	U.S.$	Can.$	U.K.£
1a	Flowers	White; blue/orange/yellow flowers; orange handles/foot	135	225.00	275.00	135.00
1b	Leaves	Mottled yellow; green/grey/yellow leaves	135	225.00	275.00	135.00
1c	Trees and rectangles	Cream; cream trees; multicoloured flowers/rectangles	135	225.00	275.00	135.00

WADE HEATH *(cont.)*

SHAPE 156, GOTHIC WARE, c.1940

This extra large Gothic ware vase has two pronged handles near the top and base.

Backstamp: "Flaxman Wade Heath England" with impressed "156"

No.	Description	Colourways	Size	U.S.$	Can.$	U.K.£
1a	Gothic ware	Creamy yellow; green/dark green	370	105.00	150.00	65.00
1b	Gothic ware	Green	370	105.00	150.00	65.00

SHAPE 211, 1934-1935

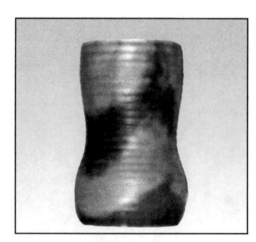

Backstamp: "Flaxmanware Handmade Pottery by Wadeheath England" with impressed "211"

No.	Description	Colourways	Size	U.S.$	Can.$	U.K.£
1	Waisted	Creamy yellow; green/dark green	165	65.00	85.00	40.00

WADE HEATH (cont.)

SHAPE 212, 1934-1935

Backstamp: **A.** Black ink stamp "Wadeheath England" with a lion and impressed "212"
B. Black ink stamp "Flaxman Wade Heath England" with impressed "212"

No.	Description	Colourways	Size	U.S.$	Can.$	U.K.£
1a	Castle	Cream; grey rim; yellow turrets; mauve/purple flowers	165	120.00	160.00	60.00
1b	Flowers	Brown; orange/yellow flowers; green leaves	165	120.00	160.00	60.00
1c	Solid colour	Pale blue	165	120.00	160.00	60.00

SHAPE 213, 1934-1935

Flowers

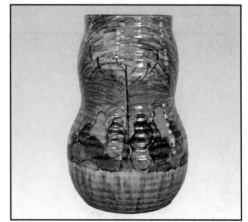

Tree

Backstamp: Black ink stamp "Wadeheath England" with a lion and impressed "213"

No.	Description	Colourways	Size	U.S.$	Can.$	U.K.£
1a	Flowers	Fawn; orange leaves; blue/red flowers	184	110.00	145.00	55.00
1b	Flowers	Mottled blue/mauve; large orange flowers; brown flying birds/trees	184	110.00	145.00	55.00
1c	Tree	Cream/brown; brown/green tree; brown rocks; green grass	184	120.00	160.00	60.00

WADE HEATH (cont.)

SHAPE 214, 1934-1935

Backstamp: Black ink stamp "Wadeheath England" with a lion and impressed "214"

No.	Description	Colourways	Size	U.S.$	Can.$	U.K.£
1a	Flowers	Mottled cream/brown; yellow leaves; orange/blue flowers	184	110.00	145.00	55.00
1b	Mottled	Mottled green	184	55.00	75.00	35.00
1c	Two tone	Pale blue/light brown	184	55.00	75.00	35.00

SHAPE 215, 1934-1937

The hand-painted vase has a cottage and trees design often seen on Wadeheath items of this era. The mottled V vase has a background of turquoise with a broad band of orange in a V shape.

Cottage and trees

Mottled V

Backstamp: Black ink stamp "Flaxman Ware Hand Made Pottery by Wadeheath England" with impressed "215" 1935-1937

No	Description	Colourways	Size	U.S.$	Can.$	U.K.£
1a	Cottage and trees	Cream/brown:/green:/grey/orange/blue flowers; green handles	190	130.00	175.00	65.00
1b	Mottled stripe	Pale blue; yellow stripe	190	110.00	145.00	55.00
1c	Mottled V	Turquoise; orange	190	130.00	175.00	55.00

WADE HEATH (cont.)

SHAPE 217, 1934-1937

There are several holes for flowers on top of the scalloped ledge in the middle of the vase.

Backstamp: A. Black ink stamp "Wadeheath England" with a lion and impressed "217", 1934-1935
B. Black ink stamp "Flaxman Ware Hand Made Pottery by Wadeheath England" with impressed "217", 1935-1937

No	Description	Colourways	Size	U.S.$	Can.$	U.K.£
1a	Flowers	Cream; orange flowers; grey shields; orange rim	225	130.00	175.00	65.00
1b	Flowers	Cream; yellow/mauve/orange flowers; green handles, shields; orange rim	225	130.00	175.00	65.00
1c	Mottled	Mottled blue	225	110.00	145.00	55.00
1d	Mottled	Mottled grey/pale blue	225	110.00	145.00	55.00

WADE HEATH (cont.)

SHAPE 243, FLAXMAN WARE, 1937-1939

Flower vase with frog

Backstamp: **A.** Black ink stamp "Wade Heath England," 1936-1940s
B. Black ink stamp "Flaxman Wade Heath England" with impressed "243"

No.	Description	Colourways	Size	U.S.$	Can.$	U.K.£
1a	Flowers	Off white; yellow pillars; pink flowers	140	120.00	165.00	60.00
1b	Solid colour	Off white	140	100.00	145.00	55.00
1c	Solid colour	Pale blue	140	100.00	145.00	55.00
1d	Solid colour	Pale green	140	100.00	145.00	55.00

WADE HEATH *(cont.)*

SHAPE 244, FLAXMAN WARE, 1937-1939

These flower holders have a flower frog inserted in the mouth. The flower holders No 1a and 1b have a poem dedicated to Mother on the front; this decorated version may have been produced for Mother's Day. The poem: "Mother, God sent the birds and sunshine to gladden all the world. He sent the foliage and flowers in radiance unfurled. He sent the sun, the moon, the stars, the pearly dew drops sweet. And then he sent you Mother dear to make it all complete."

Front, with poem

Back, with flowers

Backstamp: **A.** Black ink stamp "Flaxman Wade Heath England"
B. Black ink stamp "Wade Heath England"
C. Black ink stamp "Flaxman Ware Hand made pottery by Wadeheath England"

No.	Description	Colourways	Size	U.S.$	Can.$	U.K.£
1a	Mother Poem	Cream; yellow/orange/blue flowers; green lines; silver highlighting; black lettering	140	155.00	220.00	95.00
1b	Mother Poem	Orange flowers; green leaves, band; gold edging; brown lettering	140	155.00	220.00	95.00
1c	Mottled	Mottled brown	140	110.00	150.00	55.00
1d	Mottled	Mottled brown/green/yellow	140	110.00	150.00	55.00
1e	Solid colour	Pale blue/mauve	140	110.00	150.00	55.00

WADE HEATH *(cont.)*

SHAPE 245, 1936-c.1940

This flower holder has a flower frog in the mouth.

Backstamp: Green ink stamp "Wade Heath England"

No.	Description	Colourways	Size	U.S.$	Can.$	U.K.£
1a	Flowers	Cream; brown fins, base; blue/pink flowers	130	150.00	200.00	75.00
1b	Mottled	Mottled brown/orange	130	150.00	200.00	75.00
1c	Orcadia	Yellow/orange streaks	130	150.00	200.00	75.00

SHAPE 310, 1934-1937

This tapered vase has an embossed Art Nouveau leaf design wrapped around the body from top to bottom. The design on the flowered vase obscures the embossed leaf.

Flowers

Silver flower, leaf

Backstamp: Black ink stamped "Wadeheath England" with Lion and embossed "219"

No.	Description	Colourways	Size	U.S.$	Can.$	U.K.£
1a	Flowers	Cream; multicoloured flowers	220	185.00	255.00	60.00
1b	Silver flower /leaf	Cream; light green rim/base; silver leaf and flower	220	185.00	255.00	60.00

WADE HEATH (cont.)

SHAPE 313, FLAXMAN, HARVEST WARE, c.1948-c.1952

Cream, orange Flaxman colourway

Backstamp: **A.** Black ink stamp "Harvest Ware Wade England" with impressed "313"
B. Black ink stamp "Flaxman Wade Heath England" with impressed "313"

No.	Description	Colourways	Size	U.S.$	Can.$	U.K.£
1a	Mottled	Cream; mottled orange	225	50.00	75.00	35.00
1b	Peony	Cream; multicoloured peony flowers	225	75.00	95.00	45.00

SHAPE 314, FLAXMAN, UNKNOWN

These vases have a ribbed base and foot.

Turquoise and orange Flaxman colourway

Yellow and orange Flaxman colourway

Backstamp: Black ink stamped "Flaxman Wade Heath England" with impressed "314"

No.	Description	Colourways	Size	U.S.$	Can.$	U.K.£
1a	Flaxman	Mottled turquoise/orange	225	75.00	100.00	35.00
1b	Flaxman	Mottled yellow/orange	225	75.00	100.00	35.00

WADE HEATH (cont.)

SHAPE 315, FLAXMAN, UNKNOWN

These vases have a ribbed base and foot.

Brown Flaxman colourway

Green and orange Flaxman colourway

Backstamp: Black ink stamped "Flaxman Wade Heath England" with impressed "315"

No.	Description	Colourways	Size	U.S.$	Can.$	U.K.£
1a	Flaxman	Mottled brown	220	75.00	100.00	35.00
1b	Flaxman	Mottled green/orange	220	75.00	100.00	35.00

SHAPE 316, FLAXMAN, 1937-1939

Photograph not available
at press time

Backstamp: Black ink stamp "Flaxman Wade Heath England"

No.	Description	Colourways	Size	U.S.$	Can.$	U.K.£
1	Flaxman	Mottled beige	Unknown	100.00	135.00	45.00

WADE HEATH *(cont.)*

SHAPE 332, HARVEST WARE, c.1948-c.1953

Peony

Leaves

Backstamp: **A.** Black ink stamp "Harvest Ware Wade England" with impressed "332"
B. Black ink stamp "Wade England" with impressed "332"

No.	Description	Colourways	Size	U.S.$	Can.$	U.K.£
1a	Peony	Cream; multicoloured flowers	225	70.00	95.00	50.00
1b	Leaves	Cream; brown/coffee leaves; grey speckles	225	70.00	95.00	40.00

WADE HEATH *(cont.)*

SHAPE 333, FLAXMAN, HARVEST WARE, c.1948-c.1952 and 1961

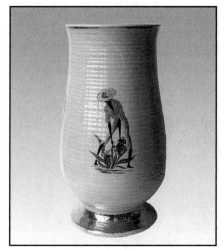

Orange and green Flaxman colourway

Tropical fruit gatherers

Backstamp: **A.** Black ink stamp "Harvest Ware Wade England" with impressed "333"
B. Black ink stamp "Flaxman Wade Heath England" with impressed "333"
C. Printed "Wade England" with impressed "333"

No.	Description	Colourways	Size	U.S.$	Can.$	U.K.£
1a	Leaves	Cream; pearlised orange rim/foot; brown leaves; pale blue berries	225	110.00	150.00	50.00
1b	Mottled	Cream/green	225	70.00	95.00	35.00
1c	Mottled	Orange/green	225	70.00	95.00	35.00
1d	Peony	Cream; multicoloured flowers	225	80.00	100.00	50.00
1e	Tropical fruit gatherers	Cream; multicoloured print; gold foot/rim	225	70.00	95.00	45.00

WADE HEATH (cont.)

SHAPE 342, HARVEST WARE, c.1948-c.1952

Leaves

Peonies

Backstamp: Black ink stamp "Harvest Ware Wade England" with impressed "342"

No.	Description	Colourways	Size	U.S.$	Can.$	U.K.£
1a	Leaves	Cream; brown leaves; pale blue berries	280	90.00	120.00	55.00
1b	Peony	Cream; multicoloured flowers	280	100.00	135.00	60.00
2	Leaves	Cream; long brown/coffee leaves; grey speckles	291	90.00	120.00	55.00

SHAPE 343, HARVEST WARE, 1937-c.1952

The aqua vase received its name from the delicate seaweed and fish design, it was in production between 1937 and 1938. The Peony series was issued c.1948-c.1952.

Aqua

Peonies

Backstamp: A. Black ink stamp "Wade Heath England" 1936-1940s
B. Black ink stamp "Harvest Ware Wade England" with impressed "343" late 1940s-early 1950s

No.	Description	Colourways	Size	U.S.$	Can.$	U.K.£
1a	Aqua	Cream/white; blue fish; orange/brown seaweed;	260	170.00	225.00	85.00
1b	Daisies	Cream; large white daisy flowers	260	170.00	225.00	85.00
1c	Leaves	Pale green; orange leaves	260	100.00	150.00	65.00
2	Peony	Cream; multicoloured flowers	225	170.00	225.00	85.00

WADE HEATH *(cont.)*

SHAPE 359, GOTHIC WARE, 1940, c.1947-c.1953

The 1940 issue was produced in matt colours. Shape 359 was reissued from 1947 to 1953 in new gloss colours, with the embossed design highlighted in pastel colours and gold lustre.

Flaxenware, matt

Gold lustre, high gloss

Backstamp: A. Black ink stamp "Gothic Wade Heath England" with impressed "359"
               B. Green ink stamp "Wade England Gothic" with impressed "359"

No.	Description	Colourways	Size	U.S.$	Can.$	U.K.£
1a	Gothic	Orange; matt	170	110.00	145.00	55.00
1b	Gothic	Pale orange; pale pink flowers; pale green leaves; gloss	170	110.00	145.00	55.00
1c	Gothic	Cream; pink/yellow flowers; blue/green leaves; gold lustre; gloss	170	110.00	145.00	55.00
2	Gothic	Cream; lilac/pink flowers; green/gold leaves; gloss	160	110.00	145.00	55.00

WADE HEATH *(cont.)*

SHAPE 360, GOTHIC WARE, c.1940-1953

The Gothic vase 1b is hand painted in black and red, which was rarely used by the Wade pottery because of firing difficulties with these colours.

Gothic ware, gold leaves

Gothic ware, black outline

Backstamp: Green ink stamp "Wade England Gothic" with impressed "360"

No.	Description	Colourways	Size	U.S.$	Can.$	U.K.£
1a	Gothic	Cream; lilac/pink flowers; green/gold leaves; gloss	215	110.00	145.00	55.00
1b	Gothic	White; black outlined leaves; red flower centres; red inside	215	110.00	145.00	55.00

WADE HEATH (cont.)

SHAPE 362, HARVEST WARE, c.1948-c.1952

The large daisy and peony designs are hand-painted, so no two are identical. A Canadian store advertised the peony vase for sale in June 1951.

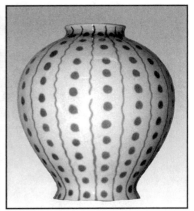

| Daisies | Daisy and bands | Spots and wavy lines |

Backstamp: A. Black ink stamp "Harvest Ware Wade England" with impressed "362"
B. Black ink stamp "Wade England" with impressed "362"

No.	Description	Colourways	Size	U.S.$	Can.$	U.K.£
1a	Daisies	Cream; purple/maroon flowers	225	100.00	135.00	65.00
1b	Daisy and bands	Grey; white band; blue/grey flowers	225	100.00	135.00	65.00
1c	Leaves	Cream; long brown/coffee leaves; grey speckles	225	100.00	135.00	65.00
1d	Peony	Cream; multicoloured flowers	225	100.00	135.00	75.00
1e	Spots, wavy lines	White; blue spots; grey lines	225	90.00	105.00	45.00

SHAPE 366, GOTHIC WARE, November 1946-1953

Gothic ware, gold leaves

Backstamp: Green ink stamp "Wade England Gothic" with impressed "366"

No.	Description	Colourways	Shape/Size	U.S.$	Can.$	U.K.£
1	Gothic	Cream; lilac/pink flowers; green/gold leaves	Ball shape/230	150.00	195.00	75.00

WADE HEATH (cont.)

SHAPE 394, HARVEST WARE, c.1948-c.1952

Backstamp: Black ink stamp "Harvest Ware Wade England" with impressed "394"

No.	Description	Colourways	Size	U.S.$	Can.$	U.K.£
1	Peony	Cream; multicoloured flowers	225	100.00	150.00	65.00

SHAPE 400, EMPRESS, c.1948-1954

In the late 1940s the Wadeheath Pottery produced these vases in mottled glazes. In 1954 a white matt colourway was introduced, and in 1952-1953 they were glazed in bright colours.

Empress

Backstamp: A. Circular ink stamp "Royal Victoria Pottery Wade England" late 1940s
B. Black ink stamp "Wade England" with impressed "400," early 1950s
C. Black ink stamp "Wade Empress England" with impressed "400," 1952-1953

No.	Description	Colourways	Size	U.S.$	Can.$	U.K.£
1a	Empress	Blue; gold stripes	225	130.00	175.00	65.00
1b	Empress	Green; gold stripes	225	130.00	175.00	65.00
1c	Empress	Maroon; gold stripes	225	130.00	175.00	65.00
1d	Empress	Mottled green	225	80.00	110.00	40.00
1e	Empress	White, matt	225	80.00	110.00	40.00

WADE HEATH (cont.)

SHAPE 402, EMPRESS, c.1948-1954

In the late 1940s the Wadeheath Pottery produced these vases in mottled glazes. In 1954 a white matt colourway was introduced, and in 1952-1953 they were glazed in bright colours.

Empress

Backstamp: **A.** Circular ink stamp "Royal Victoria Pottery Wade England" late 1940s
B. Black ink stamp "Wade England" with impressed "402" early 1950s
C. Black ink stamp "Wade Empress England" with impressed "402" 1952-1953

No.	Description	Colourways	Size	U.S.$	Can.$	U.K.£
1a	Empress	Blue; gold stripes	225	130.00	175.00	65.00
1b	Empress	Green; gold stripes	225	130.00	175.00	65.00
1c	Empress	Maroon; gold stripes	225	130.00	175.00	65.00
1d	Empress	Mottled green	225	80.00	110.00	40.00
1e	Empress	White, matt	225	80.00	110.00	40.00

WADE HEATH (cont.)

SHAPE 403, EMPRESS, c.1948-1954

In the late 1940s the Wadeheath Pottery produced these vases in mottled glazes. In 1954 a white matt colourway was introduced, and in 1952-1953 they were glazed in bright colours.

Empress

Backstamp: **A.** Circular ink stamp "Royal Victoria Pottery Wade England," late 1940s
B. Black ink stamp "Wade England" with impressed "403," early 1950s
C. Black ink stamp "Wade Empress England" with impressed "403," 1952-1953

No.	Description	Colourways	Size	U.S.$	Can.$	U.K.£
1a	Empress	Blue; gold stripes	170	130.00	175.00	65.00
1b	Empress	Green; gold stripes	170	130.00	175.00	65.00
1c	Empress	Maroon; gold stripes	170	130.00	175.00	65.00
1d	Empress	Mottled green	180	80.00	110.00	40.00
1e	Empress	White, matt	180	80.00	110.00	40.00

SHAPE 404, EMPRESS, c.1948-1954

In the late 1940s the Wadeheath Pottery produced these vases in mottled glazes. In 1954 a white matt colourway was introduced, and in 1952-1953 they were glazed in bright colours.

Photograph not available
at press time

Backstamp: **A.** Circular ink stamp "Royal Victoria Pottery Wade England," late 1940s
B. Black ink stamp "Wade England" with impressed "404," early 1950s
C. Black ink stamp "Wade Empress England" with impressed "404," 1952-1953

No.	Description	Colourways	Size	U.S.$	Can.$	U.K.£
1a	Empress	Blue; gold stripes	255	140.00	195.00	75.00
1b	Empress	Green; gold stripes	280	140.00	195.00	75.00
1c	Empress	Maroon; gold stripes	280	140.00	195.00	75.00
1d	Empress	Mottled green	255	90.00	125.00	45.00
1e	Empress	White, matt	255	90.00	125.00	45.00

WADE HEATH (cont.)

SHAPE 434, HARMONY WARE, 1957-c.1962

Shooting stars

Backstamp: **A.** Red transfer print "Wade England" with impressed "England" and "434"
B. Red transfer print "Wade England Fern" with impressed "England" and "434"
C. Black transfer print "Wade England Parasol" with impressed "England" and "434"
D. Black print "Wade England" green shooting stars and impressed "England" and "434"
E. Impressed "Wade England" and "434"

No	Description	Colourways	Size	U.S.$	Can.$	U.K.£
1a	Carnival	White; yellow/red/green flower	220	80.00	110.00	40.00
1b	Fern	White; red/black ferns	220	80.00	110.00	40.00
1c	Parasols	White; multicoloured parasols	220	80.00	110.00	40.00
1d	Shooting stars	White; multicoloured stars	220	80.00	110.00	40.00
1e	Solid colour	Black	220	50.00	70.00	25.00
1f	Solid colour	Green	220	50.00	70.00	25.00
1g	Solid colour	White	220	50.00	70.00	25.00
1h	Solid colour	Yellow	220	50.00	70.00	25.00
1i	Two tone	Green outside; peach inside	220	50.00	70.00	25.00
1j	Two tone	Grey outside; pink inside	220	50.00	70.00	25.00

WADE HEATH (cont.)

SHAPE 452, HARMONY WARE, 1957-c.1962

Shape 452 is a miniature bud vase with a deep V-shaped mouth.

Shooting stars

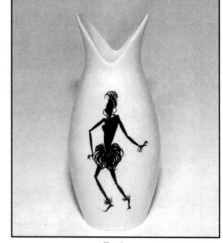

Zamba

Backstamp: **A.** Red transfer print "Wade England" with impressed "England" and "452"
B. Red transfer print "Wade England Fern" with impressed "England" and "452"
C. Black transfer print "Wade England Parasol" with impressed "England" and "452"
D. Black print "Wade England" green shooting stars and impressed "England" and "452"
E. Impressed "Wade England" and "452"
F. Impressed "Wade" and "452"

No.	Description	Colourways	Size	U.S.$	Can.$	U.K.£
1a	Carnival	White; yellow/red/green flower	126	20.00	30.00	12.00
1b	Fern	White; black/red ferns	126	20.00	30.00	12.00
1c	Parasols	White; multicoloured parasols	126	20.00	30.00	12.00
1d	Shooting stars	White; black and multicoloured stars	126	20.00	30.00	12.00
1e	Solid colour	Black	126	10.00	15.00	5.00
1f	Solid colour	Green	126	10.00	15.00	5.00
1g	Solid colour	White	126	10.00	15.00	5.00
1h	Solid colour	Yellow	126	10.00	15.00	5.00
1i	Two tone	Black outside; yellow inside	126	10.00	15.00	6.00
1j	Two tone	Green outside; peach inside	126	10.00	15.00	6.00
1k	Two tone	Grey outside; pink inside	126	10.00	15.00	6.00
1l	Zamba	White; black prints	126	65.00	75.00	30.00

WADE HEATH (cont.)

SHAPE 458, HARMONY WARE, 1957-1958

These vases are similar to shape 434, but are slightly narrower.

Ballet transfer print

Parasols transfer print

Backstamp: **A.** Black and red transfer print "Ballet Wade of England" and impressed "England" with "458"
B. Black and red transfer print "Ballet Wade of England" with impressed "England"
C. Red transfer print "Wade England" with impressed "England" and "458"
D. Red transfer print "Wade England Fern" with impressed "England" and "458"
E. Black transfer print "Wade England Parasol" with impressed "England" and "458"
F. Black print "Wade England" green shooting stars and impressed "England" and "458"
G. Impressed "Wade England" and "458"

No.	Description	Colourways	Size	U.S.$	Can.$	U.K.£
1a	Ballet	White; black/yellow print; black inside	177	130.00	175.00	65.00
1b	Carnival	White; yellow/red/green flower	177	50.00	70.00	25.00
1c	Fern	White; black/red ferns	177	50.00	70.00	25.00
1d	Parasols	White; multicoloured parasols	177	50.00	70.00	25.00
1e	Shooting stars	White; multicoloured stars	177	50.00	70.00	25.00
1f	Solid colour	Black	177	30.00	45.00	15.00
1g	Solid colour	Green	177	30.00	45.00	15.00
1h	Solid colour	White	177	30.00	45.00	15.00
1i	Solid colour	Yellow	177	30.00	45.00	15.00
1j	Two tone	Green outside; peach inside	177	30.00	45.00	15.00
1k	Two tone	Grey outside; pink inside	177	30.00	45.00	15.00

WADE HEATH (cont.)

SHAPE 459, 1957

This vase features black dancers in rhythmic poses silhouetted on a white glazed background. Care has to be taken when washing as the black paint inside flakes off.

Zamba transfer print

Backstamp: **A.** Red or black transfer print "Wade England" with impressed "England" and "459"
B. Red or black transfer print "Wade England"
C. Red or black transfer print "Wade England" with impressed "England"

No.	Description	Colourways	Size	U.S.$	Can.$	U.K.£
1	Zamba	White; black print	285	150.00	200.00	85.00

WADE HEATH *(cont.)*

SHAPE 460, 1957-1958

Shape number 460 was issued with three designs, Ballet, Fantasia and Zamba. All are transfer prints. Care must be excersized in cleaning the black inside of the Zamba vase.

Fantasia transfer print

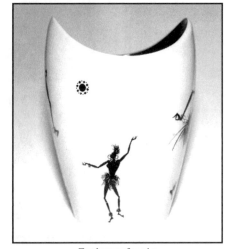

Zamba transfer print

Backstamp: A. Black and red transfer print "Ballet Wade of England" and impressed "England" and "460"
B. Black and red transfer print "Ballet Wade of England" with impressed "England"
C. Black transfer print "Fantasia by Wade of England copyright Walt Disney Productions" with impressed "England 460"
D. Red or Black transfer print "Wade England" with impressed "England" and "460"
E. Red or Black transfer print "Wade England"

No.	Description	Colourways	Size	U.S.$	Can.$	U.K.£
1a	Ballet	White; black/yellow print; black inside	185	120.00	135.00	65.00
1b	Fantasia	Grey outside; black, white, pink print; pink inside	185	200.00	300.00	150.00
1c	Zamba	White; black print	185	160.00	215.00	85.00

WADE HEATH (cont.)

SHAPE 464, 1957

This vase features black dancers in rhythmic poses silhouetted on a white glazed background. Care must be exercised when cleaning the inside of the vase as the paint tends to flake.

Zamba transfer print

Backstamp: A. Red or black transfer print "Wade England" with impressed "England" and "464"
B. Red or black transfer print "Wade England"
C. Red or black transfer print "Wade England" with impressed "England"

No.	Description	Colourways	Size	U.S.$	Can.$	U.K.£
1	Zamba 464	White; black print	235	160.00	200.00	70.00

WADE HEATH (cont.)

SHAPE 467, 1957-1958

The Ballet Series vase was issued between 1957 and 1958 and the Zamba Series vase in 1957.

| Ballet transfer print | Zamba transfer print |

Backstamp: **A.** Black and red transfer print "Ballet Wade of England" and impressed "England" with "467"
B. Black and red transfer print "Ballet Wade of England" with impressed "England"
C. Red or black transfer print "Wade England"
D. Red or black transfer print "Wade England" with impressed "England"
E. Red or black transfer print "Wade England" with impressed "England" and "467"

No.	Description	Colourways	Size	U.S.$	Can.$	U.K.£
1a	Ballet	White; black/yellow print; black inside	105	60.00	90.00	45.00
1b	Zamba	White; black print; black inside	105	60.00	90.00	45.00

SHAPE 468, 1957-1958, 1961

Ballet transfer print

Backstamp: **A.** Black and red transfer print "Ballet Wade of England" and impressed "England" with "468"
B. Black and red transfer print "Ballet Wade of England" with impressed "England"
C. Black transfer print "Fantasia by Wade of England - copyright Walt Disney Productions" with impressed "England 468"

No.	Description	Colourways	Size	U.S.$	Can.$	U.K.£
1a	Ballet	White; black/yellow print; black inside	245	150.00	200.00	75.00
1b	Fantasia	Grey outside; black/white/pink print; pink inside	228	290.00	400.00	195.00

WADE HEATH (cont.)

SHAPE 469, MINIATURE VASE, 1957

Zamba transfer print

Backstamp: A. Red or black transfer print "Wade England" with impressed "England" and "469"
          B. Red or black transfer print "Wade England"
          C. Red or black transfer print "Wade England" with impressed "England"

No.	Description	Colourways	Size	U.S.$	Can.$	U.K.£
1	Zamba	White; black print	125	40.00	55.00	22.00

SHAPE 477, 1957-1961

The Ballet series was produced between 1957 and 1958 and the Fantasia series was available during 1961 only.

Photograph not available
at press time

Backstamp: A. Black and red transfer print "Ballet Wade Of England" and impressed "England" with "477"
          B. Black and red transfer print "Ballet Wade Of England" with impressed "England"
          C. Black transfer print "Fantasia by Wade of England - copyright Walt Disney Productions" impressed "England 477"

No.	Description	Colourways	Size	U.S.$	Can.$	U.K.£
1a	Ballet	White; red mouth; black/yellow print	228	100.00	135.00	50.00
1b	Fantasia	Grey outside; black/white/pink print; pink inside	228	200.00	300.00	150.00
1c	Fantasia	Pink outside; black/white/pink print; grey inside	228	200.00	300.00	150.00

WADE HEATH (cont.)

SHAPE 478, 1957-1958

The Zamba vase features black dancers in rhythmic poses silhouetted on a white glazed background. Care must be exercised when cleaning the inside of the vase as the paint tends to flake.

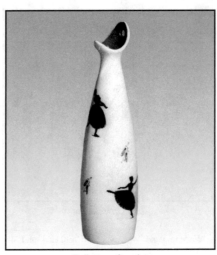

Ballet transfer print

Backstamp: A. Black and red transfer print "Ballet Wade of England" and impressed "England" with "478"
B. Black and red transfer print "Ballet Wade of England" with impressed "England"
C. Red or black transfer print "Wade England" with impressed "England" and "478"
D. Red or black transfer print "Wade England"
E. Red or black transfer print "Wade England" with impressed "England"

No.	Description	Colourways	Size	U.S.$	Can.$	U.K.£
1a	Ballet	White; black/yellow print; red inside	300	100.00	135.00	50.00
1b	Zamba	White; black print; red inside	300	100.00	135.00	65.00

WADE HEATH (cont.)

SHAPE 483, 1957-c.1965
Ballet Transfer Prints, 1957-1962

Ballet transfer print

Backstamp: A. Black and red transfer print "Ballet Wade of England" and impressed "England with "483"
B. Black and red transfer print "Ballet Wade of England" with impressed "England"

No.	Description	Colourways	Size	U.S.$	Can.$	U.K.£
1	Ballet	White; black/yellow print; black inside	110	30.00	40.00	15.00

Black Frost Transfer Prints, 1957-c.1962

The black frost series of vases was in production c.1957-1962 and consists of white frosted transfer prints of wild flowers on a black vase, there are a number of variations of flowers to be found.

Black Frost colourway

Backstamp: Red print "Wade England"

No.	Description	Colourways	Size	U.S.$	Can.$	U.K.£
1	Black Frost	Black; white flowers; gold rim	110	20.00	30.00	10.00

WADE HEATH (cont.)

SHAPE 483 (cont.)

The rim of these vases is decorated with 22-karat gold.

Floral transfer prints

Backstamp: A. Red transfer print "Wade England"
 B. Black transfer print "Wade England"

Floral Transper Prints, c.1958-c.1965

No.	Description	Colourways	Size	U.S.$	Can.$	U.K.£
1a	Pink rose	White; pink flower; gold inside	110	20.00	30.00	10.00
1b	Red rose	White; red flower; gold inside	110	20.00	30.00	10.00
1c	Wild violet	White; violet flowers; gold inside	110	20.00	30.00	10.00
1d	Yellow rose	White; yellow flower; gold inside	110	20.00	30.00	10.00

Pixie Transfer Print

No.	Description	Colourways	Size	U.S.$	Can.$	U.K.£
1	Pixie on mushroom	White; green/red pixie; gold inside	110	20.00	30.00	10.00

WADE HEATH (cont.)

SHAPE 483 (cont.)
Souvenir Transfer Prints, c.1958-c.1962

The mouth of these vase can be found in black, gold and red, care has to be taken when washing the black and red mouth vases as the paint wears off.

Souvenir transfer prints

Backstamp: **A.** Red transfer print "Wade England"
B. Red transfer print "Wade England" with impressed "483"
C. Red transfer print "A Wade Product"

No.	Description	Colourways	Size	U.S.$	Can.$	U.K.£
1a	Balmoral, stags head	White; brown print; red inside	110	20.00	30.00	10.00
1b	Big Ben	White; black/blue print; black inside	110	20.00	30.00	10.00
1c	Braemar, stags head	White; brown print	110	20.00	30.00	10.00
1d	Eastbourne, Pixie	White; red/green pixie; black inside	110	20.00	30.00	10.00
1e	Eros, Piccadilly Circus	White; black/blue print; black inside	110	20.00	30.00	10.00
1f	Jersey arms	White; red/yellow print; yellow lettering; gold inside	110	20.00	30.00	10.00
1g	London arms	White; multicoloured print; gold inside	110	20.00	30.00	10.00
1h	New Brunswick shield	White; multicoloured print; gold inside	115	20.00	30.00	10.00
1i	Nova Scotia shield	White; multi coloured print; gold inside	115	20.00	30.00	10.00
1j	Paignton, Pixie	White; green/red pixie; black lettering Paignton; gold inside	110	20.00	30.00	10.00
1k	Prince Edward Island	White; multicoloured print; gold inside	115	20.00	30.00	10.00
1l	Tower Bridge	White; black/blue print; black inside	110	20.00	30.00	10.00
1m	Trafalgar Square	White; black/blue print; black inside	110	20.00	30.00	10.00
1n	Trafalgar Square	Black; white print	110	20.00	30.00	10.00

WADE HEATH (cont.)

SHAPE 484, 1957-c.1965
Ballet Transfer Prints, 1957-1958

Ballet transfer print

Backstamp: **A.** Black and red transfer print "Ballet Wade of England" and impressed "England" with "484"
B. Black and red transfer print "Ballet Wade of England" with impressed "England"

No.	Description	Colourways	Size	U.S.$	Can.$	U.K.£
1	Ballet	White; black/yellow print; red inside	110	30.00	40.00	15.00

Floral Transfer Prints, c.1958-c.1965

Pink and red rose floral print

Wild violets floral print

Backstamp: **A.** Red transfer print "Wade England"
B. Black transfer print "Wade England"

No.	Description	Colourways	Size	U.S.$	Can.$	U.K.£
1a	Pearlised	Pearlised orange; gold mouth	110	20.00	30.00	10.00
1b	Pink rose	White; pink flower; gold inside	110	20.00	30.00	10.00
1c	Red rose	White; red flower; gold inside	110	20.00	30.00	10.00
1d	Yellow rose	White; yellow flower; gold inside	110	20.00	30.00	10.00
1e	Wild Violets	White; violet flowers; gold inside	110	20.00	30.00	10.00

WADE HEATH (cont.)

SHAPE 484 (cont.)
Souvenir Transfer Prints, c.1958-c.1962

Photograph not available
at press time

Backstamp: A. Red transfer print "Wade England"
B. Red transfer print "Wade England" with impressed "484"

No.	Description	Colourways	Shape/Size	U.S.$	Can.$	U.K.£
1a	London	White; multicoloured print; gold inside	110	15.00	20.00	10.00
1b	Dawlish	White; red sailboat print; gold inside	110	15.00	20.00	10.00
1c	Eros, Piccadilly	White; multicoloured print; gold inside	110	15.00	20.00	10.00
1d	Hastings	White; red sail boat; gold inside	110	15.00	20.00	10.00
1e	New Brunswick	White; multicoloured print; gold inside	110	15.00	20.00	10.00
1f	Paignton pixie	White; red/green pixie; gold inside	110	15.00	20.00	10.00
1g	Prince Edward Island	White; multicoloured print; gold inside	110	15.00	20.00	10.00
1h	Remember? Guernsey	White; multicoloured print; gold inside	110	15.00	20.00	8.00
1i	Remember? London	White; multicoloured print; gold inside	110	15.00	20.00	8.00
1j	Tower Bridge	White; black/blue print; black inside	110	15.00	20.00	8.00
1k	Trafalgar Square	White; black/blue print; black inside	110	15.00	20.00	8.00

SHAPE 513, 1957-c.1962

The Black Frost design used on these vases is similar to that used by Wade Heath in the 1930s.

Black Frost transfer print

Backstamp: Red print "Wade England"

No.	Description	Colourways	Size	U.S.$	Can.$	U.K.£
1	Black Frost	Black; white flowers; gold rim	143	50.00	70.00	25.00

WADE HEATH (cont.)

TOPLINE VASES, 1963

TOPLINE is a series of contemporary shapes and decoration by freelance designer Michael Caddy and produced for only a short time in 1963. All the vases are cylindrical in shape, some have a foot while others have a long neck or, a foot and short neck. The concave lid vase has a pierced lid for inserting flower stems.

The multicoloured prints are of vintage vehicles, horse drawn carriages or cars. There has been some confusion as to which are Topline and which are Veteran Cars, all Topline vehicles have people included in the design, and the veteran cars have no people.

The short foot vase has been found in two sizes. The larger vase can be found with or without a pierced concave lid for the flower stems.

SHAPE 528, 1963

| Abstract, black foot | Abstract, gold foot | Feather medallion, gold foot | Black Frost transfer print |

Backstamp: Red print "Wade England"

No.	Description	Colourways	Size	U.S.$	Can.$	U.K.£
1a	Abstract	White; gold abstract panels; black bands, foot	108	60.00	80.00	30.00
1b	Abstract	White; purple/gold abstract panels; black foot	108	60.00	80.00	30.00
1c	Duryea phaeton 1904	White; multicoloured print; black foot	108	50.00	70.00	25.00
1d	Feather	Black; white feather medallion; gold foot	108	50.00	70.00	25.00
1e	Leaf	Black; white leaf medallion; gold foot	108	50.00	70.00	25.00
1f	Leaf	White; black leaf medallion; gold foot	108	50.00	70.00	25.00
2a	Abstract	White; gold abstract panels; black bands, foot	160	60.00	80.00	30.00
2b	Abstract	White; purple abstract panels; black band; gold foot	160	60.00	80.00	30.00
2c	Abstract	White; purple and gold abstract panels; black foot	160	60.00	80.00	30.00
2d	Abstract	Yellow; black abstract panels; black foot	160	60.00	80.00	30.00
2e	Feather	Black; white leaf medallions; pierced lid; gold foot	165	50.00	70.00	25.00
2f	Leaf	Black; white leaf medallions; gold foot	160	50.00	70.00	25.00
2g	Leaf	Black; white leaf medallions; pierced lid; gold foot	160	50.00	70.00	25.00
2h	Multi-prints	White; multicoloured prints; black foot	160	50.00	70.00	25.00
3	Black Frost	Black; white flowers; gold rim; pierced lid	165	90.00	120.00	45.00

WADE HEATH (cont.)

TOPLINE VASES (cont.)
SHAPE 530, 1963

The long neck vase has been found in one size only.

Abstract

Benz 1898

Governess cart, 1900

No.	Description	Colourways	Size	U.S.$	Can.$	U.K.£
1a	Abstract	White; gold abstract panels, rim; black neck	165	70.00	95.00	35.00
1b	Abstract	White; purple abstract panels; black neck; gold rim	165	70.00	95.00	35.00
1c	Abstract	White; purple/gold abstract panels; black neck; white rim	165	70.00	95.00	35.00
1d	Benz 1898 / Governess cart 1900	White; multicoloured print; black neck; gold rim	165	60.00	80.00	30.00
1e	Feather	White; white feather medallion; gold neck; black rim	165	60.00	80.00	30.00
1f	Leaf	White; black/silver-grey leaf medallion; black neck; gold rim	165	60.00	80.00	30.00
1g	Stanhope Phaeton 1900	White; multicoloured print; black neck; gold rim	165	60.00	80.00	30.00

WADE HEATH *(cont.)*

TOPLINE VASES *(cont.)*
SHAPE 531, 1963

The short neck vase with foot has been found in one size only.

Duryea Phaeton 1904/Tricycle 1888

Feather medallion

No.	Description	Colourways	Size	U.S.$	Can.$	U.K.£
1a	Abstract	White; gold abstract panels; black neck, foot	98	50.00	70.00	25.00
1b	Abstract	White; purple/gold abstract panels; black neck, foot	98	50.00	70.00	25.00
1c	Abstract	White; purple abstract panels; black neck; gold foot	98	50.00	70.00	25.00
1d	Duryea phaeton 1904/ Tricycle 1888	White; multicoloured print; black neck, foot	98	40.00	55.00	20.00
1e	Leaf	White; black/silver-grey leaf medallion; black neck; gold foot	98	40.00	55.00	20.00
1f	Leaf	Black; white leaf medallion; black neck; gold foot	98	40.00	55.00	20.00
1g	Stanhope Phaeton 1900	White; multicoloured print; black neck, foot	98	40.00	55.00	20.00

WADE HEATH *(cont.)*

BLACK FROST VASES, 1957-c.1962

The Black Frost design used on these vases is similar to that used by Wade Heath in the 1930s.

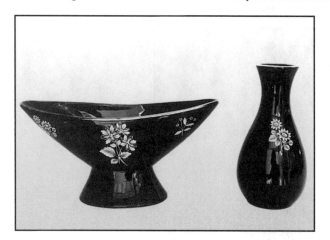 

Backstamp: Red print "Wade England"

No.	Description	Colourways	Size	U.S.$	Can.$	U.K.£
1	Boat shape	Black; white flowers; gold rim	113	80.00	110.00	40.00
2	Small bulbous	Black; white flowers; gold rim	125	50.00	70.00	25.00
3	Tapered neck	Black; white flowers; gold rim	170	70.00	95.00	35.00

WADE HEATH (cont.)

BLUE-RIMMED MINIATURE BUD VASES, 1959-c.1965
Curved foot

The Dickens vases are decorated with transfer prints of characters from Charles Dickens's novels. See also the Charles Dickens dishes page 73.

Roses

Backstamp: A. Red transfer print "Wade England" on base, with a silhouette of Dickens's head on the back of the vase
B. Red or black printed "Wade England"

No.	Description	Colourways	Size	U.S.$	Can.$	U.K.£
1a	Crinoline lady	White; blue rim; multicoloured print	115	20.00	30.00	10.00
1b	Flower spray	White; blue rim; multicoloured flowers	115	20.00	30.00	10.00
1c	Little Nell	White; blue rim, base; multicoloured print	115	20.00	30.00	10.00
1d	Roses	White; blue rim; pink roses	115	20.00	30.00	10.00
1e	Uriah Heep	White; blue rim, base; multicoloured print	115	20.00	30.00	10.00

WADE HEATH (cont.)

BLUE RIMMED MINIATURE BUD VASES, 1959-1960
Round Footed

The Dickens vases are decorated with transfer prints of characters from Charles Dickens's novels. See also the Charles Dickens dishes on page 73. The New Brunswick crest vase has a small wild violets print on the back.

Dickens Little Nell, front and back views

Backstamp: **A.** Red transfer print "Wade England" on base
B. Red or black printed "Wade England"

No.	Description	Colourways	Size	U.S.$	Can.$	U.K.£
1a	Flower	White; orange rim; pink flower	115	20.00	30.00	10.00
1b	Flower	White; yellow rim; pink flower	115	20.00	30.00	10.00
1c	Little Nell	White; blue rim, base; multicoloured print	115	20.00	30.00	10.00
1d	Little Nell	White; grey rim, base; multicoloured print	115	20.00	30.00	15.00
1e	Mr. Micawber	White; blue rim, base; multicoloured print	115	20.00	30.00	10.00
1f	Mr. Pickwick	White; blue rim, base; multicoloured print	115	20.00	30.00	10.00
1g	New Brunswick shield	White; gold foot; multicoloured print	115	20.00	30.00	10.00
1h	Wild violets	White; blue rim; violet flowers	115	20.00	30.00	10.00

WADE HEATH *(cont.)*

BLUE RIMMED MINIATURE BUD VASES, 1959-1960
Round No Foot

The Dickens vases are decorated with transfer prints of characters from Charles Dickens's novels. See also the Charles Dickens dishes page 73.

Backstamp: **A:** Red transfer print "Wade England" on base
B. Red or black printed "Wade England"

No.	Description	Colourways	Size	U.S.$	Can.$	U.K.£
1a	Ballerina	White; blue rim; multicoloured print	115	20.00	30.00	10.00
1b	Crinoline lady	White; blue rim; multicoloured print	115	20.00	30.00	10.00
1c	Mr. Pickwick	White; blue rim, base; multicoloured print	115	20.00	30.00	10.00

CHELSEA SERIES VASE, 1962

This vase is similar in style to the Empress vases.

Photograph not available
at press time

Backstamp: Red transfer print "Wade England"

No	Description	Colourways	Size	U.S.$	Can.$	U.K.£
1	Chelsea	Black matt; gold highlights	171	60.00	85.00	35.00

WADE HEATH (cont.)

CLARENCE AND CLARA BUD VASES

These miniature bud vases, which were called "Buddies" on the package, were painted to look like cats. Clarence has his eyes open; Clara's eyes are closed.

Backstamp: Red transfer print "Wade England"

No.	Description	Colourways	Size	U.S.$	Can.$	U.K.£
1a	Clarence	White; black/blue/red face; eyes open; red inside	110	42.00	60.00	22.00
1b	Clara	White; black/red face; eyes closed; red inside	110	42.00	60.00	22.00

SOUVENIR CLARA BUD VASE

Photograph not available
at press time

A souvenir Clara vase has been found with the Oxfordshire (UK) town with the name of Henley-on-Thames printed on it.

No.	Description	Colourways	Size	U.S.$	Can.$	U.K.£
1	Clara, Henley-on-Thames	White; black/red face; eyes closed; black lettering; red inside	110	42.00	60.00	22.00

DIAMOND-SHAPED FLOWER HOLDER, 1936-1940s

This diamond-shaped flower holder has fins on each side and a fitted flower frog in the top.

Photograph not available
at press time

Backstamp: Black ink stamp "Wadeheath England" with a lion

No.	Description	Colourways	Size	U.S.$	Can.$	U.K.£
1	Diamond	Cream; black fins; orange base, flower; orange/black/yellow bands	171	150.00	200.00	75.00

WADE HEATH (cont.)

DON SHAPE, 1933-1934

These round flower holders have a flared, wavy rim and a flower frog in the neck. The brightly coloured splash design looks almost like crocus flowers. The cottage vase is a hand-painted design, the pattern number 4216 and sample is handwritten on the base, this may have been a vase sent to a wholesaler or could be a sales representatives sample.

| Cottage | Orcadia | Splash |

Backstamp: **A.** Red ink stamp "Wadeheath England" with a lion
B. Red ink stamp "Wadeheath England 4216" Sample with a lion
C. Orange ink stamp "Wadeheath Orcadia Ware"

No.	Description	Colourways	Size	U.S.$	Can.$	U.K.£
1a	Cottage	White; yellow rim; multicoloured cottage/tree	141	190.00	255.00	95.00
1b	Jigsaw	Cream; red/blue/orange jigsaw design	141	170.00	235.00	85.00
1c	Orcadia	Orange/brown streaks	141	125.00	180.00	75.00
1d	Orcadia	Orange/green streaks	141	125.00	180.00	75.00
1e	Orcadia	Orange/green / purple/blue streaks	141	125.00	180.00	75.00
1f	Rings	Cream; brown/orange rings	141	125.00	180.00	75.00
1g	Splash	Orange/brown blue/green/mauve splashes	141	125.00	180.00	75.00

WADE HEATH (cont.)

EDWARDIAN VASES, 1986-1990

These vases have a flared neck and a wavy rim. The floral fayre design consists of small pink flowers; the fuchsia design is of fuchsias and leaves, the Queensway design is of large white flowers. For matching items in these patterns please see Edwardian photograph frames on page 268 and planters on page 275.

Floral fayre

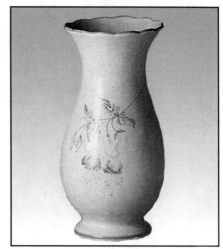

Fuchsia

Backstamp: Red "Wade England" with two red lines

No.	Description	Colourways	Size	U.S.$	Can.$	U.K.£
1a	Floral fayre	White; pink/green print	Small/153	20.00	30.00	10.00
1b	Fuchsia	White; pink/yellow/grey print	Small/153	20.00	30.00	10.00
1c	Queensway	White; white/green	Small/153	20.00	30.00	10.00
2a	Floral fayre	White; pink/green print	Medium/190	30.00	40.00	15.00
2b	Fuchsia	White; pink/yellow/grey print	Medium/190	30.00	40.00	15.00
2c	Queensway	White; white/green print	Medium/190	30.00	40.00	15.00

WADE HEATH (cont.)

EGYPTIAN THEME VASES, 1999-2000

These pot-shaped vases have the same Egyptian designs as used on the wall plates that were sold at the Christmas Extravaganza in 1997. They have an ancient Egyptian theme in muted colours, of papyrus reeds, fans, and flying ducks. The original cost was £3.00 and they were available from the Wade factory shop.

Backstamp: Unmarked

No.	Description	Colourways	Size	U.S.$	Can.$	U.K.£
1	Reeds, fans, ducks	White; gold rim; multicoloured prints	Small/105	8.00	12.00	5.00
2a	Reeds, fans, ducks	White; gold rim; multicoloured prints	Large/130	10.00	15.00	5.00
2b	Flower	White; gold rim; multicoloured prints	Large/130	10.00	15.00	5.00

FANTASIA SERIES VASES, 1961

Narrow, long neck

Round, short neck

Round, long neck

Backstamp: Black transfer print "Fantasia by Wade of England - copyright Walt Disney Productions"

No.	Description	Colourways	Size	U.S.$	Can.$	U.K.£
1	Narrow/long neck	Pale blue; black, white, pink print; gold rim	275	200.00	300.00	150.00
2	Round/short neck	Pale blue; black, white, pink print; gold rim	225	200.00	300.00	150.00
3	Round/long neck	Pale blue; black, white, pink print; gold rim	185	200.00	300.00	150.00

WADE HEATH *(cont.)*

HEXAGONAL VASE 1999

This six-sided vase has a design of pale pink dog roses, which are outlined in white.

Backstamp: Semi circular "Royal Victoria Pottery Staffordshire Wade England"

No.	Description	Colourways	Size	U.S.$	Can.$	U.K.£
1	Dog rose	Pale grey; pale pink/white flowers	155	8.00	10.00	5.00

IMPRESSED BANDS VASE

This vase has seven rows of impressed bands around the body

Backstamp: Brown ink "Wade Heath England"

No.	Description	Colourways	Size	U.S.$	Can.$	U.K.£
1	Impressed bands	Yellow	230	55.00	75.00	35.00

WADE HEATH (cont.)

JACOBEAN AND KAWA VASES, 1990-1992

Backstamp: **A.** Red print "Wade England" with two red lines and "Jacobean"
B. Gold print "Wade England" with two gold lines and "Kawa"
C. Red print "Wade England" with two red lines

No.	Description	Colourways	Size	U.S.$	Can.$	U.K.£
1a	Jacobean	White; red/black print	Small/Unknown	35.00	50.00	25.00
1b	Kawa	White; pastel pink/green print; gold highlights	Small/Unknown	35.00	50.00	25.00
2a	Jacobean	White; red/black print	Medium/Unknown	42.00	65.00	30.00
2b	Kawa	White; pastel pink/green print; gold highlights	Medium/Unknown	42.00	65.00	30.00
3a	Jacobean	White; red/black print	Large/254	55.00	75.00	35.00
3b	Kawa	White; pastel pink/green print; gold highlights	Large/254	55.00	75.00	35.00

WADE HEATH (cont.)

MINIATURE VASES 1 AND 3, 1933-1934

Although shown in a late 1930s Wade Heath sales catalogue as vase 1 and vase 3, these small hand decorated vases would be better classed as posy bowls.

Peony, Vase 1

Leaves, Poppies, Vase 3

Backstamp: **A.** Green ink stamp "Harvest Ware Wade England" c. late 1940s-c. Early 1950
B. Green ink stamp "Wade Heath England" Round W c. 1937-c.1940
C. Black ink stamp "Wade Heath England" Crossed W c. early to mid 1940s

Vase 1

No.	Description	Colourways	Size	U.S.$	Can.$	U.K.£
1a	Daisy pointed leaves	Cream; copper lustre; mauve flowers;	60	45.00	60.00	25.00
1b	Vase 1 Peony	Cream; maroon/purple flowers; green brown leaves	60	45.00	60.00	25.00

Vase 3

No.	Description	Colourways	Size	U.S.$	Can.$	U.K.£
2a	Copper lustre	Copper lustre	60	45.00	60.00	25.00
2b	Leaves	White; silver lustre rim; highlights; mauve/green leaves	60	45.00	60.00	25.00
2c	Poppy	Cream; maroon/purple flowers; green brown leaves	60	45.00	60.00	25.00

MINIATURE-HANDLES VASE, 1937

This round vase has miniature handles near the top and a rolling scroll design around the base.

Photograph not available
at press time

Backstamp: Black ink stamp "Flaxman Ware Hand Made Pottery by Wadeheath England," 1935-1937

No.	Description	Colourways	Size	U.S.$	Can.$	U.K.£
1	Miniature handles	Mottled green/grey	229	70.00	95.00	35.00

WADE HEATH (cont.)

MINIATURE-RIBBED VASE, 1933-1934

This miniature vase has ribs around the body

Backstamp: Black ink stamp "Wade England"

No.	Description	Colourways	Size	U.S.$	Can.$	U.K.£
1a	Mottled	Mottled blue/orange	95	45.00	60.00	25.00
1b	Mottled	Mottled cream/yellow	95	45.00	60.00	25.00

MISCELLANEOUS POT-SHAPED VASES, c. 1940s

To date no shape number has been found for these vases nor a design name. The vase with red flowers has an impressed Made in England backstamp.

Art Nouveau

Flowers

Backstamp: **A.** Impressed "Made in England" with ink stamp "Wade England"
B. Ink stamp "Wadeheath England"

No.	Description	Colourways	Size	U.S.$	Can.$	U.K.£
1a	Art Nouveau	Green; brown/yellow/green flower leaf design	155	50.00	70.00	35.00
1b	Flowers	Green; red flower; green leaves	155	50.00	70.00	35.00

WADE HEATH *(cont.)*

ORCADIA WARE VASES, 1933-1935

Orcadia Ware was produced in vivid streaked glazes that were allowed to run over the rims and down the inside and the outside of the vases.

Style 1 is an art nouveau style with high shoulders that narrow to a flared foot. The square-topped flower holder, style 4, has fins on each side and a flower frog in the neck. Style 6 has a wide mouth tapering to the waist.

Round shape

Square shape

Straight sided shape

Pot shape

Waisted shape

Backstamp: **A**. Orange ink stamp "Wades Orcadia Ware British Made"
B. Orange ink stamp "Wadeheath Orcadia Ware"
C. Orange ink stamp "British Roskyl Pottery"

No.	Description	Colourways	Size	U.S.$	Can.$	U.K.£
1	Art nouveau	Orange/green	180	150.00	200.00	75.00
2	Pot shape	Blue/orange/green/blue	135	150.00	200.00	75.00
3	Round	Green/orange streaks; blue base	175	150.00	200.00	75.00
4	Square flower holder	Orange/green	170	190.00	255.00	95.00
5a	Straight sides	Orange/yellow	190	150.00	200.00	75.00
5b	Straight sides	Green/orange streaks; blue base	190	150.00	200.00	75.00
6a	Waisted	Blue/orange/green/blue	145	150.00	200.00	75.00
6b	Waisted	Orange/green	145	150.00	200.00	75.00

WADE HEATH (cont.)

OVOID SHAPE VASES, c. late 1970s

The red glaze used on the Ovoid Bands vase is a colour not often used by Wade because of firing problems.

| Ovoid bands | Ovoid flowers |

Backstamp: Red transfer print "Wade England"

No.	Description	Colourways	Size	U.S.$	Can.$	U.K.£
1	Ovoid bands	Red; black/white bands; yellow inside	180	70.00	100.00	48.00
2	Ovoid flowers	Green; multicoloured wild flowers	200	70.00	100.00	55.00

REGENCY SERIES MINIATURE VASE, 1959-1961

The miniature Regency vase is a scaled down version of the Empress Vase, see page 336.

Regency

Backstamp: **A.** Red transfer print "Wade England"
B. Black transfer print "Wade England"

No.	Description	Colourways	Size	U.S.$	Can.$	U.K.£
1	Regency	White; gold highlights	Miniature/110	30.00	40.00	15.00

WADE HEATH (cont.)

ROMAN AMPHORA VASES, 1937-1939

Vase No. 2 has been reported with a very faint impressed number on the base that could be 327, I would be pleased to hear from anyone who can confirm this.

Impressed flower handles

Ribbed handles

Three-ring handles

Backstamp: Black ink stamp "Flaxman Wade Heath England"

No.	Description	Colourways	Size	U.S.$	Can.$	U.K.£
1	Impressed flower handles	Pale mottled green/grey	Miniature/100	70.00	95.00	35.00
2	Ribbed handles	Mottled orange/grey	Miniature/100	70.00	95.00	35.00
3a	Three-ring handles	Light brown	Miniature/95	70.00	95.00	35.00
3b	Three-ring handles	Orange	Miniature/95	70.00	95.00	35.00
3c	Three-ring handles	Pale blue	Miniature/95	70.00	95.00	35.00

ROSE TRELLIS VASES, 1986-1990

Backstamp: Red print "Wade England" with two red lines

No.	Name	Description	Size	U.S.$	Can.$	U.K.£
1	Rose trellis	White; dark pink/green print	Small/159	20.00	30.00	10.00
2	Rose trellis	White; dark pink/green print	Large/190	40.00	55.00	20.00

WADE HEATH *(cont.)*

SILHOUETTE SERIES VASES, 1962

First issued in January 1962, these unusual-shaped vases have two blue panels, and two matt-black panels with either a giraffe or a lion on them. The giraffe vase was introduced in January 1962, the lion vases in summer 1962. The original price was 5/6d.

Backstamp: Embossed "Wade Porcelain made in England"

No.	Description	Colourways	Size	U.S.$	Can.$	U.K.£
1	Giraffe	Blue/black; blue giraffe	108	60.00	80.00	30.00
2a	Lion	Blue/black; blue lion	108	60.00	80.00	30.00
2b	Lion	Blue/black; white lion	108	60.00	80.00	30.00

SOUVENIR BUD VASES, c.1958-c.1962

This is the same shape vase as the blue-rimmed miniature Dickens bud vases, although a new mould made these vases slightly smaller. The New Brunswick vase has been found with a transfer print of wild Violet flowers on the back.

New Brunswick shield, front and back

Backstamp: Red transfer print "Wade England"

No.	Description	Colourways	Shape/Size	U.S.$	Can.$	U.K.£
1a	New Brunswick shield	White; gold foot; multicoloured print	Round/112	20.00	30.00	12.00
1b	New Brunswick shield	White; gold foot; multicoloured print violet flowers on back	Round/112	20.00	30.00	12.00
1c	Nova Scotia shield	White; gold foot; multicoloured print	Round/112	20.00	30.00	12.00

WADE HEATH (cont.)

SPONGED SHELL DESIGN

This flask-shaped vase has an unusual sponged shell-like design.

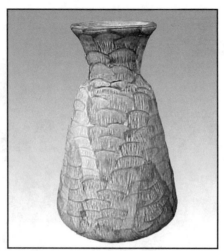

Backstamp: Black ink "Wadeheath England" with lion

No.	Description	Colourways	Size	U.S.$	Can.$	U.K.£
1	Vase	Blue/green/orange	153	60.00	90.00	45.00

TAPERED VASES, 1998/99

The designs on these Tapered vases varied. The Nouvelle design was originally used on the Gallery collection jugs which were produced in 1995. They were available at the Wade factory shop during 1999.

Santa Claus

Nouvelle

Backstamp: Red print "Wade England"

No.	Description	Colourways	Size	U.S.$	Can.$	U.K.£
1a	Nouvelle	White; orange/green/yellow/black	225	30.00	40.00	15.00
1b	Santa Claus	White; multicoloured print	225	30.00	40.00	15.00

WADE HEATH (cont.)

TROPICAL FRUIT GATHERER VASES, 1961

The large vase has ribs running down the body, whereas the small vase does not.

Backstamp: Red transfer print "Wade England"

No.	Description	Colourways	Shape/Size	U.S.$	Can.$	U.K.£
1a	Banana gatherer	White; multicoloured print	Small/112	20.00	30.00	10.00
1b	Coconut gatherer	White; multicoloured print	Small/112	20.00	30.00	10.00
1c	Date gatherer	White; multicoloured print	Small/112	20.00	30.00	10.00
1d	Pineapple gatherer	White; multicoloured print	Small/112	20.00	30.00	10.00
1e	Prickly pear gatherer	White; multicoloured print	Small/112	20.00	30.00	10.00
1f	Sugar cane cutter	White; multicoloured print	Small/112	20.00	30.00	10.00
2	Banana gatherer	Cream; gold rim, foot; multicoloured print	Large/242	70.00	95.00	35.00

WADE HEATH (cont.)

VIKING VASES, 1959-1965, 1976-1982

First issued in September 1959, these vases were produced in a Scintillite, high-gloss finish. These vases were produced both in England and Ireland. The original price was 4/11d each. Versions 1c and 1d were reissued from 1976 to 1982.

Backstamp: **A.** Embossed "Wade Porcelain Made in England"
B. Embossed "Wade Porcelain Made in Ireland"

No.	Description	Colourways	Size	U.S.$	Can.$	U.K.£
1a	Viking vase	Brown/blue/grey	80	40.00	55.00	20.00
1b	Viking vase	Dark brown/grey blue	80	40.00	55.00	20.00
1c	Viking vase	Honey	80	40.00	55.00	20.00
1d	Viking vase	Honey brown/grey green	80	40.00	55.00	20.00

WADE IRELAND

A large range of Wade Ireland vases was introduced and reissued throughout its 38 years of production. Only approximate dates can be given for Wade Ireland products in the typical blue-green glazes, as very often the original moulds, which included impressed and embossed backstamps, were reissued a decade later with no change to the backstamp.

With the exception of the small Shamrock range, and Mourne vases, all the vases are in the easily recognisable Irish Wade mottled blues and brownish green glazes. The vases are listed by shape number first, followed by the series/shape name if known. Almost all the Wade Ireland vases have a shape number (*I.P.* stands for Irish porcelain; *S.R.* for Shamrock Range; *C* Mourne Range and *CK* Celtic Kells). Vases found without shape numbers or names are listed in order of shape, in the miscellaneous section at the end of this listing.

IRISH PORCELAIN

SHAPE C.345, MOURNE, 1971-1976

This series of porcelain vases is completely different from previously produced Irish Wade. The vases have an impressed orange or yellow flower on the front and back. The C.345 vase has been found in an unusual honey glaze.

Grey/green glaze   Honey glaze

Backstamp: Embossed "Made in Ireland Porcelain Wade eire tira dheanta"

No.	Description	Colourways	Size	U.S.$	Can.$	U.K.£
1a	Mourne	Grey/green; orange sunflower	95	65.00	85.00	40.00
1b	Mourne	Honey; orange sunflower	95	65.00	85.00	40.00

IRISH PORCELAIN (cont.)

SHAPE C.346, MOURNE, 1971-1976

Backstamp: Embossed "Made in Ireland Porcelain Wade eire tira dheanta"

No.	Description	Colourways	Size	U.S.$	Can.$	U.K.£
1	Mourne	Grey/green; yellow flower	100	65.00	85.00	40.00

SHAPE C.347, MOURNE, 1971-1976

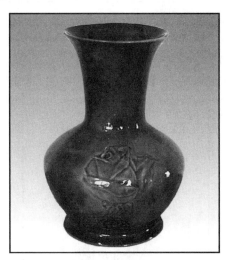

Backstamp: Embossed "Made in Ireland Porcelain Wade eire tira dheanta"

No.	Description	Colourways	Size	U.S.$	Can.$	U.K.£
1	Mourne	Grey/green; orange rose	190	65.00	85.00	40.00

IRISH PORCELAIN (cont.)

SHAPE C.350, Mourne, 1971-1976

This vase has been found without the flower design.

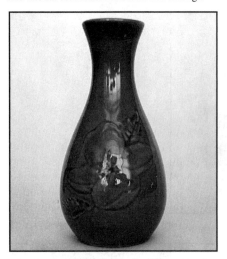

Backstamp: A. Embossed "Made in Ireland Porcelain Wade eire tira dheanta"
B. Embossed "Wade Made in Ireland" with shamrock and crown design

No.	Description	Colourways	Size	U.S.$	Can.$	U.K.£
1a	Mourne	Grey/green; orange flower	170	65.00	85.00	40.00
1b	Mourne	Grey/brown	170	65.00	85.00	40.00

SHAPE NO. C.K.3 AND C.K.5, CELTIC URNS, 1965

The Celtic porcelain urns were produced in two sizes, both have an embossed design of twisted cords and knots on the lid and urn.

C.K. 5, small urn

Backstamp: A. Embossed" Celtic Porcelain by Wade Ireland" in an Irish knot wreath
B. Black transfer print "Celtic Porcelain made in Ireland by Wade Co. Armagh"

No.	Description	Colourways	Size	U.S.$	Can.$	U.K.£
1	Urn, large	Mottled blue-green	Large/293	100.00	135.00	60.00
2	Urn, small	Mottled blue-green	Small/146	90.00	120.00	50.00

IRISH PORCELAIN (cont.)

SHAPE I.P.93, 1950-c.1985

The Barrel vase has two rows of knurls and a row of shamrock leaves around the centre. It was first produced in the 1950s, then again in the 1970s and 1980s. The Giant Finn MacCaul was produced from the early 1960s to the 1980s.

Backstamp: A. Impressed "Irish Porcelain" curved over a shamrock with "Made in Ireland" impressed in a straight line underneath
B. Black print "Irish Porcelain" over a shamrock with "Wade County Armagh"

No.	Description	Colourways	Size	U.S.$	Can.$	U.K.£
1a	Barrel	Blue/green	101	20.00	30.00	10.00
1b	The Giant Finn MacCaul	Blue-grey; multicoloured print	101	40.00	55.00	20.00

SHAMROCK RANGE

IRISH PORCELAIN (cont.)

SHAPE S.R.09, 1983-1986

Wade Ireland produced this vase with a design of shamrock leaves on it. It is a bud vase similar in shape to the Mourne vase. It was from the same mould as the 1981 Royal Wedding vase.

For an illustration of this vase
see page 382

Backstamp: Green printed "Made in Ireland eire tir A dheanta Porcelain Wade" over a shamrock and crown design

No	Description	Colourways	Size	U.S.$	Can.$	U.K.£
1	Vase	White; green shamrocks	220	30.00	40.00	15.00

SHAPE S.R.10, 1983-1986

There is a design of shamrock leaves on this round vase.

For an illustration of this vase
see page 382

Backstamp: Green printed "Made in Ireland eire tir A dheanta Porcelain Wade" over a shamrock and crown design

No	Description	Colourways	Size	U.S.$	Can.$	U.K.£
1	Vase	White; green shamrocks	Unknown	30.00	40.00	15.00

SHAPE S.R.11, 1983-1986

There is a design of shamrock leaves on type 1a of this oval vase. Type 1b is a plain glazed vase.

For an illustration of this vase
see page 382

Backstamp: **A.** Green printed "Made in Ireland eire tir A dheanta Porcelain Wade" over a shamrock and crown design (1a)
B. Embossed "Irish Porcelain Made in Ireland" over a clover leaf and seashell (Seagoe) 1989-1993 (1b)

No	Description	Colourways	Size	U.S.$	Can.$	U.K.£
1a	Vase	White; green shamrocks	115	30.00	40.00	15.00
1b	Vase	Brown/blue/grey	115	40.00	55.00	20.00

SHAPE S.R.19, 1983-1986

Wade Ireland produced this urn with a design of shamrock leaves on it.

For an illustration of this vase
see page 382

Backstamp: Unknown

No	Description	Colourways	Size	U.S.$	Can.$	U.K.£
1	Urn	White; green shamrocks	202	30.00	40.00	15.00

IRISH PORCELAIN (cont.)

BULBOUS, 1959-1993

This vase has the characteristic Wade Ireland glaze of grey-blue, grey-green/brown. The vase has a raised circular design.

Backstamp: Embossed "Wade Porcelain Made in Ireland" and crown design

No.	Description	Colourways	Size	U.S.$	Can.$	U.K.£
1	Bulbous vase circles	Brown/blue/grey	115	40.00	55.00	20.00

CURVED NECK , c.1988

This unusual shaped vase curves in at the neck and has a bowl shaped body. The shape name or number of this vase has not been found.

Backstamp: Embossed "Irish Porcelain Wade Made in Ireland" with "Shamrock" and crown design

No.	Description	Colourways	Size	U.S.$	Can.$	U.K.£
1	Curved neck vase	Greenish grey	190	40.00	55.00	25.00**

IRISH PORCELAIN (cont.)

GRAPEVINE MINIATURE VASE

This Wade Ireland vase is unusual in that it is decorated in white and gold rather than the normal grey-blue colours used by the Irish pottery.

Grapevine

Backstamp: Black transfer print "Made in Ireland by Wade"

No.	Description	Colourways	Size	U.S.$	Can.$	U.K.£
1	Grapevine	White; gold grapevine, rim	85	35.00	50.00	25.00

POT-SHAPED VASE 1959-late 1960s

These vases have the characteristic Wade Ireland glaze of grey-blue, grey-green/brown, with a transfer prints in the centre, the designs are often seen on the Wade Ireland ashtrays. The shape name or number of these vases has not been found.

Colleen and cottage   Flying ducks   Flying pheasants

Backstamp: Ink stamp "Irish Porcelain Wade Co. Armagh"

No.	Description	Colourways	Size	U.S.$	Can.$	U.K.£
1a	Colleen and cottage	Blue/grey; multicoloured print "Ireland;" black lettering	100	40.00	55.00	20.00
1b	Flying ducks	Blue/grey; multicoloured print	100	40.00	55.00	20.00
1c	Flying pheasants	Blue/grey; multicoloured print	100	40.00	55.00	20.00
1d	The Giant Finn MacCaul	Blue/grey; multicoloured print	100	40.00	55.00	20.00

IRISH PORCELAIN (cont.)

TALL VASES, 1959-1980s

Vase 1a has two rows of impressed knurls and 1b has one row of impressed and one row of raised knurls. The shape numbers of these vases have not been found.

Impressed design

Raised design

Backstamp: A. Embossed "Wade Porcelain Made in Ireland" with crown design
B. Impressed "Irish Porcelain Made in England" inside an arch (1a)

No.	Description	Colourways	Size	U.S.$	Can.$	U.K.£
1	Impressed knurls	Brown/blue/grey	195	65.00	85.00	35.00
2	Raised knurls	Brown/blue/grey	190	65.00	85.00	35.00

WADE
(IRELAND) LTD
ONE OF THE WADE GROUP

Registered Office:

WATSON STREET
PORTADOWN
CO. ARMAGH BT 63 5AH
NORTHERN IRELAND

TELEPHONE:
(0762) 332288
TELEX: 747128

SHAMROCK RANGE
1. SR09 Bud Vase
3. SR11 Oval Vase

2. SR10 Round Vase
5. SR19 Shamrock Urn

SHEET S4

4. SR20 Shamrock Cooking Pot

WALL DECORATIONS
1935-1993

The earliest plaques and wall decorations were made by Wade Heath in the 1930s, followed by Gothic Ware wall pockets in 1940, then wall masks. In the late 1940s Wade produced Regency and Romance wall plates and a series of ribbed wall plaques. Beginning in the 1950s, transfer prints were commonly used on wall decorations.

This section is divided into plaques, wall masks, wall plates and wall pockets. The items are listed in alphabetical order with the exception of the section on wall pockets.

Wade Heath
Plaques
Wall Masks
Wall Plates
Wall Pockets
Wade Ireland
Cameos
Plaques

BACKSTAMPS

Ink Stamps	*Transfer Prints*

 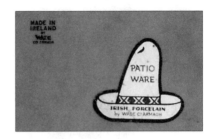

Wade Heath wall decorations were marked with black and green ink stamps from 1935 until circa 1940. Items from Wade Ireland can be found with ink stamps from 1960 until 1964.

From 1953 to 1991, most plaques and wall decorations were marked with transfer-printed backstamps.

Embossed Backstamps

Beginning in 1958 the exotic fish wall plaques were marked with an embossed backstamp. In 1960 embossed backstamps from Wade England and Wade Ireland were used on the yacht wall plaques.

WADE HEATH

PLAQUES

DISPLAY PLAQUES, 1993-2000

During 1993 dealers who purchased a quantity of Whimsey-in-the-Vale models (see *The Charlton Standard Catalogue of Wade Whimsical Collectables*) were able to purchase the Royal Victoria Pottery plaque to display with them. Since 1997 the plaques have been available at Wade shows and at the Wade factory shop.

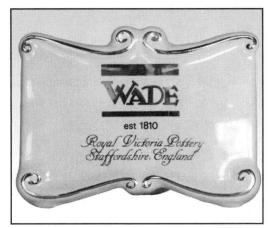

Royal Victoria Pottery plaque

Backstamp: Unmarked

No.	Description	Colourways	Size	U.S.$	Can.$	U.K.£
1	Royal Victoria pottery plaque	White; gold lettering	65 x 94	25.00	30.00	12.00

EXOTIC FISH, 1958-1959

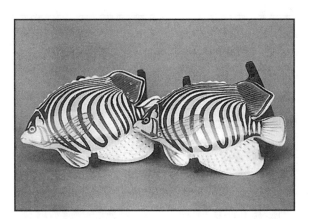

Backstamp: Embossed "Wade Porcelain Made in England"

No.	Description	Colourways	Size	U.S.$	Can.$	U.K.£
1a	Exotic fish	Blue head; white/orange body; pink tail	65 x 95		Rare	
1b	Exotic fish	Green head; green/pink body; yellow tail	65 x 95		Rare	
1c	Exotic fish	Green head; white/pink body; yellow tail	65 x 95		Rare	
1d	Exotic fish	Green head; white/maroon body; pink tail	65 x 95		Rare	
1e	Exotic fish	Green head; white/maroon body; yellow tail	65 x 95		Rare	
1f	Exotic fish	Grey head; white/pink body; green tail	65 x 95		Rare	
1g	Exotic fish	Pink head; white/yellow body; green tail	65 x 95		Rare	

WADE HEATH (cont.)

SEAGULL PLAQUE, 1960

This model of a flying seagull was produced as a bathroom wall decoration.

Backstamp: Unmarked

No.	Description	Colourways	Size	U.S.$	Can.$	U.K.£
1	Seagull	White; black wing tips; yellow beak, feet	225 x 80	90.00	120.00	45.00

WEE WILLIE WINKIE PLAQUES, 1959-1960

These four nursery wall plaques were only produced for a short time. They depict scenes from the children's nursery rhyme, "Wee Willie Winkie," on the recessed face. Each plaque has a different illustration and two lines from the rhyme. There is a recessed hole in the back for hanging on a wall. They were originally sold with black and gold "Genuine Wade Porcelain" labels on the backs. These plaques are extremely hard to find.

Backstamp: Black transfer print "Wade England"

No.	Description	Colourways	Size	U.S.$	Can.$	U.K.£
1a	Wee Willie Winkie runs through the town	White; multicoloured print	133	200.00	265.00	100.00
1b	Upstairs and downstairs in his night gown	White; multicoloured print	133	200.00	265.00	100.00
1c	Tapping at the window, peeping through the lock	White; multicoloured print	133	200.00	265.00	100.00
1d	Are the children in their beds, it's past 8 o'clock	White; multicoloured print	133	200.00	265.00	100.00

WADE HEATH (cont.)

WILDFOWL PLAQUES, 1960

This set includes four duck wall plaques in natural colours. A loop is provided for hanging.

Mallard drake

Shoveller drake

Pintail

Shoveller, female

Backstamp: A. Black transfer print "Wildfowl by Wade of England" and model name
B. Black transfer print "Wildfowl by Wade of England," model name and signature of Peter Scott
C. Unmarked

No.	Description	Colourways	Size	U.S.$	Can.$	U.K.£
1	Mallard drake	Grey; green head; brown neck; white/beige wings; orange feet	230 x 245	150.00	200.00	75.00
2	Pintail	Green/black head; beige/grey/white wings; grey feet	240 x 205	150.00	200.00	75.00
3	Shoveller drake	White/black body; black/green head; beige/white wings	190 x 220	150.00	200.00	75.00
4	Shoveller female	Grey/brown body; green head	175 x 200	150.00	200.00	75.00

WADE HEATH (cont.)

YACHT PLAQUES, 1960

These brightly coloured racing yachts, designed for decoration in a bathroom, have a number on their sails. A set has been seen which have a print of a sailor on the sail but have no backstamp; it is believed these may have been a prototype design. At some time in late 1960, the production of these plaques was moved to Wade Ireland. The original price was 9/11d.

Backstamp: **A.** Embossed "Wade England" in recess
B. Embossed "Wade Ireland" in recess

No.	Description	Colourways	Size	U.S.$	Can.$	U.K.£
1a	Yacht, no. 7	Blue hull; brown roof; white/grey striped sails	Small/85 x 20	65.00	85.00	30.00
1b	Yacht, no. 7	Dark green hull; dark blue roof; pink sails	Small/85 x 20	50.00	70.00	25.00
1c	Yacht, no. 7	Green hull; blue roof; beige/mauve sails	Small/85 x 20	50.00	70.00	25.00
2a	Yacht, no. 3	Blue hull; brown roof; white/grey striped sails	Medium/110 x 26	66.00	85.00	30.00
2b	Yacht, no. 3	Blue hull; dark green roof; pale green sails	Medium/110 x 26	50.00	70.00	25.00
2c	Yacht, no. 3	Dark blue hull; dark green roof; pale green sails	Medium/110 x 26	50.00	70.00	25.00
3a	Yacht, no. 9	Blue hull; brown roof; white/grey striped sails	Large/115 x 30	65.00	85.00	30.00
3b	Yacht, no. 9	Red hull; yellow roof; blue sails	Large/115 x 30	50.00	70.00	25.00
3c	Yacht, no. 9	Red hull; brown roof; dark blue sails	Large/115 x 30	50.00	70.00	25.00
	Set of three	(small, medium and large)		150.00	200.00	75.00

MISCELLANEOUS

WADE HEATH (cont.)

PICTURE FRAMES, c.1988

This plain, oval frame has a foot at the back to enable it to stand. A photograph is meant to be glued into the recessed face.

Photograph not available
at press time

Backstamp: Unmarked

No.	Description	Colourways	Size	U.S.$	Can.$	U.K.£
1	Photo holder	Blue/grey	105 x 85		Unknown	

TEENAGE POTTERY CAMEOS, 1960

First issued in 1960, the original price was 12/6.

Backstamp: Embossed "Wade Porcelain Made in England"

No.	Description	Colourways	Size	U.S.$	Can.$	U.K.£
1a	Cliff Richard	Maroon; gold edge, multicoloured print	95 x 70	160.00	215.00	80.00
1b	Marty Wilde	Maroon; gold edge, multicoloured print	95 x 70	160.00	215.00	80.00

WALL MASKS

WADE HEATH (cont.)

FACE MASKS c.1938-c.1948

These wall masks have been found in three glaze types—cellulose, matt and high gloss. The masks all have cellulose glazed backs, with a backstamp from the late 1930s. This suggests the cellulose glaze was used first, then the unsold masks were reglazed in a matt or high-gloss glaze at a later date and again offered for sale.

Dyllis

Frolic

Sonia

Pan

Backstamp: Black ink stamp "Wade Figures," a red leaping deer over "Made in England" and the model name hand-written in black

No.	Description	Colourways	Size	U.S.$	Can.$	U.K.£
1a	Dyllis	Black hair; cream face; pink flowers; cellulose glaze	180 x 95	300.00	400.00	175.00
1b	Dyllis	Black hair; cream face; pink flowers; high-gloss glaze	180 x 95	375.00	500.00	195.00
2a	Frolic	Green; matt glaze	180 x 160	375.00	500.00	195.00
2b	Frolic	Pale yellow; high-gloss glaze	180 x 160	375.00	500.00	195.00
3a	Pan	Cream; matt glaze	180 x 115	375.00	500.00	195.00
3b	Pan	Green; matt glaze	180 x 115	375.00	500.00	195.00
4a	Sonia	Black hair; flesh-coloured face; pink flowers; cellulose glaze	220 x 110	300.00	400.00	175.00
4b	Sonia	Black hair; flesh-coloured face; pink flowers; high-gloss glaze	220 x 110	375.00	500.00	195.00

WALL PLATES

WADE HEATH (cont.)

APPRENTICE PLATE, c.1962

Apprentices in the Wade Potteries were sometimes allowed to let their 'Imaginations' run wild on such things as bowls, plates and tankards, practising their skills at hand painting or applying transfers on items which may be sold later in the Factory shop. The plate illustrated has multiple transfers of characters used on Wade Heath Childrens' Nursery wares of the late 1940s-1957. Some of the characters on this plate are Noddy, Big Ears, the Naughty Golliwog, Prudence the Cat, Muffin the Mule and other Muffin Characters, Quack Quacks, Hansel and Gretel, and Gingy the Bear from the 1957 Snippets series.

Backstamp: None

No.	Description	Colourways	Size	U.S.$	Can.$	U.K.£
1	Apprentice Plate	White; multicoloured prints	254		Rare	

BABY'S BIRTHDAY PLATES, c.1970

These Baby's Birthday wall plate, with a design of a cuckoo clock and a stork holding a baby on a set of scales, was intended as birth commemorative. The time of birth and the baby's weight could be hand painted on the clock and the scales.

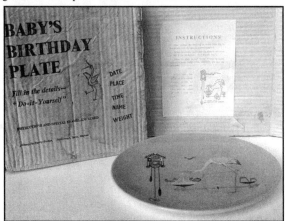

Backstamp: Black transfer print "Wade England, Made in England", Red printed "Cherry Pie Potteries, Farnborough, Hampshire England, Limited Edition"

No.	Description	Colourways	Size	U.S.$	Can.$	U.K.£
1a	Baby's birthday plate	Blue; white/black/yellow print	240	50.00	70.00	25.00
1b	Baby's birthday plate	Pink; white/black/yellow print	240	50.00	70.00	25.00

WADE HEATH *(cont.)*

CHARGERS: WALL PLATES

SHAPE 398, c.1935-1939 -c.1948

A small number of heavy, ribbed wall plaques were produced from 1935 to 1939. The peony plaque was produced c.1948. Owing to their high production costs, not many of these plaques were made. There are three holes in the back for hanging. The Chaffinch and the Autumn Lady plaques are larger than the other plaques listed which may be due to a new mould being made. The Chaffinch plaque is signed and dated 'A. Fereday 1939'

Heron

Corn flowers and poppies

Blue bird

Autumn lady

Backstamp: A. Black ink stamp "Flaxman Ware Hand Made Pottery by Wadeheath England. A. Fereday 1939"
B. Black ink stamp "Flaxman Ware Hand Painted Pottery by Wadeheath England"
C. Black ink stamp "Harvest Ware Wade England" with impressed "398"

No.	Description	Colourways	Size	U.S.$	Can.$	U.K.£
1a	Bluebird	Green; bluebird on branch; blue flowers; brown/green leaves	265	145.00	195.00	85.00
1b	Butterflies	Creamy yellow; yellow/orange butterflies, flowers; green leaves	265	145.00	195.00	85.00
1c	Corn flowers and poppies	Yellow plaque; blue cornflowers; red poppies	265	145.00	195.00	85.00
1d	Cottage	Cream; brown cottage, trees; blue/orange flowers; green leaves/grass	265	145.00	195.00	85.00
1e	Criss Cross	Off white/ mottled orange; blue criss cross lines	265	145.00	195.00	85.00
1f	Heron	Dull yellow; brown heron, chrysanthemums; green leaves	265	145.00	195.00	85.00
1g	Hellebore flowers	Dull yellow; dark purple flowers; brown hills; green trees	265	145.00	195.00	85.00
1h	Owl and moon	Pale blue; brown owl; green tree; grey moon	265	145.00	195.00	85.00
1i	Peony	Cream; bright mauve/red/green flowers	265	145.00	195.00	85.00
1j	Rabbits and sunset	Pale blue; dark brown rabbits; dull yellow sun; green trees	265	145.00	195.00	85.00
2a	Autumn lady	Creamy yellow; black hair/trees; orange/ brown spotted dress, leaves	325	145.00	195.00	85.00
2b	Chaffinch	Creamy yellow; white/black marked bird; green leaves; yellow flower	325	145.00	195.00	85.00

WADE HEATH (cont.)

CHRISTMAS WALL PLATES 1997

Sold at the Wade Christmas Extravaganza in November 1997, these plates have multicoloured transfer prints of Christmas scenes.

Children building a snowman

Noel

Two Robins on Ivy branch

Santa Claus

Teddy Santa at fireplace

Teddy Santa in sleigh

Backstamp: Red printed "Wade"

No.	Description	Colourways	Size	U.S.$	Can.$	U.K.£
1a	Carol singers	White; multicoloured print	254	10.00	12.00	6.00
1b	Children building snowman	White; multicoloured print	254	10.00	12.00	6.00
1c	Clowns, baby animals	White; multicoloured print	254	10.00	12.00	6.00
1d	Noel	White; multicoloured print	254	8.00	10.00	4.00
1e	Poinsettia	White; multicoloured print	254	10.00	12.00	6.00
1f	Robin and window	White; multicoloured print	254	10.00	12.00	6.00
1g	Two Robins on ivy branch	White; multicoloured print	254	10.00	12.00	6.00
1h	Santa Claus	White; multicoloured print	254	10.00	12.00	6.00
1i	Teddy Santa at fireplace	White; multicoloured print	254	10.00	12.00	6.00
1j	Teddy Santa in sleigh	White; multicoloured print	254	10.00	12.00	6.00

WADE HEATH (cont.)

COUNTRYMEN WALL PLATES, 1959-1963

The prints on this series of wall plates are known as 'Countrymen' they were also used on ashtrays, bowls, dishes and tankards. All the Countrymen plates have a wide band of colour round the rim. For Foxhunting scene plates without the colour band see decorative wall plates.

Huntsmen

Poodle

Terrier

Backstamp: Black or Red transfer print "Wade England"

No.	Description	Colourways	Size	U.S.$	Can.$	U.K.£
1a	Horses' Heads	White; red rim; white and brown horse' heads	210	35.00	45.00	20.00
1b	Huntsmen	White; red rim; multicoloured print	210	35.00	45.00	20.00
1c	Poodle dog	White; red rim; grey	210	35.00	45.00	20.00
1d	Schnauzer dog	White; green rim; grey dog	210	35.00	45.00	20.00
1e	Terrier dog	White; red rim; brown and white dog	210	35.00	45.00	20.00

DECORATIVE WALL PLATES 1997

Egyptian Pharaoh cat

Fox Hunting

Backstamp: Red printed "Wade"

No.	Description	Colourways	Size	U.S.$	Can.$	U.K.£
1a	Dog and cat heads	White; multicoloured print	254	10.00	15.00	8.00
1b	Egyptian pharaoh cat	White; light brown cat; multicoloured print	254	10.00	15.00	8.00
1c	Egyptian pharaoh dog	White; orange dog; multicoloured print	254	10.00	15.00	8.00
1d	Egyptian ducks	White; multicoloured print	254	10.00	15.00	8.00
1e	Fox hunting	White; multicoloured print	254	10.00	15.00	6.00

WADE HEATH *(cont.)*

ENGLISH LIFE WALL PLATES, 1992-1993

Only six plates were issued in the English Life Series. Each plate was produced in two sizes and was white with multicoloured transfer print of village shops, etc., similar to those of the English Life teapots.

Backstamp: Black transfer print "English Life Collector Plates, designs by Barry Smith and Barbara Wootton Exclusively for Wade U.K."

No.	Description	Caption	Size	U.S.$	Can.$	U.K.£
1a	Antique shop	"Second-hand Rose"	Small/190	10.00	15.00	8.00
1b	Antique shop	"Second-hand Rose"	Large/240	20.00	30.00	12.00
2a	Fish and chip shop	"Three penny worth please"	Small/190	10.00	15.00	8.00
2b	Fish and chip shop	"Three penny worth please"	Large/240	20.00	30.00	12.00
3a	Flories flowers	"Say it with flowers"	Small/190	10.00	15.00	8.00
3b	Flories flowers	"Say it with flowers"	Large/240	20.00	30.00	12.00
4a	Post office	"Please write Soon"	Small/190	10.00	15.00	8.00
4b	Post office	"Please write soon"	Large/240	20.00	30.00	12.00
5a	Primrose Junction	"All change please"	Small/190	10.00	15.00	8.00
5b	Primrose Junction	"All change please"	Large/240	20.00	30.00	12.00
6a	The Queen Victoria	"Time gentleman please"	Small/190	10.00	15.00	8.00
6b	The Queen Victoria	"Time gentleman please"	Large/240	20.00	30.00	12.00

WADE HEATH (cont.)

MILLENNIUM PLATTER , 1999-2000

Produced as part of the Millennium set these hexagonal platters were produced in two colourways.

Backstamp: Printed "Wade England" between two lines

No.	Description	Colourways	Size	U.S.$	Can.$	U.K.£
1a	Black/gold	Black; gold decorative prints	270	35.00	50.00	25.00
1b	Blue/silver	Dark blue; silver decorative prints	270	35.00	50.00	25.00

MIRROR WALL PLATES, c.1950

The first mirror has a decorative brass rim framing a Wade dinner plate decorated with spring flowers and has a brass framed mirror riveted to the centre of the plate. The second mirror is framed in solid brass and riveted into the centre of a Regency-style plate. The mirrors and the Brass rims were added later by an unknown company, which may have been the Peerage Brass Company.

Decorative mirror   Plain mirror

Backstamp: Gold transfer circular printed "Royal Victoria Pottery, Wade England"

No.	Description	Colourways	Size	U.S.$	Can.$	U.K.£
1	Decorative mirror plate	White plate; multicoloured flowers decorative brass frame; mirror	365	75.00	95.00	40.00
2	Plain mirror plate	Pale green plate; plain brass frame; mirror	265	35.00	45.00	20.00

WADE HEATH (cont.)

NURSERY RHYME WALL PLATES, 1997

Produced for the Wade Christmas Extravaganza held at Trentham Gardens in November 1997, these plates have a multicoloured nursery rhyme print in the centre. Other designs are known to exist.

Humpty Dumpty

Little Miss Muffet

Backstamp: Red printed "Wade Made in England"

No.	Description	Colourways	Size	U.S.$	Can.$	U.K.£
1a	Humpty Dumpty	White plate; multicoloured print of children and Humpty Dumpty	254	10.00	12.00	5.00
1b	Little Miss Muffet	White plate; multicoloured print of Little Miss Muffet	254	10.00	12.00	5.00

WADE HEATH (cont.)

REGENCY WALL PLATES, c.1940-c.1950

These plates have a fluted rim (which is the Regency shape), some have a wide solid colour band, while others have a mottled coloured band which is called 'Powdered Ware'. 'Powdered Ware,' 'Springtime' (parrot tulip) and the 'Richmond Lass' (rose) are also found on Wade tablewares.

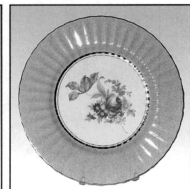

| Richmond Lass (rose) | Springtime | Peony and tulip |

Backstamp: Green ink stamp "Wade England"

No.	Description	Colourways	Size	U.S.$	Can.$	U.K.£
1a	A Somerset cottage	Dark blue band; multicoloured print	265	35.00	45.00	22.00
1b	Assorted flowers	Maroon band; pink/yellow/blue flowers	265	35.00	45.00	22.00
1c	Assorted flowers	Powdered pale grey band; pink/yellow/blue flowers	265	35.00	45.00	22.00
1d	Assorted flowers	Turquoise band; pink/yellow/blue flowers	265	35.00	45.00	22.00
1e	Daisies	Maroon band; pink/purple daises; small blue/yellow flowers	265	35.00	45.00	22.00
1f	Daisies	Powdered green band; pink/purple daisies; small blue/yellow flowers	265	35.00	45.00	22.0 0
1g	Daisies	Turquoise band; pink/purple daisies; small blue/yellow flowers	265	35.00	45.00	22.00
1h	Fruits and berries	White band; purple/red/blue fruits, berries	265	35.00	45.00	22.00
1i	Peony and daisies	Royal blue band; pink peony; purple/yellow daisies	265	35.00	45.00	22.00
1j	Peony and fuchsia	Maroon band; pink peony; yellow purple fuchsia, small blue/yellow/purple flowers	265	35.00	45.00	22.00
1k	Peony and fuchsia	Powdered blue band; pink peony; yellow purple fuchsia, small blue/yellow/purple flowers	265	35.00	45.00	22.00
1l	Peony and fuchsia	Powdered grey band; pink peony; yellow purple fuchsia, small blue/yellow/purple flowers	265	35.00	45.00	22.00
1m	Peony and fuchsia	Turquoise band; pink peony; yellow purple fuchsia, small blue/yellow/purple flowers	265	35.00	45.00	22.00
1n	Peony and tulip	Powdered green band; large pink flowers; small purple/blue flowers	265	35.00	45.00	22.00
1o	Plums	White band; purple/blue fruit	265	30.00	40.00	15.00
1p	Richmond Lass (rose)	Powdered blue band; pink flower and buds	265	35.00	45.00	22.00
1q	Richmond Lass (rose)	Powdered green band; pink flower and buds	265	35.00	45.00	22.00
1r	Richmond Lass (rose)	Powdered yellow band; pink flower and buds	265	35.00	45.00	22.00
1s	Springtime (tulip)	Powdered green band; pink tulip/peony; small blue/yellow flowers	265	35.00	45.00	22.00
1t	Springtime (tulip)	White band; pink tulip/peony; small blue/yellow flowers	265	35.00	45.00	20.00

WADE HEATH (cont.)

ROMANCE WALL PLATES, c.1940-c.1950
Romance Round Wall Plates

Lady curtsying

Couple beside well

Couple seated

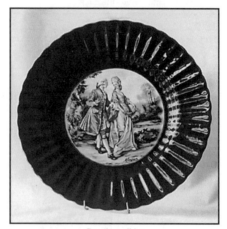

Couple walking

Backstamp: A. Green ink stamp "Wade England"
B. Gold transfer print "Royal Victoria Pottery, Wade England"

No.	Description	Colourways	Size	U.S.$	Can.$	U.K.£
1a	Lady curtsying	Dark blue band; multicoloured print	265	36.00	50.00	25.00
1b	Lady curtsying	Dark green band; multicoloured print	265	36.00	50.00	25.00
1c	Lady with bouquet	Maroon band; multicoloured print	265	36.00	50.00	25.00
1d	Couple beside well	Dark green band; multicoloured print	265	36.00	50.00	25.00
1e	Couple beside well	Maroon band; multicoloured print	265	36.00	50.00	25.00
1f	Couple beside well	Yellow band; multicoloured print	265	36.00	50.00	25.00
1g	Couple seated	Dark green band; multicoloured print	265	36.00	50.00	25.00
1h	Couple seated	Maroon band; multicoloured print	265	36.00	50.00	25.00
1i	Couple walking	Dark blue band; multicoloured print	265	36.00	50.00	25.00
1j	Couple walking	Maroon band; multicoloured print	265	36.00	50.00	25.00

WADE HEATH (cont.)

Romance Star Shaped Wall Plate

This eight-pointed wall plaque carries the same multicoloured print of a "Georgian couple beside a well" as was used on the Romance wall plate. The plate was also issued as a Royal Commemorative for the Coronation of H. M. Queen Elizabeth II (see *The Charlton Standard Catalogue of Wade, Volume One, General Issues*).

Backstamp: Green ink stamp "Wade England"

No.	Description	Colourways	Size	U.S.$	Can.$	U.K.£
1	Couple beside well	Dark blue band; multicoloured print	235	45.00	60.00	35.00

SOMERSET COTTAGE WALL PLATE, c.1950

This plate has a print of a thatched cottage in a garden of flowers, the outer band has two varieties of decoration.

Backstamp: Gold transfer print "Royal Victoria Pottery, Wade England"

No.	Description	Colourways	Size	U.S.$	Can.$	U.K.£
1a	A Somerset cottage	Maroon band; multicoloured print	265	36.00	50.00	25.00
1b	A Somerset cottage	Dark blue band; gold decoration; multicoloured print	265	36.00	50.00	25.00

WADE HEATH (cont.)

SOUVENIR WALL PLATES, 1957-c.1960
Canadian Provinces Wall Plates

This series of white wall plates with multicoloured transfer prints depict items related to each province. They were produced for the Canadian tourist industry and were not sold in England.

| British Columbia | Dominion of Canada | Province of Alberta, Canada |
| "Canada's Evergreen playground" | | |

Backstamp: Red transfer print "Wade England"

No.	Description	Description	Size	U.S.$	Can.$	U.K.£
1a	British Columbia	Map; R.C.M.P.; totem pole; dogwood; Arms	240	25.00	35.00	20.00
1b	British Columbia	Map; R.C.M.P.; totem pole; dogwood; Arms "Canada's Evergreen Playground"	240	25.00	35.00	20.00
1c	Dominion of Canada	Map; maple leaves; Dominion of Canada	240	28.00	35.00	35.00
1d	Gaspesie, P.Q. Canada	Map; maple leaf; seagulls	240	25.00	35.00	20.00
1e	Historic Nova Scotia	Flag; provincial flower; history of flag	240	25.00	35.00	20.00
1f	Maritime lobster and trap	Lobster trap; Arms	240	25.00	35.00	20.00
1g	New Brunswick, Canada	Map; provincial flower; Arms	240	25.00	35.00	20.00
1h	Niagara Falls	Niagara Falls	240	25.00	35.00	20.00
1i	Niagara Falls	White; gold rim; multicoloured print; black lettering;, Arms; "Discovered in 1678 by Father Louis Hennensin"	240	25.00	35.00	20.00
1j	Nova Scotia, Canada	Map; provincial flower; Arms	240	25.00	35.00	20.00
1k	Nova Scotia	Map; provincial flower; ships wheel; "Canada's Ocean Playground"	240	25.00	35.00	20.00
1l	Prince Edward Island	Map; provincial flower; Arms	240	25.00	35.00	20.00
1m	Alberta	Map; R.C.M.P.; Indian chief	240	25.00	35.00	20.00
1n	Ontario	Map; Parliament buildings; Arms; trillium; "Province of Ontario"	240	25.00	35.00	20.00

WADE HEATH (cont.)

Great Britain Souvenir Wall Plates

The first plate has a reproduction of an early 17th-century map of the Isle of Wight in the centre. The others illustrate tourist attractions of England and of Wales. Plate 4 has four-points and resembles a Catherine Wheel.

Welsh lady with spinning wheel

Four-point Welsh lady "Cymru Am Byth"

Backstamp: **A.** Black transfer print "Royal Victoria Pottery Wade England"
B. Gold circular print "Royal Victoria Pottery Wade England"
C. Red transfer print "Wade England"

No.	Description	Colourways	Size	U.S.$	Can.$	U.K.£
1	Isle of Wight map	White; multicoloured prints	240	30.00	40.00	15.00
2	London map	White; red band; multicoloured prints	205	30.00	40.00	15.00
3	Wales and Bristol Channel map	White; red band; multicoloured print	205	30.00	40.00	15.00
4	Welsh Lady	White; gold flowers; multicoloured print; black lettering, Cymru Am Byth (Wales For Ever)	200	33.00	45.00	24.00
5	Welsh Lady with spinning wheel	White; gold flowers; multicoloured print	240	33.00	45.00	22.00

WADE HEATH (cont.)

Nassau, Bahamas, Wall Plate

This wall plate has a multicoloured transfer print of the Island of New Providence. It was produced for the tourist industry and were not sold in England.

Backstamp: Red transfer print "Wade England"

No.	Description	Description	Size	U.S.$	Can.$	U.K.£
1	Nassau	Map; compass point; flags and leaves; "The Island of New Providence Nassau Bahamas"	240	25.00	35.00	20.00

VETERAN CAR WALL PLATES, c.1965

In the latter half of the long running Veteran Car Series, Wade Ireland produced the last sets of the Veteran Car tankards with coloured transfers of competition cars. The same transfers are in the centre of these souvenir plates, which were produced for the tourist trade.

Photograph not available
at press time

Backstamp: Black transfer print "An RK product by Wade of Ireland"

No.	Description	Colourways	Size	U.S.$	Can.$	U.K.£
1a	Fiat F2, 1907	White; red/yellow print	180	30.00	40.00	15.00
1b	Dusenbourg, 1933	White; blue/black print	180	30.00	40.00	15.00
1c	Wolseley, 6hp, 1904	White; red/black/cream print	180	30.00	40.00	15.00
1d	Austin Seven, 1926	White; red/black print	180	30.00	40.00	15.00

WADE HEATH (cont.)

WELLYPHANT WALL PLATE, 1991

This wall plate was part of an intended series, called Wellyphant World. It was designed by Stuart Hampson and issued in a limited edition of 5,000.

Backstamp: **A.** Black transfer print "Wellyphant World, a limited edition of 5,000 designed by Stuart Hampson,
B. "Wade Made in England"

No.	Description	Colourways	Size	U.S.$	Can.$	U.K.£
1	Wellyphant	White; red/yellow prints	190	50.00	70.00	25.00

ZAMBA WALL PLATE, c.1957

This wall plate features black dancers in rhythmic poses silhouetted on a white glazed background.

Backstamp: Black or Red transfer print "Wade England"

No.	Description	Colourways	Size	U.S.$	Can.$	U.K.£
1	Zamba	White; black prints	240	50.00	70.00	28.00

WALL POCKETS

Wall pockets are flat-backed vases that have a hole in the back top edge so they can be hung on a wall. They are glazed inside to hold water.

SHAPE 159, GOTHIC WARE, 1940, NOVEMBER 1946-1953

These triangular-shaped wall pockets are decorated with an embossed design of swirling leaves and tulips characteristic of Gothic Ware.

Backstamp: **A.** Black ink stamp "Gothic Wade Heath England" and impressed "159"
 B. Gold transfer print "Wade made in England - hand painted - Gothic" and impressed "159"

No.	Description	Colourways	Size	U.S.$	Can.$	U.K.£
1a	Gothic	Cream; lilac/pink flowers; green/gold leaves	165 x 165	70.00	90.00	35.00
1b	Gothic	Creamy orange; pale pink flower; pale green leaves	165 x 165	60.00	80.00	30.00
1c	Gothic	Pale yellow	165 x 165	60.00	80.00	30.00

WADE HEATH (cont.)

SHAPE 223, LEAVES AND FLOWERS, 1935-c.1940

These wall pockets have a panelled front with an embossed design of flowers and leaves.

Green Flaxman

Yellow Flaxman

Backstamp: A. Black ink stamp "Flaxman Wade Heath England Made in England"
B. Black ink stamp "Flaxman Hand Made Pottery by Wade Heath England"

No.	Description	Colourways	Size	U.S.$	Can.$	U.K.£
1a	Flowers and leaves	Mottled green	175	50.00	70.00	25.00
1b	Flowers and leaves	Mottled yellow	175	50.00	70.00	25.00

SHAPE 224, ROUND TOP, 1935-c.1940

These wall pockets have an embossed design of flowers around the top.

Backstamp: Black ink stamp "Wadeheath Ware England"

No.	Description	Colourways	Size	U.S.$	Can.$	U.K.£
1a	Round top	Mottled blue/orange	180 x 153	50.00	70.00	25.00
1b	Round top	Mottled orange/yellow/brown; blue/orange/pink flowers	180 x 153	50.00	70.00	25.00
1c	Round top	Mottled white/blue/yellow	180 x 153	50.00	70.00	25.00

WADE HEATH (cont.)

SHAPE 225, FLEUR-DE-LIS, 1935-c.1940

Backstamp: Black ink stamp "Flaxman Wade Heath England," with impressed "225"

No.	Description	Colourways	Size	U.S.$	Can.$	U.K.£
1	Fleur-de-lis	Pale yellow	220 x 118	50.00	70.00	25.00

SHAPE 226, FAN, 1935-c.1940

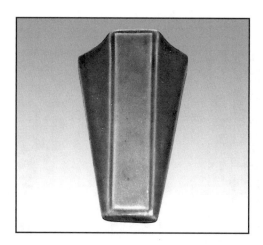

Backstamp: Black ink stamp "Wadeheath Ware England," with impressed "226"

No.	Description	Colourways	Size	U.S.$	Can.$	U.K.£
1a	Fan	Cream; violet/blue flowers; green leaves	Medium 145 x 90	60.00	80.00	35.00
1b	Fan	Mottled blue/orange	Medium/145 x 90	51.00	70.00	25.00
1c	Fan	Mottled orange/grey	Medium/145 x 90	51.00	70.00	25.00
1d	Fan	Mottled green/orange	Medium/145 x 90	40.00	55.00	20.00
2	Fan	White; turquoise criss-cross stripes	Large/150 x 150	60.00	80.00	30.00

WADE HEATH *(cont.)*

SHAPE 228, BLOCKS, 1935-c.1940

These wall pockets resemble a tower of building blocks when viewed upside down.

Flowers

Mottled brown and orange

Backstamp: Black ink stamp "Flaxman Wade Heath England," with impressed "228"

No.	Description	Colourways	Size	U.S.$	Can.$	U.K.£
1a	Flowers	Cream/yellow/blue/pink/green	138	85.00	125.00	50.00
1b	Mottled	Mottled brown/orange	138	60.00	80.00	35.00
1c	Mottled	Mottled turquoise/brown	138	60.00	80.00	35.00

SHAPE 229, TULIP, 1935-c.1940

Red and yellow tulip with green leaves

Yellow tulip with green leaves

Backstamp: Black ink stamp "Wadeheath Ware England" with impressed number "229"

No.	Description	Colourways	Size	U.S.$	Can.$	U.K.£
1	Tulip	Red/yellow tulip; green leaves	155 x 95	90.00	120.00	55.00
2	Tulip	Yellow tulip; green leaves	165 x 95	90.00	120.00	55.00

WADE HEATH (cont.)

SHAPE 249, BASKET WARE, 1935-c.1940

Backstamp: Black ink stamp "Wade Heath England," with impressed shape number "249"

No.	Description	Colourways	Size	U.S.$	Can.$	U.K.£
1	Basket ware	Cream; grey/pink/yellow flowers; green leaves	145 x 185	51.00	70.00	30.00

SHAPE 281, ROSE, 1935-c.1940

Photograph not available
at press time

Backstamp: Black ink stamp "Wade Heath England," with impressed shape number "281"

No.	Description	Colourways	Size	U.S.$	Can.$	U.K.£
1	Rose	Yellow; pink roses; green leaves	205 x 100	90.00	120.00	55.00

WADE HEATH *(cont.)*

SHAPES, NUMBERS UNKNOWN, 1935-2000
Japanese Garden, 1998-2000

Backstamp: Printed "The Gallery Collection Japanese Garden inspired by original 1930's Wade Heath Designs Wade Made in England 31"

No.	Description	Colourways	Size	U.S.$	Can.$	U.K.£
1	Japanese Garden	Mottled yellow/green/lilac	205	25.00	35.00	10.00

Round Top, 1935-c.1940

Round top

Backstamp: Black ink stamp "Flaxman Ware hand made Pottery by Wade Heath England"

No.	Description	Colourways	Size	U.S.$	Can.$	U.K.£
1	Daffodil	Grey daffodils; green leaves	205 x 100	90.00	120.00	55.00
2	Round top	Mottled yellow/green/lilac	140 x 88	30.00	40.00	15.00

WADE HEATH *(cont.)*

Scrolls, 1935-c.1940

Scrolls

Backstamp: Black ink stamp "Wade Heath England"

No.	Description	Colourways	Size	U.S.$	Can.$	U.K.£
1	Scrolls	Mottled green/grey	180 x 153	50.00	70.00	30.00

Sombrero, 1935-c.1940

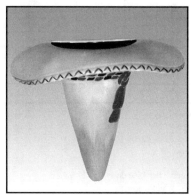

Sombrero

Backstamp: Black ink stamp "Wade Heath England"

No.	Description	Colourways	Size	U.S.$	Can.$	U.K.£
1	Sombrero	Yellow; orange/black stitching, tassel	165	80.00	100.00	50.00

WADE IRELAND

CAMEOS

CAMEO PORTRAITS, c.1988-c.1990

A number of oval Victorian ladies cameo portraits were produced by Wade Ireland, possibly at the same time as the Gray Fine Art plaques (see *The Charlton Standard Catalogue of Wade, Volume One, General Issues*). The cameos can be found in two sizes 65mm and 85mm, they can have a plain or plaited rim, a pierced hole for hanging or have a ring glued to the back, and others have a slotted porcelain stand for the cameo to sit in.

Some cameos were used on the lids of trinket boxes (see Boxes section) or set into unglazed pottery frames, the boxes and the frames were not produced by Wade.

Variations in design can be found such as the Longhaired lady who has been found with and without a 'cross and chain necklace'. Most variations though are in colours and size.

Backstamp: Unmarked

No.	Description	Colourways	Size	U.S.$	Can.$	U.K.£
1a	Hair band	Green background, dress	65	30.00	40.00	15.00
1b	Long pearl necklace, shawl	Brown; blue-grey dress	65	30.00	40.00	15.00
1c	Short pearl necklace, folded hands	Green; grey dress	65	30.00	40.00	15.00
1d	Sombrero	Brown background, hat; blue dress	65	30.00	40.00	15.00
1e	White wig	Brownish green; white wig	65	30.00	40.00	15.00
2a	Hair band	Green background, dress	85	30.00	40.00	15.00
2b	Hair in bun	Beige; green dress	85	30.00	40.00	15.00
2c	Hair in bun	Green-brown; blue-grey dress	85	30.00	40.00	15.00
2d	Hat white frill	Grey; grey hat; brown shawl	85	30.00	40.00	15.00
2e	Hat with white band	Green; blue-grey coat dress	85	30.00	40.00	15.00
2f	Holding flowers	Green; blue-grey dress; yellow flowers	85	30.00	40.00	15.00
2g	Holding flowers	Blue-grey background, dress; yellow flowers	85	30.00	40.00	15.00
2h	Holding flowers	Blue-grey; brown dress; yellow flowers	85	30.00	40.00	15.00
2i	Knotted collar	Green; blue-grey dress	85	30.00	40.00	15.00
2j	Pearl and cross necklace	Brown; dark grey-blue dress	85	30.00	40.00	15.00
2k	Lace shawl on head	Grey; white head shawl	85	30.00	40.00	15.00
2l	Long hair, cross and chain necklace	Grey-brown; blue-grey dress	85	30.00	40.00	15.00

No.	Description	Colourways	Size	U.S.$	Can.$	U.K.£
2m	Long hair, no cross and chain necklace	Blue-grey background, dress	85	30.00	40.00	15.00
2n	Long pearl necklace, frilled collar	Browny green; blue-grey dress	85	30.00	40.00	15.00
2o	Long pearl necklace, no collar	Brown; blue-grey dress	85	30.00	40.00	15.00
2p	Ostrich feathers	Green-brown; blue-grey dress	85	30.00	40.00	15.00
2q	Shawl, buttoned blouse	Green; blue-grey shawl	85	30.00	40.00	15.00
2r	Short pearl necklace	Grey; brown hair	85	30.00	40.00	15.00
2s	Short pearl necklace	Brown	85	30.00	40.00	15.00
2t	Sombrero	Brown background, hat; green dress	85	30.00	40.00	15.00
2u	Sombrero	Grey; brown hat/dress	85	30.00	40.00	15.00

CAMEO FRAMES

These plaques are set into an unglazed pottery or plaster frame which were not produced by Wade.

Backstamp: None

No.	Description	Colourways	Size	U.S.$	Can.$	U.K.£
1	Hairband	Off white; gold rim; grey background; brown dress; blue grey shawl	125	30.00	40.00	15.00
2	Hairband, necklace	Grey; Cream Hairband and dress; brown necklace; grey shawl	65	20.00	30.00	10.00
3	Long pearl necklace	Olive green rim; white border; dark grey background; long pearl necklace; grey blue dress	80	50.00	70.00	25.00

IRISH PORCELAIN (cont.)

CAMEO STANDS, c.1988-c.1990

No.	Description	Colourways	Size	U.S.$	Can.$	U.K.£
1	Cameo stand	Grey/blue/green	20 x 105	10.00	14.00	5.00

IRISH PORCELAIN (cont.)

PLAQUES

BOTTLES AND JARS, 1963-1964

These plaques which were made to appear like carved wood were produced at the same time as the pearlstone plaques. They have a contemporary design of glass bottles and jars.

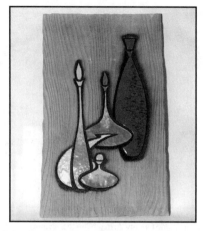

Backstamp: **A.** Black ink stamp "Made in Ireland by Wade Co Armagh"
B. Black ink stamp "Made in Ireland by Wade Co Armagh" and a gold foil label shaped like a sombrero with "Patio Ware Irish Porcelain by Wade Co Armagh" flat back

No.	Description	Colourways	Size	U.S.$	Can.$	U.K.£
1	Bottles and jars	Brown; red/green/blue/orange jars	415 x 255	420.00	550.00	275.00

DISPLAY PLAQUES

The Irish Porcelain plaque, produced c.1960, was meant to be displayed with Wade Ireland figures.

Backstamp: Unmarked

No.	Description	Colourways	Size	U.S.$	Can.$	U.K.£
1	Irish Porcelain plaque	Green/grey	135 x 98	40.00	55.00	20.00

IRISH PORCELAIN (cont.)

IRISH SCENES, c.1960

This series of square wall plaques with an embossed design of Irish knots around the rim was produced by Wade Ireland with multicoloured transfer prints of various Irish scenes, they can be found in the typical Irish blue/grey/green glazes or white.

Backstamp: A. Black ink stamp "Irish Porcelain Wade County Armagh" with a shamrock leaf
B. Unmarked

No.	Description	Colourways	Size	U.S.$	Can.$	U.K.£
1a	City Hall, Belfast	White; multicoloured print	72	50.00	70.00	25.00
1b	Colleen and cottage	Grey-green; multicoloured print	75	50.00	70.00	25.00
1c	Colleen and cottage	White; multicoloured print	72	50.00	70.00	25.00
1d	Giants Causeway	Grey-green; multicoloured print	72	50.00	70.00	25.00
1e	Giants Causeway	White; multicoloured print	72	50.00	70.00	25.00
1f	Ireland	White; multicoloured print	72	50.00	70.00	25.00
1g	Irish fisherman	Grey-green; multicoloured print	72	50.00	70.00	25.00
1h	Irish fisherman	White; multicoloured print	72	50.00	70.00	25.00
1i	Irish jaunting car	Grey-green; multicoloured print	75	50.00	70.00	25.00
1j	Irish jaunting car	White; multicoloured print	72	50.00	70.00	25.00

IRISH PORCELAIN (cont.)

PEARLSTONE WALL PLAQUES, 1963-1964

It is interesting to note that these plaques were originally designed and produced in 1958-1959, by the 'Hagen Renaker' Pottery in San Dimas, California, but because of problems with the production process were soon discontinued. Iris Carryer daughter of Sir George Wade was formerly the Art Director at Wade Ireland, but had left in late 1966 for a new life in the USA with her husband Straker Carryer. Together they founded Carryer Craft of California. Iris soon began an association with Hagen Renaker, she and Jim Renaker agreed that the Hagen Renaker moulds would be sent to Wade Ireland for a trial period in the early 1960s.

As with the Hagen Renaker plaques numerous problems arose with most of the plaques cracking during the cool down period after firing. Because of the problems, production of the plaques was discontinued almost as soon as it began. The original Hagen Renaker names for the fish are given in the listing.

Two styles of backs are found on these plaques. One has large irregular hollows in the back for setting into a stone fireplace or wall by filling with cement. It also has holes into which wire or cord could be strung for hanging, if preferred. Other plaques with Patio Ware labels have a flat back with a large hole on the top horizontal edge for hanging on a wall hook and small holes on the vertical edge for hanging with wire.

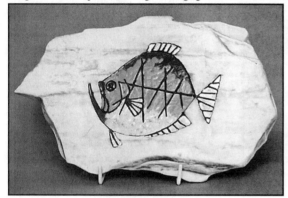

Snapper

Barracuda and Pompano fish

Stallion, running

Stallions, running side-by-side

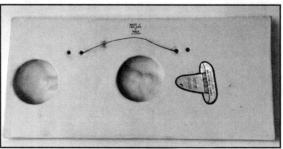

Backstamp

IRISH PORCELAIN (cont.)

Stallions running, facing right

Stallions running, facing left

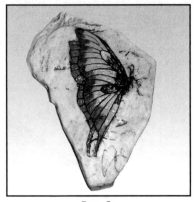

Butterfly

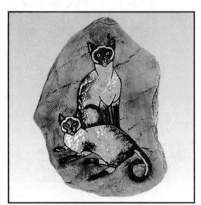

Siamese cats

Backstamp: **A.** Black ink stamp "Made in Ireland by Wade Co Armagh," hollowed back
B. Black ink stamp "Made in Ireland by Wade Co Armagh" and a gold foil label shaped like a sombrero with "Patio Ware Irish Porcelain by Wade Co Armagh" flat back
C. Unmarked

No.	Description	Colourways	Size	U.S.$	Can.$	U.K.£
1	Bison	Stone; brown bison	185 x 300		Rare	
2	Butterfly	Stone; orange; green; yellow; brown butterfly	210 x 340		Rare	
3a	Barracuda	Creamy beige; turquoise fish	180 x 300		Rare	
3b	Barracuda	Dark grey; turquoise/white fish	180 x 300		Rare	
4	Pompano	Beige; white/orange/grey fish with red spots	185 x 300		Rare	
5a	Snapper	Beige; red/white/black fish	205 x 425		Rare	
5b	Snapper	Beige; pink/green/black/white fish	205 x 425		Rare	
6	Siamese cats	Stone; chocolate brown/cream cats; blue eyes	400 x 290		Rare	
7a	Stallion, running	Beige/cream; green stallion; yellow mane, tail	310 x 400		Rare	
7b	Stallion, running	Beige/cream; turquoise stallion; white mane, tail	310 x 400		Rare	
8	Stallions, running, facing left	Beige/cream; green stallions; white manes, tails	150 x 325		Rare	
9	Stallions, running , facing right	Beige/cream; green stallions; white manes, tails	150 x 325		Rare	
10	Stallions, running side-by-side	Beige/cream; brown stallions; white manes, tails	195 x 290		Rare	

INDICES

ALPHABETICAL INDEX

SHAPE NUMBER INDEX

If you want to know what is happening in the world of collecting Wade!
then you must join the only

Official International Wade Collectors Club

Membership offers, besides the pleasure of sharing a hobby, such intangibles as greater appreciation of Wade collectables through initiation into techniques of designing, modelling and production. You can find out about new products - designed to charm and capture the heart.

2002 Club membership pieces are all characters from the Peter Pan range.

Annual Membership Benefits

Membership figure:	•	exclusive to club members only.
Membership pin:	•	designed to compliment the membership figure.
Membership certificate:	•	personalised complete with date of membership.
Membership card:	•	entitles you to 10% discount at fairs/Wade shop on selected items.
Quarterly magazine:	•	Full of news on limited editions, club news, fairs and events, articles on old Wade, and sales and wants. **PLUS** the opportunity to purchase members only limited editions

Enrol a friend: Why not introduce a friend to the club? They will receive all the benefits of membership and you will BOTH be sent 'Ruffles', a great bonus gift. Call us for details.

Fees: Annual Membership (12 mos from receipt) £12.00 / US $42.00
Two year membership (24 mos from receipt) £45.00 / US $78.00
Family membership (12 mos from receipt - 4 family members) £85.00 / US $128.00

Membership Application Form

Simply photocopy this form and send it to: **The Official International Wade Collectors Club,**
Wade Ceramics Ltd, Westport Road, Burslem, Stoke-on-Trent, St6 4Ap, England
Tel: (01782) 255255 E-mail; club@wade.co.uk; www.wade.co.uk

Please enrol me as a member   ❑ 1 year (£25)   ❑ My cheque for .... Pounds payable to Wade Ceramics
                                      ❑ 2 year (£45)   is enclosed

Title .... First Name ....

Last Name ....

Address ....

....

....

Post/Zip Code ....

Tel No ....

❑ Debit my credit/charge card

❑ Visa   ❑ Mastercard   ❑ Amex

❑ Switch   ❑❑❑❑❑❑❑❑❑❑❑❑❑❑❑❑❑❑

The sum of ....

Card expires on month ❑❑   year ❑❑

Issue number (switch only) ....

Signature ....

Please allow 28 days for processing your membership.